DIRTY POLITICS

DIRTY

POLITICS

Bruce L. Felknor

W · W · NORTON & COMPANY · INC · *New York*

Published simultaneously in Canada by
George J. McLeod Limited, Toronto

PRINTED IN THE UNITED STATES OF AMERICA

1 2 3 4 5 6 7 8 9 0

For my wife Edith,
and for Susan, Sarah,
and Bruce, Jr.

Contents

Introduction

AMONG the political memorabilia at the Smithsonian Institution is a tiny figure of a pig. When its snout is turned toward the light, the viewer may peer through a lens at the opposite end and behold the likeness of a nineteenth-century candidate for President of the United States.

Fortunately, political artifacts of the sheer vulgarity of the above reach a smaller proportion of the electorate today than they did a hundred years ago. For one thing, high prices prevent mass distribution of three-dimensional objects as campaign throwaways. However, plain and fancy lying about candidates for high public office has tended to become more persuasive and more damaging.

American history has seen a continuing communications revolution that has made it possible for political argument to reach virtually the entire electorate instantaneously. Until recently, the citizen's compliance has been necessary; he has had to tune in the program or pick up the paper to receive the argument. But the technological revolution rolls on, and it is possible now for a machine to telephone one citizen or many and deliver a political pitch. Nothing the citizen can do will force that machine to relinquish the line until the message is completed.

A review of ethics and the mores they are supposed to govern has been forced on many areas of modern society, but the American concept of the ethics of political persuasion remains what it was a generation ago. Dirty campaigns have disturbed and galvanized masses occasionally and sensitive individuals often. Nevertheless, efforts to restrain scurrilous electioneering without impeding honest argument have been spotty. Legal restraints are limited usually to such matters as libel and identification, and responsible victims of the wildest campaign slanders usually have shunned—and wisely—any effort to legislate campaign morality.

In 1950 the Congressional elections were fought out in a spectacular descent into the gutter. Protesting a "nightmare of immersion in billingsgate," the New York Times editorialized: "So complete is the character assassination in some cases that those who reach public office will have lost the confidence of the voters who put them there. The most serious result of all, perhaps, is that if this sort of thing continues, it will become increasingly difficult to get decent men and women to stand for public office because of the unjustified abuse suffered en route . . .

". . . When almost everyone is calling everybody else a liar and a thief, the result becomes a standoff. There is, then, no black and white of reputation in the public mind, only a muddy gray."

The 81st Congress which was chosen in that 1950 election appointed a subcommittee, headed by Senator Paul H. Douglas of Illinois, to study ethics in government. Testifying before the committee, Senator William Benton of Connecticut reinforced the somber apprehensions of the Times editorial quoted above. He put the case succinctly: "One of the gravest problems the American people face is the public cynicism about politics and government. We are paying a frightful cost for this unjustified cynicism. Many decent—including many prominent—citizens shy away from assuming civic responsibilities because they mistakenly believe politics and government are generally corrupt and evil. Our entire society suffers."

Senator Benton offered a remedy: "a non-partisan continuing commission of distinguished private citizens" which would study campaign conduct, report the facts, and recommend standards of responsibility for election campaigns.

Meanwhile, the Senate elections subcommittee, headed by Iowa's Guy Gillette, was investigating complaints of unfairness in the 1950 campaigns. Senator Benton offered similar recommendations to the Gillette subcommittee. In its report the subcommittee adopted the Benton proposal and called for "a continuing committee of eminent members of both parties, working jointly for higher and cleaner standards of campaigning," and suggested that such an effort could do "as much as the enactment of laws to rid this nation of abuses which are reaching alarming proportions."

The Douglas ethics subcommittee agreed, and pointed a direction for a continuing committee: "Progress depends also upon critical listeners who ask for evidence, are skeptical about unsupported assertions, and realize that name-calling, 'smears,' appeals to bigotry, and emotionalism generally are prima facie evidence that the speaker has frequently nothing more substantial with which to support his position."

The Iowa solon and some of his associates, notably his own administrative assistant, Stewart E. McClure, drew up in the course of their deliberations a model code of fair campaign practices.

Shortly before the 1954 Congressional elections, a group of "eminent members of both parties" came together to constitute the Fair Campaign Practices Committee, under the leadership of Anna Lord Strauss, of New York, recently president of the League of Women Voters of the United States. Miss Strauss and her colleagues, including publishers Palmer Hoyt of the Denver Post and Barry Bingham of the Louisville Times and Courier-Journal, and Charles P. Taft of Cincinnati, adopted, with slight modifications, the Gillette subcommittee's Code of Fair Campaign Practices; they summoned a press conference at which the document was endorsed by Republican national chairman Leonard W. Hall and Democratic chairman Stephen A. Mitchell. The fledgling committee also mailed off copies of the Code (See Appendix I) to every Congressional candidate, with the request that he pledge publicly to abide by it and return a signed copy to the Committee.

The Code-signing press conference was enlivened by a dispute between the two party leaders as to whose partisans would be most apt to disregard the Code, and the entire effort was greeted with sardonic editorials which acknowledged the need for improvement but voiced much skepticism about the effectiveness of the available instrument. The Committee subsided with Election Day, to re-emerge at the beginning of 1956 on a permanent basis.

Charles P. Taft, the lawyer and churchman, son of a President and Chief Justice, brother of "Mr. Republican" Robert A. Taft, became chairman and I was named executive director. With year-round activity it became possible to study weaknesses in the original concept of the Committee, to probe for the causes of unfair campaigning and explore possible remedies.

In time the Code was abandoned as a pledge and was advanced purely as a reasonable standard by which candidates and voters and the press might gauge campaign tactics. State-by-state post-mortems of election campaigns were initiated to discover where and when and how unfair campaigns were waged and what made them succeed or fail. An experiment in teaching aids for high schoools was begun and this evolved into pamphlets and newsletters, first for the schools and later for wider consumption.

Hard-headed politicians were added to the Committee board both to bring realistic political counsel and to counteract possible editorial mockery about "do-gooders." Over the next decade the Committee slowly achieved what two party leaders, Democrat John Bailey and Republican William E. Miller, once called "its impartial and increasingly effective role as the conscience of American politics."

During that decade, as executive director of the Committee, I have had a literally unique opportunity to study, full-time, the conduct of American election campaigns in terms of political ethics. I have come to know political pros and amateurs, bigots and zealots, demagogs and charlatans, idealists and pragmatists, radicals, moderates, conservatives and reactionaries. I have learned that smear campaigns are the monopoly of cynical or desperate human beings, not of Republicans and Democrats. I have discovered that impartiality is easy to come by if one's deepest loyalty is to the integrity of the political system, and that thoughtful and honest partisans despise trickery and deceit for or against their own party—when they can recognize it.

This book is the story of dirty campaigning and political chicanery in America. It begins with the time when politics was the concern of an elite few and news traveled slowly, and closes with today, when every citizen may vote and news travels at the speed of light.

This is a personal book, whose observations are my own and not those of the Fair Campaign Practices Committee, which could not speak out thus if it would, for the tax law under which the Committee is an exempt educational organization forbids public statements about candidates for office.

I am indebted to Emmet John Hughes for suggesting that I write such a book, to Noel E. Parmentel for goading me into actually writing it, and to Carol Houck for editing it deftly, relentlessly, and compassionately.

For a wealth of general assistance I am grateful to my incomparable secretary, Roz Hosenball, and for typing to Laurie Felknor. For the illustrations appearing between pages 128 and 129 I am indebted to the Fair Campaign Practices Committee and the Smithsonian Institution, and especially to Wilcomb Washburn and Keith Melder; and for photographic assistance and advice to Dick Dorgan. The frontispiece, my favorite political cartoon, is Whitney Darrow's, from the *New Yorker*. I also acknowledge with thanks the contributions of George E. Agree, Herbert E. Alexander, Totton J. Anderson, Barry Bingham, Hugh Bone, Samuel C. Brightman, Argyll Campbell, John Chancellor, Maureen Drummy, Elizabeth R. Gatov, Louis Harris, Albert B. Hermann, Frank H. Jonas, Stanley Kelley, Jr., Roger Kent, Stewart E. McClure, Wesley McCune, Henry Mandel and associates, Stephen A. Mitchell, Templeton Peck, Arthur L. Peterson, Wayne Phillips, William B. Prendergast, Woodruff M. Price, Alan Reitman, Robert Riggs, Joseph Roos, Richard M. Scammon, Thomas N. Schroth, John T. Swing, and last (only alphabetically), Charles P. Taft, who may be the best citizen I have known.

Bruce L. Felknor
March, 1966

DIRTY POLITICS

CHAPTER 1

Mud on the
White House

IN THE beginning, American Presidential politics was pure and
simple. George Washington was the obvious and unanimous
choice for the Presidency of a grateful Republic. In 1789 the new
nation did not have a national anthem: the people improvised
one to the tune of *God Save the King:* "God save great Washington."

Then as Washington's two administrations progressed, some
colleagues and friends fell away, and others found reason to re-
sent his conduct of this or that affair of state. Hostilities developed, and suspicions.

The very architect of victory over the British Crown came to
be denounced as pro-British. Washington's resentment of and response to the remarkable mischiefs of the French minister, Citizen Genet, were portrayed by some as ingratitude to the land of
Lafayette, then torn with its own revolution. The President's
determination to prevent the development of an American king-
ship, so favored by Tories and many Federalists, became warped
in some minds into a Washington yearning for a throne. His characteristic aloofness and even the stiffness of his bows were
ascribed to regal pretensions rather than to his angular personal-

ity and the process of aging. The fact that Washington was child-less did not deter the alarmists: it was rumored that an hereditary Presidency could be passed along through the issue of the President's brother, Lund Washington.

So George Washington, the first President and the only one ever elected unanimously, became also the first victim of the envy-ridden lies, and half-truths, and accusations that every successor to his high office would suffer in some degree.

Washington's dream of a one-party nation foundered on the Federalist mistrust of common, unlettered citizens as participants in government, and on emerging anti-Federalist sentiment that was beginning to crystallize into a Democratic-Republican Party. John Adams was a patrician and a Federalist to the marrow. Anti-Federalist writers taxed him with contempt for the "canaille multitude," but in fact he mistrusted the people less than many of his fellow-Federalists. Notable among these hard-liners was the brilliant, far-sighted, hot-headed, base-born aristocrat of the Federalist Party, Alexander Hamilton.

The election of 1796 pitted Adams and his colleague, Thomas Pinckney, against the Democratic-Republicans Thomas Jefferson and Aaron Burr. The Federalist press condemned the egalitarian leanings of Jefferson. The rival Republicans denounced the well-born Adams and what they feared were his dynastic ambitions; unlike Washington, Adams had sons, and they offered a greater threat of hereditary succession than did Jefferson's daughters.

In this first campaign for the Presidency the first downright lie—a false statement of "fact"—appeared about an American Presidential candidate. The *Independent Chronicle* of Boston said that Adams, although professing loyalty to Washington during the Revolution, actually had connived to remove the General from command of the Revolutionary armies. The real facts were that Washington's leadership had been attacked by a group that briefly included Adams' second cousin Sam. However, the Federalist John Adams had argued long and successfully to persuade his Republican kinsman to abandon the cabal.

The campaign of 1796 introduced many varieties of innu-endo, distortion and falsehood that were to persist in American politics. Some enemies described Adams as pro-British while others claimed he was pro-French. This pair of epithets was about as compatible as "pro-American" and "pro-Soviet" would be today. Adams was labeled vain and jealous, and numerous anecdotes were invented or magnified about his celebrated temper.

For his part, Jefferson was dubbed a coward and a drunkard. He was said to be the son of a half-breed squaw by a mulatto father. He was "Mad Tom," and a "philosopher," the derisive eighteenth-century equivalent of "egghead." Today, Jefferson would be thought of as a Unitarian; then he was called an atheist, and lurid word-pictures were painted of him and his friend, the British atheist Tom Paine, lolling about "fraternizing and philoso-phizing against the Christian religion." A story that Jefferson had arranged a government sinecure for a favored political hatchet man was perhaps the original accusation of "cronyism."

Jefferson was also attacked as a Jacobin, in an era when every packet ship carried news of The Terror in far-away France. Today the corresponding term would be "Communist." Jefferson had been Washington's, and the nation's, first Secretary of State, and now in the campaign of 1796 he was said to have presided over a State Department riddled with Jacobins [Communists].

The dominant strain in political campaign excesses, calumny, was well-represented in 1796. Another strain, manipulation, did not come into play until the electors had been chosen. Due to the vagaries of the electoral system in this early year, Election Day and its returns shed no light on who actually would be President. There were sixteen states and 138 electors, of whom about one-sixth had been chosen "at large" in statewide general elections. The remainder was divided almost evenly between electors chosen by vote in individual districts and those named by state legislatures. Electors were not committed publicly to any candi-date. Each elector voted for two men; the candidate with the highest tally became President, and the Vice Presidency went to the candidate with the second-highest vote.

Jefferson held Adams in respect and affection, and refused to campaign against him with the electors. Alexander Hamilton, however, found his personal distaste for his fellow-Federalist Adams stronger than his political fear of Jefferson's democratic leanings. Hamilton set out to influence every elector he could reach, seeking to downgrade Adams with the Federalists in the Electoral College. His hope was that Adams' running mate, Federalist Thomas Pinckney, would be elected President and that Adams would be relegated to the Vice Presidency. Hamilton was the first political strategist to visualize the Vice Presidency as a burying ground for politicians who were in the way. And because of him, intra-party bitterness became a major political problem in the very first Presidential contest.

Hamilton's efforts to sidetrack Adams were worse than in vain. The Federalist Adams won the Presidency with three electoral votes to spare, and the Republican Jefferson beat out Federalist Pinckney to become Vice President.

The experience of the Electoral College of 1797 made evident the dangerous possibility that political rivals could occupy the Presidency and the Vice Presidency.[1] As a result, the first electoral reform would come to pass in 1804 as the Twelfth Amendment. It stipulated that President and Vice President would be voted on separately within the Electoral College.

By 1800 Republican hostility to Adams had intensified, not least because of his ill-conceived advocacy of the Alien and Sedi-

---

[1] The accident of 1796–1797 invites conjecture as to what might have occurred in later years without the Twelfth Amendment. If, in 1964, the Rockefeller-Scranton-Lodge forces had lobbied against Goldwater with the electors, who would have been Johnson's Vice President? Goldwater? Humphrey? Miller? Visualize a 1961 administration of Kennedy and Nixon, or, indeed, an Eisenhower-Stevenson regime. Suppose the combination in 1948 had been Truman and Dewey, or Wallace, or Thurmond. If the 1948 election, by some wild quirk, had gone in the Electoral College to Thurmond and Wallace, or in 1964 to Goldwater and Humphrey, the disparity, the polar difference, between the Chief Executive and his deputy would have been quite like the ideological gulf that separated President John Adams and Vice President Thomas Jefferson, for all their mutual esteem.

tion Acts of 1798. The growing western frontier was becoming heavily Republican and the Acts, suspending trial by jury and giving vast and punitive powers to the Executive, speeded the trend. All the old canards against Adams were revived, and the rancor aroused by his mistakes in office was nourished enthusiastically by the Democratic-Republican Party.

Jefferson again opposed Adams. The anti-Jefferson smears of 1796 were reiterated and embroidered upon, and new ones added. Some Federalists saw Jefferson's election as sure to bring on a civil war. Lurid Federalist propaganda ascribed to Jefferson depraved tastes and appetites. It was said that his election would bring on a national orgy of rape, incest, and adultery. Furthermore, although Jefferson was a slaveholder, he strongly disapproved of the practice of slavery. His considerate treatment of his own slaves and his distaste for the system now became "documentation" for stories among planters that he would abolish the institution if elected.

Some Federalists also maintained that Jefferson's "smears" and "slanders" against the Adams Administration were sapping public confidence in the United States Government. In the political jargon of our day, Jefferson was a "peddler of gloom and doom," or "fright and fear."

The Electoral College of 1801 encountered a problem which reinforced the need for electoral reform, already demonstrated in 1797. There were 73 Republican electors, a majority, and all of them enthusiastically cast their ballots for Jefferson and his running mate, Aaron Burr. The resulting deadlock between Jefferson and Burr threw the election into the House of Representatives, where Alexander Hamilton again used his influence—very considerable in the House—to manipulate the outcome of a Presidential election. Hamilton counted Jefferson far less dangerous than Burr, and his view prevailed: Jefferson became President.[2]

In 1804 Jefferson sought a second term and swamped the

[2] Hamilton's antipathy for Burr, and, more important, the ardor with which he expressed it in the House, was one reason for the duel three years later in which the third Vice President took the life of the Federalist genius.

Federalists in a campaign from which that party never recovered. Four years later he retired from public life, admired extravagantly and hated extravagantly. In *Ordeal of the Presidency*,[3] David Cushman Coyle notes that implacable hatred of Jefferson persisted long after he had left office, and draws an interesting parallel with the emotions of the Roosevelt-haters of a later era. Coyle also observes that Jefferson was the first President to foresee the calumny he would have to endure before he sought the office, and that he was able to regard it philosophically for the eighteen years he lived after leaving it.

The War of 1812 and the ensuing "Era of Good Feeling," in which inter-party rancors dwindled with the gradual decay of the Federalist Party, interrupted the growth of the political smear in America. The "good feeling" began to evaporate with the election of 1824, in which John Quincy Adams lost the popular and electoral vote to Andrew Jackson but won the Presidency in the House of Representatives.

Speaker of the House Henry Clay and one other candidate had won enough electoral votes to deprive Jackson of the required majority, although he had 99 votes to Adams' 84. Thus the choice of the President fell to the House. There Speaker Clay lobbied effectively with his colleagues on Adams' behalf, and the House elected Adams. The new President thereupon determined that the best qualified man for Secretary of State was Henry Clay, and appointed him.

The charge of buying the Presidency for a Cabinet post rose immediately, and dogged Adams to the end of his career. When Andrew Jackson, Virginia-born migrant to Tennessee, political leader in that pioneer state, war hero and man of the people, ran against Adams again in 1828, his supporters harped incessantly on the Adams-Clay "deal."

John Quincy Adams himself had refrained from personal attacks on Jackson, but few of his advocates were as temperate. Jackson was seen as a wild man of the frontier, a bloodthirsty, trigger-happy knave and brawler. His wife, Rachel, had married

[3] Public Affairs Press, Washington, D.C., 1960.

him after divorce had ended an unhappy earlier marriage. Then it was discovered that her first husband had not obtained a divorce after all. The divorce was secured and the Jacksons were remarried. However, Adams' backers plagued Mrs. Jackson with pious taunts and publicly condemned her as an adulteress.

Others said Jackson's mother had been a prostitute who married a Negro, and they buttressed the allegation with the tale that Jackson's older brother had been sold as a slave.[4]

The most notorious of the numerous anti-Jackson tracts was the "Coffin Handbill," a flyer decorated with drawings of eighteen coffins, each representing a supposedly innocent victim of Old Hickory's callous cruelty. In truth, most of the "victims" were soldiers under his command who had been court-martialed and executed for mutiny and desertion. One was a man Jackson had slain in self-defense, and for whose death he had been tried. Here the author of the handbill turned to innuendo: "But finding means to convince the petit jury that he committed the act in self-defense, he was acquitted."

Another anti-Jackson handbill may have been the first forgery to attain substantial circulation in a Presidential campaign. This was a carefully edited extract from court-martial records, doctored to make the Coffin Handbill executions seem useless, arbitrary and simply cruel. Falsely titled "Official Record from the War Department," it bore the spurious imprimatur, "Ordered to be Printed by the Congress."

For their part, roistering Jackson adherents mocked the patrician bearing and demeanor of John Quincy Adams, spread word along the frontier that he despised the common folk, and pointed to his personal austerity to support charges of stinginess.

The frontier and most of the South rallied to Jackson and he beat Adams decisively. But the joy of victory for the new President was demolished by his wife's death of a heart attack, brought on, many contemporary and later observers believed, by her deep sensitivity to the "adulteress" charges.

---

[4] Negro blood had been ascribed to Jefferson, and later would be to Lincoln and Harding.

In the election of 1832, Old Hickory confronted arch-conservative Henry Clay, the architect of his 1824 defeat by Adams. Jackson made short work of the Speaker, but not without acquiring a few new scars. The President had determined to break the stranglehold on the Federal government of Nicholas Biddle's immensely powerful Bank of the United States. He had chosen and dismissed a succession of Treasury Secretaries until he found one who would obey his order to deposit Federal funds in other banks. And early in the election year of 1832, Jackson had vetoed legislation to renew the Bank's federal charter. This insistence on obedience, and the "autocratic" act of killing the charter-renewal, added the epithet "king" to the President's substantial collection. Some journals called him a Caesar and one suggested that the republic was in need of a Brutus.[5]

Jackson's relentless determination to root out incompetent officeholders, and his vetoing of public works projects in the interest of government economy were reminiscent of Jefferson, and, similarly, they caused a continuing uproar. Jackson replaced many dismissed officials by sharing the "spoils of victory" with his fellow victors in the new Democratic-Republican Party, and this distribution of the "spoils" heightened the outcry.

Jackson all but totally alienated the wealthy and conservative citizens. Most of the vulgar mass, however, was solidly behind Old Hickory. When the vote was in, the well-born and the conservative abandoned hope, although the *Boston Courier* saw a glimmer of light. With the Electoral College yet to meet, there was "one comfort left: God has promised that the days of the wicked shall be short; the wicked [Jackson] is old and feeble, and he may die before he can be elected. It is the duty of every good Christian to pray to our Maker to have pity on us."

After the campaign excesses of the Jackson era, the slanderers of Presidential candidates slipped into a period of inactivity.

[5] A Brutus appeared in the person of a crazed house painter, Richard Lawrence, who triggered a brace of pistols at the President as he emerged from a funeral in the Capitol. Both weapons misfired. Lawrence was found insane and placed in an asylum. His hallucinations had told him that he was King and Jackson an impostor.

Only one campaign between 1836 and 1860 involved a memorable piece of chicanery. In 1844 the Tennessee Democrat James K. Polk was opposed for the Presidency by Virginia's Henry Clay, who by now was a Whig. Just before Election Day the *Chronicle*, of Ithaca, New York, published an excerpt from one Baron Roorback's journal of "A Tour Through the Western and Southern States." The good baron told of watching the purchase of 43 slaves by James K. Polk, "the present Speaker of the House of Representatives,[6] the mark of the branding iron and the initials of his name, on their shoulders, distinguishing them . . ."

Though the election was at hand, other newspapers that shared the Ithaca *Chronicle's* Whig leanings found time to reprint this report of the Democrat's inhumanity. In actual fact, the sale never was made, the branding scene never took place, and there was no Baron Roorback. Polk won, but the deception hurt his cause. The word Roorback became a common noun, known to generation after generation of political practitioners and students: roorback, noun, any false or damaging story about a political candidate published too late in a campaign to permit effective refutation.

Following the Roorback incident the smear front was quiet until 1861. Abraham Lincoln's 1860 Presidential campaign against Stephen A. Douglas gave no hint of the vilification that was to rise about him and hover over him until his death. The Democrats were too busy fighting one another. In a foretaste of events just ahead, Southern state delegations seceded from the Democratic National Convention. The Loyal Democrats named Douglas. The seceders put up John C. Breckenridge. Stragglers from the now-defunct Whigs and the American (Know-Nothing) Party coalesced as the Constitutional Union Party and nominated John Bell. The four-year-old Republican party chose Lincoln, drafted a platform with wide appeal, and waited for the opposition to kill one another off, which promptly came to pass.

---

[6] The journal presumably was dated at least five years earlier, since in 1839 Polk left the Congress and the Speaker's Chair to run successfully for governor of Tennessee.

Immediately upon Lincoln's election, the brickbats began to fly. Influential newspapers, clergymen, and political leaders, north and south, began to view with horror the work of the electorate. The first of a series of actual and reported assassination plots was discovered and evaded. With inauguration, secession, and war, the abuse intensified and spread.

The calumniators took note of the President's wife. One of the most searing episodes of American history occurred midway in Lincoln's first term, when a Senate committee met secretly to consider widespread rumors that the First Lady was a Confederate sympathizer, possibly an agent. The President appeared suddenly before the committee unbidden and unannounced. He said quietly: "I, Abraham Lincoln, President of the United States, appear of my own volition before this committee of the Senate to say that I, of my own knowledge, know that it is untrue that any of my family hold treasonable communication with the enemy."

In 1864 the Republicans convened under a National Union banner, renominated the President and chose as his running mate a pro-war Democrat from Tennessee, Andrew Johnson. The Democrats named that cocky, offensive, highly political and often insubordinate soldier, General George B. McClellan, and drew up a platform calling for immediate cessation of hostilities. McClellan repudiated that fruit of Copperhead influence, but continued sedulously to court the substantial defeatist vote in the North.

The campaign was bitter. A month before Election Day one Ohio editor viewed the verbal carnage with distaste:

"The vulgar language of Republicans and Democrats is disgusting. Stump orators vie in scurrility and obscene allusions. Surely the friends of Mr. Lincoln do not expect to gain votes by calling all the friends and supporters of Gen. McClellan traitors and Copperheads; and we know that the course [sic] epithets applied to Mr. Lincoln are hurting the cause of Gen. McClellan a great deal."

The coarse epithets applied to Mr. Lincoln were remarkable both in volume and in viciousness. Those excesses have been so fully chronicled that only highlights need be recalled here.

The quickest summary is a negative one: Lincoln was not called a ladies' man. And none of the slanderous smear words that gained wide circulation throughout the Union began with the letters Q, X, Y or Z.

Otherwise, every letter of the alphabet was called into play against the wartime President. A fragmentary but representative list of epithet includes: Ape, Buffoon, Coward, Drunkard, Execrable, Fiend, Ghoul, Hopeless, Ignoramus, Jokester (in the face of war tragedies), Knave, Lunatic, Murderer, Negro, Outlaw, Perjurer, Robber, Savage, Traitor, Usurper, Vulgar, Weakling.

Lincoln won re-election, with a bare 55 per cent of the popular vote and an electoral landslide, although he won New York's 33 electors by less than one per cent of that state's three-quarters of a million votes. The returns focused attention on the Vice President-elect, who had received only incidental mention during the campaign. Copperheads, perhaps exhausted by their maligning of Lincoln, and also possibly more comfortable with a known devil than a strange one, now voiced their dread "that only one frail life stands between this insolent, clownish drunk [Johnson— although the same phrase had been used to describe Lincoln] and the Presidency."

The apprehensions were justified. On Good Friday, forty days after his inauguration, Lincoln was shot. The next day the "insolent, clownish drunk" was President, and then, indeed, by the very grace of the demon rum. For Vice President Johnson's assassin-designate in the Lincoln plot had consumed too much bottled courage before the fateful moment and slept a drunken sleep past the appointed hour—a few yards away from Andrew Johnson's hotel room.

Andrew Johnson, shortly to be maligned as "King Andy I," inherited the calumny as well as the office from Lincoln. Immediately on taking the oath of office, Johnson began to implement Lincoln's conciliatory reconstruction policies with only minor changes. The radical Republicans in Congress resisted and hampered him at every turn, blueprinting a harsh Congressional formula for reconstruction. Johnson took to the hustings in 1866 in an effort to elect moderates to the Congress. His tour became a series of harangues and the attempt was a complete failure. The Radicals won solid domination of both Houses of Congress and proceeded virtually to seize the reins of the executive and dominate the reconstruction effort completely.

The tide continued to run their way and the Republicans had no difficulty in electing General Ulysses Grant in 1868, though with a narrow plurality of only 300,000.

In 1872, despite widespread and convincing cries of corruption, Grant was able to win re-election, over Horace Greeley, who was accused of favoring free love and Fourierism (creeping socialism). Greeley died after the election but before the Electoral College met. In the confusion over whom the Greeley electors should name, Grant, with a popular majority of only some 700,000, won a lopsided electoral victory, 286 to 42 for his nearest competitor.

Mounting concern over the corruption of the Grant administration, coupled with Southern determination to end the reconstruction and flagging Northern interest in supporting it, set the stage for the election of 1876. The bizarre story of Hayes' victory over Tilden is reviewed in Chapter 7.

The Hayes Presidency did see the end of the reconstruction. In the Republican convention of 1880, "Stalwarts," trying to capitalize on waning "bloody shirt" sentiment, sought to nominate General Grant for a third term, President Hayes having declined to run. Reformers, the "Half-Breed" faction, managed to nominate one of their own, James A. Garfield. To appease the Stalwarts, the convention made a Stalwart, Chester A. Arthur, the Vice Presidential nominee. Garfield served as President nearly four months when Charles J. Guiteau, a Stalwart who had been refused an appointment by Garfield, murdered him, to make way, he said, for the Stalwart Vice President Arthur.

James G. Blaine, the leading "Half-Breed" reformer and sometime Speaker of the House, had figured in Presidential politics for several years, but also in wide talk of financial irregularities. He beat President Arthur out of the Republican nomination in 1884, thus alienating one faction of reform Republicans. These supported the Democratic nominee, and shortly came to be called mugwumps.

Blaine's loyalists did not waver either in their admiration of the "Plumed Knight" from Maine or in their contempt for the Democratic candidate, a vigorous reformer, Governor of New York and former mayor of Buffalo, Grover Cleveland. The campaign degenerated into a sea of mud.

Not all of the contumely of 1884 was unfair. Much of the verbiage was colorful and imaginative.[7] Many of the slurs were based solidly in fact. To a large degree Blaine and Cleveland and their splinter party rivals were not smeared; they were simply exposed. Not all of the vilification, however, met the test of relevancy to the office.

Cleveland was described as a drunken saloon lounger and the epitome of immorality. A bachelor, he was accused of fathering the illegitimate child of a widow with whom he was known to be friendly. The situation seemed to demand more candor than courtliness, and Cleveland admitted the intimacy but denied the paternity. Few believed the denial, but there is little evidence that the image of human fallibility cost him many votes. Woman suffrage was a generation in the future.

Nevertheless, Republicans sought the puritan vote with cartoons depicting an infant labeled "one more vote for Cleveland," and torchlight paraders chanting "Ma, Ma, where's my pa? Gone to the White House, ha, ha, ha!"

Democrats deflated the Plumed Knight with their own torchlight chant, "Blaine, Blaine, James G. Blaine! The continental liar from the State of Maine!" Democratic literature made the most (and a great deal was possible) of a celebrated set of letters from a bookkeeper named Mulligan, which detailed some corrupt and otherwise improper dealings by Blaine.[8] The reformer, the

---

[7] Mark Twain, for instance, said of Greenback Party nominee Benjamin Butler, "When he smiles it is like the breaking up of a hard winter." (Butler had been the original "waver of the bloody shirt," doing so to illustrate Southern brutality in a speech in Congress.)

[8] The letters never became public; in House testimony Mulligan re-

Plumed Knight, the symbol of integrity, was thus portrayed as dishonest and a hypocrite, and with telling effect.

Here were two tainted symbols of reform and rectitude. Blaine was tarred with conflict of interest, use of his position to enrich himself and lying to defend himself. Cleveland was a confessed adulterer (albeit in a liaison between his bachelor self and a widow) and the accused progenitor of a nameless child. Which condition should disqualify a reform leader and presumed moralist? Bastardy or dastardy?

Other irrelevant and illegitimate issues intruded. Blaine, whose mother was a devout Roman Catholic, was labeled an anti-Catholic and a persecutor of the foreign-born in city areas where multitudes of Catholics and foreign-born lived.

Assiduous application of this smear by the Democrats set the stage for a fateful sneer at Catholics by one of Blaine's own partisans. The Reverend Samuel D. Burchard was, like Cleveland's father, a Presbyterian minister. Burchard was an ardent Blaine man, and on the Wednesday before Election Day he led a delegation of New York City clergymen to call on the Plumed Knight in the Fifth Avenue Hotel. Bitterness toward Rome was the Protestant pastime of the day; "ecumenism" literally had not entered the language. In Blaine's presence, Burchard rang out a malediction on Cleveland and his party, "whose antecedents are Rum, Romanism and Rebellion."

The aphorism reflected the views of many Protestants of the day, but it was uttered in a public place and in the hearing of reporters, who noted that Blaine's majestic beard did not so much as quiver at the slur on his mother's co-religionists.[9] The word spread so quickly that a repudiation by Blaine—even if one had been forthcoming—surely could not have caught up with the Burchard remark in the six days left before election. Hordes of

ferred to them and prepared to introduce them as evidence, but Blaine managed to acquire them first. He used them in his own defense, by reading excerpts out of context and chronology, persuading no one but his most unshakable adherents.

[9] Blaine told a friend later that he was stunned and angered at the remark but quickly decided that the reporters probably had not heard it, and that repudiation would only spread the story.

Democrats of Catholic faith protested—and these were the very strength of Tammany Hall, which was trying to throw the election to Republican Blaine because of Cleveland's long and potent opposition to the corrupt New York City Democratic organization.

The Catholic defections were enough to give Cleveland a New York State plurality of one-tenth of one per cent—a 1,149 vote margin in a total vote of 1,125,000. If even 575 Catholic votes for Blaine were switched by the Reverend Mr. Burchard's slur on Romanism—and that is virtually certain—the remark cost Blaine the Presidency of the United States. For New York's 36 electoral votes gave Cleveland a tally of 219 to 182 in the Electoral College. If Cleveland had lost the New York delegation, he would have lost the White House, 183 to 218.

Another New York governor, the flamboyant Theodore Roosevelt, became President in 1901 when William McKinley was assassinated just six months after he and Vice President Roosevelt had been inaugurated.

As T.R.'s inherited term in the White House ended in 1904, American business was beginning to view the Rough Rider with distaste. But although he was nominated and elected easily in 1904, in the campaign and afterward he was vilified extensively. He was described as ruthless, cowardly, a bluff, a braggart, a trigger-happy maniac, a traitor to his class, the enemy of business and of freedom, obsequious to Negroes and arrogant to well-born whites. Mark Twain even sought to deflate Teddy's vaunted stature as a rugged outdoorsman. In a venomous sketch, he drew in acid "overwhelming circumstantial evidence" that a bear the President had shot was really a dairy cow standing mute in a clearing, tears streaming down her kind, bovine face. Others depicted Roosevelt as smearing the Constitution, the Court, and his own office with mud. He was cartooned as a militarist, as a windbag, and, presumably because of his liberal attitude toward other ethnic groups, as a standard caricature of a Jewish merchant.

On the night he was elected, Teddy had declared he would

not run again. In 1908 he was as good as his word, and William Howard Taft won the Republican nomination, and beat the Democrats' William Jennings Bryan by more than a million votes. In the campaign, Taft, a Unitarian, came in for some backhanded jibes about his religion, which was not sufficiently orthodox for many of puritanical tastes.

Four years later Woodrow Wilson was seen as too much the Puritan and was taunted as a visionary and an intellectual snob. In his campaign for a second term in 1916 ("He Kept Us Out Of War!") he was caricatured as spineless by the hard-nosed press, despised as pro-British by Irish-Americans, and hated as anti-German by German-Americans.

In a campaign with a variety of vicious aspects, Wilson's allies stamped the germanophile label indelibly on Republican nominee Charles Evans Hughes. This Justice of the United States Supreme Court was cartooned in an uhlan helmet so often that his visage with its parted beard became confused in many minds with that of Kaiser Wilhelm.

Indeed, Hughes and his running mate were forced to certify to their loyalty to the United States again and again. Great banners carried humiliating but necessary rebuttals: "Absolute and Unqualified Loyalty to Our Country—Hughes and Fairbanks!"

The 1916 election was so close that Hughes joined that small company of men who have gone to bed President-elect and awakened defeated candidate. Overnight the California vote piled up a margin of 3,000 for Wilson and pushed his Electoral College tally into the win column.

Wartime persecution of German-Americans ignited a slow, smoldering fire of resentments and hostilities in the middle west that would flame up as political complications in future decades. Prohibition, given its final push by war-related needs to preserve grain, and to punish brewers with German names, offered organized crime its historic breakthrough, creating underground problems of political influence and social impact that have yet to be plumbed. Then, under the comforting banner of normalcy, Harding succumbed to manipulators, Coolidge marked time, and

Hoover, sensitive and able, tried vainly to harness the young science of economics in time to stave off chaos. The American political system was ready for one of those watersheds of history, after which human affairs can never again be the same.

The first casualty was Herbert Clark Hoover, Iowa boy, self-made man, engineer, humanitarian, war relief administrator, patriot, Quaker, Cabinet member and 31st President of the United States. Trapped by problems for which there was no solution in human experience, he was politically destroyed in the campaign of 1932, when the Democrats made his name a synonym for depression, misery, and blind reaction.

Indeed, political smear in the 1932 campaign was largely defamation of Hoover as callous, indifferent, heedlessly helpless against the ravages of the great Depression.

Franklin D. Roosevelt, on the other hand, offered the nation an alternative to ruin, from a base of manifestly conservative, even aristocratic, breeding and bearing. Somehow his proposals to adjust production to consumption did not, during the campaign, seem redolent of socialism, partly no doubt because he, like Hoover, was opposed by a Socialist slate and a Communist one. His magnificent voice and magnificent assurance offered some hope and confidence to the wealthy and to the poor.

The poor rallied to him, but many of the wealthy remained chary. Some opposition to Roosevelt crystallized around Hoover's denunciation of the radicalism of the New Deal proposals, but the incumbent was tardy with ringing phrases. Not until a week and a day before the election did Hoover say: "The grass will grow in the streets of a hundred cities, a thousand towns; the weeds will overrun the fields of a million farms."

Roosevelt's determination to seek repeal of the Prohibition amendment also generated some antagonism, but he swamped Hoover, carrying all but six states. His inaugural address allayed the lingering dread of the wealthy, but only temporarily. David Cushman Coyle, in *Ordeal of the Presidency*,[10] vividly recounts the situation.

[10] P. 345.

"Behind the intense hatred of the wealthy was the memory of their deadly fear in early 1933, when every god in their Olympus had failed them, and they saw ruin, perhaps bloody revolution, staring them in the face. In those despairing weeks before Inauguration Day bars of gold were lugged on board at least one yacht in Newport Harbor in the hope that, come the Revolution, the family might escape and find, somewhere in the South Seas, a haven where gold would still buy food and safety. Then came March 4 and the magnificent Roosevelt radio voice assured the nation that it had nothing to fear but fear; and many of the shaken souls looked up in admiration and gratitude to their brave rescuer—a man of their own class, too.

"Once the terrified ones were rescued, however, and found that their savior had scant respect for their old gods, and even thought they should pay increased taxes on their reviving incomes, the memory of their tearful relief and adoration on Inauguration Day turned to gall. They had been fooled—worse still, had fooled themselves. That they could not forgive. To be stripped of self-confidence was a shattering blow, and the natural reaction was anger. Roosevelt was in the line of fire—the more so because, with all his mistakes, he was not so comprehensively wrong as they had been."

By 1936 Roosevelt was the enemy of the people—the people of privilege and myopia. The Republicans named Alf M. Landon of Kansas to topple the new monarch. Prominent alienated Democrats supported Landon, including Al Smith and John W. Davis, victims of the Republicans in the Presidential campaigns of 1928 and 1924 respectively. The 1936 campaign moved Alexander Woollcott to write: "I think if I'd been lost like Stefansson [the Arctic explorer] for several years and returning had heard only the arguments against Mr. Roosevelt, I should have decided, on the strength of them alone, to vote for him. I had heard the same arguments before—the same words from the same people. Then they were launched against Theodore Roosevelt and later against Woodrow Wilson. The last time they were triumphant they ushered in normalcy and Warren Harding."

Landon started out on a high plane. Many of his advisors and spokesmen left it quickly. By September it was becoming fashionable to call Roosevelt a Communist, among other epithets. And as defeat loomed more surely for the Kansan he grew weary and shrill.

Landon carried Maine and Vermont. In those days, Maine was counted a bellwether state, since it voted—usually "right"—in September, the rest of the nation in November. "As Maine goes, so goes the nation," went the political tradition of the time. James A. Farley, then Democratic national chairman, did the legend in: "As Maine goes, so goes Vermont."

Although Republican U. S. Grant had sought nomination for a third term in 1880, when it became apparent in 1940 that Franklin Roosevelt might do the same thing Republicans were horrified at this callous departure from the principle of Washington. Some Democrats shared the concern, notably Jim Farley, who on this issue parted company with the man he had done so much to elect.

It is not easy to review the Roosevelt years for election campaign attacks on the President, because the slurs of passionate Roosevelt-haters went on year in and year out, and year-round. Roosevelt saw early supporters turn to implacable enemies; witness Father Coughlin in 1932 (Roosevelt or Ruin) and in 1936 (Roosevelt was anti-God, a liar). He saw opposition harden into fanaticism. Slurs about cynicism gave way to accusations of bolshevism; experiment where tradition had failed was seen as fiendish surgery on all that was fine in the economy and the nation.

He also saw fanaticism among his supporters, particularly in the 1940 campaign. To be sure, there was some light-hearted and deft harpooning, too. The irrepressible Harold Ickes, whose occupational disease was said to be hyperbole, deflated Wendell Willkie's homespun image by describing him as the barefoot boy from Wall Street. But more obscure and less responsible Roosevelt partisans made Willkie out as pro-German, and some even called him a Nazi, on the eve of American involvement in World War II.

In the mid-1930's Hitler had explored the possibility of intruding into American domestic politics, and by the close of the decade his regime was financing the German-American Bund and related activities. These augmented the discords sounded by native fascist types, such as William Dudley Pelley and his Silvershirts, the Reverend Gerald B. Winrod and his Defenders of the Christian Faith, and a variety of others. Some of these were longtime anti-Semites; others found it an easy jump from white to Nordic supremacy. Third Reich philosophies echoed in the 1940 campaign. Roosevelt was constantly portrayed as a Jew, as Willkie was occasionally. Both were members of the "International Jewish Conspiracy" seen at every hand by paranoids of that day, as of this. Some anti-Semites described the President as Franklin Rosenfeld, President of the Jewnited States, and former Governor of Jew York. The Roosevelt slanders sickened the Republican nominee. When he was offered the endorsement of Father Coughlin, by now a high priest of the hate-Roosevelt sect, Willkie rebuffed the anti-Semite in what was and remains the classic repudiation of unsought vicious support. "I have no place in my philosophy for such beliefs," he declared. "I don't have to be President of the United States, but I do have to make my beliefs clear . . . to live with myself. I am not interested in being President of the United States to compromise with my fundamental beliefs."

In 1944 Willkie was dead and the GOP nominee was New York's Thomas E. Dewey. Smears of the kind Willkie had repudiated (but could not stop) resumed—or continued. At the Democratic Convention Roosevelt had been quoted as telling a questioner, "Clear it with Sidney [Hillman, a labor leader and a Jew]."

The quotation spread like a blob of mercury on a linoleum floor, and was as impossible to contain. It was recited more often than not with a leer and a wink and a fancied Jewish accent. In a multiple guilt-by-association ploy, some Republicans circulated cards reading, "Browder, Hillman and the Communists will vote. Will you?"

Other literature identified Roosevelt with Brutus and Benedict Arnold, and the first of a hardy series of leaflets identifying the Democratic Party with war began to appear; the art work accompanying the text invariably pictured either flag-draped coffins or battlefield death scenes.

The 1944 campaign was the setting for at least one perfect squelch. Roosevelt was beset by whispered and printed criticisms that he had diverted a Navy ship to bring home his Scotty dog, Fala, left behind on a Presidential trip to Alaska. Early in the campaign the President undertook to lay the matter to rest, and into the bargain, to goad Dewey into losing his temper. "The Republican leaders have not been content to make personal attacks upon me, or my wife, or my sons," he told a cheering audience. "They now include my little dog, Fala. [The Roosevelt voice went into a taunting sing-song here.] Unlike members of my family, Fala resents this . . . I am accustomed to hearing malicious falsehoods about myself, but I think I have a right to object to libelous statements about my dog."

Ickes kept up the pressure on Dewey, impaling him with the barbed epithet, "the little man on the wedding cake." The reference to Dewey's physical stature was of course no more fair or relevant than anti-Roosevelt jibes and speculations about the degree to which the President was crippled.

When Roosevelt died the calumnies continued. The 80th Congress was elected in November of 1946. It was the first to be controlled by the Republicans since the Hoover Administration. It organized in January of 1947 and by March, before the second anniversary of Roosevelt's death, it managed to pay its disrespect to the memory of the late President by starting on its way the Twenty-Second Amendment to the Constitution, limiting any future President to two elected terms.[11]

At the same time, the 80th Congress also changed the succession law to interpose two *elected* officials, the Speaker of the House and the President Pro Tempore of the Senate, ahead of the Secretary of State in Presidential succession. Thus was it possible

[11] The amendment became law with ratification by the 36th state in 1951.

to legislate after death what the Roosevelt haters could not accomplish before: never again could a Roosevelt usurp a third or fourth term; and two human lives now stood between the elected Vice President and the Cabinet members of any future Roosevelt.

At the time of Roosevelt's death, seeds that had been planted since the Civil War were stirring beneath the surface, and would shortly break through as troublesome political weeds. Among these was the growing unrest of Negroes, whose lot in the South had not improved appreciably since the end of the Reconstruction era. Another was the second-class citizenship that had been imposed on Americans of German extraction in the First World War.

A third was the impetus that Hitler-era anti-Semitic propaganda had given to American haters of the Jew. In nineteenth-century America, German Jews, for example, were discriminated against as Germans and aliens more than as Jews. In 50 years centered on 1900, vast migrations of Jewish people from eastern Europe had brought in eight times as many Jews as the immigration of the preceding hundred years. On top of this flood, refugees from the Nazis had poured into the United States. The haters now had something to work on. It is hard for an American born since 1900 to realize that rabid, militant American anti-Semitism grew up with him: it is a child of the enlightened twentieth century.

More recently, infiltration by Communists into government posts in the New Deal and the war years had gone partly unnoticed and partly unchecked. These factors, coupled with social and economic dislocations, and with the ubiquity of radio and the imminence of television and the tape recorder, would change the face of American politics.

This was the background against which Harry S. Truman took the oath of office on April 12, 1945.

At the end of his second year in the White House, Truman promulgated an executive order providing for investigation of the loyalty of Federal employees in the executive branch. Implementation of the order got under way in August of 1947 with a loyalty check, aimed at the discovery and removal of disloyal and subversive employees. This guaranteed for Truman the ardent hostility of the Communists and fellow-travelers.

When the President announced that he would seek election in his own right, the left wing enmity began to take shape in a front operation under the name of the Progressive Party. Henry Wallace, a pro-Hoover Republican who had been Roosevelt's first Secretary of Agriculture and was Truman's predecessor as Vice President, was beguiled and maneuvered into running for President on the Progressive ticket.

Meanwhile, militant Southerners rebelled at the strong civil rights plank in the Democratic platform of 1948 and walked out of the convention to set up their own States Rights Party. The Dixiecrats, as they were quickly dubbed, named Senator Strom Thurmond of South Carolina to run against Truman.[12]

The Republicans, for the second time, nominated Thomas E. Dewey of New York. So Truman entered the campaign facing a tough Republican, who had held Franklin D. Roosevelt to the narrowest victory of his career,[13] as well as challengers from the right and left wings of his own party.

The contest between Truman and Dewey was innocent of the deep malice that characterized the attacks on Truman and his administration from the Wallace and Thurmond camps. The major candidates were well-matched in hyperbole and invective and pithiness of speech. They offered a bitter, old-style, give-em-hell campaign that made diverting, often exciting, listening and reading. Neither suffered from the sterility of speech and barrenness of image that sap the fun of electioneering. Neither leveled at the other serious, unsupported charges carefully calculated to destroy a public character.

When the polls closed, Thurmond and Wallace had cut away from the President's total more than two million votes, cast by the

---

[12] Thurmond proved to be a slow-change political chameleon who sixteen years later was finally to abandon the ante-bellum states' rights party, the Democrats, in favor of the mid-Twentieth Century one of the Goldwater Republicans.

[13] Dewey won 46.2 per cent of the two-party vote in 1944.

bigots and the babes-in-the-woods of the unlikely coalition that Truman had inherited from Roosevelt.[14]

The one group that kept its eye on the ball, the uncommitted voters, pondered records and facts. Truman won less than half of the total vote, but he beat Dewey with a plurality of more than two million, and got a clear electoral majority of 309 to 189 for Dewey.[15] He won the White House on his own, and, minority President though he was, if Roosevelt and Landon had not killed off the *Literary Digest* [16] in 1936, Truman and Dewey would have done it in 1948, because almost every expert in the land except Harry Truman knew he was doomed.[17]

When Truman was elected, the nation had conducted 41 Presidential elections in 160 years. Only six of these campaigns had been spectacularly dirty: Jackson's first election, Lincoln's second, the Hayes-Tilden debacle, and Cleveland's first election; and in the twentieth century, Roosevelt's third campaign and the Hoover-Smith clash of 1928. The latter will be examined in the next chapter in comparison with the Kennedy-Nixon campaign of 1960. Six other campaigns—Jefferson's two elections, the Wilson-Hughes contest of 1916, and the first, second and fourth Roosevelt campaigns—contained substantial elements of viciousness and unfairness, but do not qualify as real mud baths. The record to this point in history was not bad.

However, a new and malevolent era was about to begin,

[14] Wallace polled 1,157,000 votes but won no electors; Thurmond, with his localized appeal, won only 22,000 more votes but garnered 39 electors—from Alabama, Louisiana, Mississippi and South Carolina, plus one maverick from Tennessee.

[15] Truman won 48.2 per cent of the total vote. There were eight candidates, four of them minor ones who together polled fewer than 300,000 votes. Truman won 49.7 per cent of the Truman-Dewey-Wallace-Thurmond vote and 52.2 per cent of the Truman-Dewey vote.

[16] Which succumbed after its vaunted poll showed Landon the sure winner.

[17] A "post-election special" issue of *U.S. News & World Report* headlined "What President Dewey Will Do." It appeared on newsstands late election night, while Dewey's headquarters in New York's Roosevelt Hotel wondered what was holding up the farm vote that would put him in.

ushering with it a different kind of attack on distinguished American leaders. Now, on a wholesale basis, election campaigns would echo with shrill and frenzied denunciation of Presidents and candidates for President on charges of conspiring to overthrow, or undermine, the United States. Treason would be a constant campaign issue, and citizens would question the loyalty of Presidents.

CHAPTER 2

The Loyalty
of Presidents

BY THE summer of 1948, former Communist agents had been testifying about espionage, and coincident with the election campaign the House Committee on Un-American Activities had been pursuing a sensational investigation. Whittaker Chambers had charged that Alger Hiss, long a highly-placed government functionary, had been his associate in a Communist spy ring. The House Committee had been reluctant to dig far into the matter because of Hiss's persuasive manner and impeccable references. Finally it did so, but only because of the persistence of a freshman Congressman from California named Richard Milhous Nixon. A month after the 1948 election, Hiss was indicted on perjury counts arising from the investigation. A year later, after a first trial ended in a hung jury, he was convicted. Another former government employee, Judith Coplon, and a Soviet diplomatic aide, Valentin Gubichev, were brought to trial on attempted espionage charges.

Then, early in 1950, a lackluster first term Senator from Wisconsin, Joseph R. McCarthy, who had been groping for an issue around which to build his 1952 campaign for re-election, settled on the issue of Communists in government. In February he delivered his famous "card-carrying Communists in the State Department" speech in Wheeling, West Virginia.

There had been carelessness in the Roosevelt administration about Communist infiltration and influence. The leftist intellectual ferment in the nation's campuses and organizations of social concern had permeated, to some degree, most of the people whose education, training, and conviction made them possible administrators of the great social and economic experiments of the New Deal. It was inevitable that *some* Communists and more fellow-travelers would slip, fall, or bring one another into positions of some political importance in the 1930's. Others infiltrated the government during the wartime alliance with Stalin.

Now the Wisconsin senator and his supporters saw Communists behind every tree. The cold light of retrospect has demonstrated that some of McCarthy's targets *were* Communists and that a number of others *must* have been. McCarthy, however, never proved such guilt against even one of the people he attacked. Those who did come to trial were found by more responsible agencies, operating with all the frustrating restraints for the investigator posed by our Constitution and system of jurisprudence in order to protect all of us. By any reasonable test—including the Constitution and that radical, revolutionary, subversive, democratic manifesto, the Declaration of Independence—McCarthyism ruined innocent careers and lives in a flailing and virtually indiscriminate hunt for the guilty.

Hordes of Americans rallied to McCarthy's spy hunt. Among them were white Anglo-Saxon Protestants whose old American names were waning in power and influence. There were children of immigrants, whose war service and rising economic power had not assuaged their thirst for status. Irish-Americans, so long contributors to the society yet still denied full equality, rallied to the Wisconsin Senator, one of their own. German-Americans, whose parents and grandparents had been humiliated and harassed by their neighbors in two world wars, rallied to McCarthy now as they had to Old Bob LaFollette in opposition to American entry into the wars and the League of Nations. Fundamentalist Catholics and fundamentalist Protestants, as Richard Hofstadter has noted, "subordinated their old feuds (and for the first time in our history) to unite in opposition to what they usually described as 'godless' elements."[1]

So the audience was ready for McCarthy, and the Wisconsin Senator, who had virtually stumbled on the Communists-in-government issue, was ready for it.

He was a demagogue of the second water, able to summon passion and outrage in his hearers, and grateful and dedicated loyalty in his adherents. He lacked the long-range view and focus that might have made him dangerous for a longer period. He rode the opportunities of the moment. In the light of his initial unconcern with the problem, no one is likely to have been more surprised than he at the depth and genuineness of the cause for concern, or at the political pay-off waiting for him in what really was a quite superficial exploration of the subject.

It is said that McCarthy awakened America to the problem of Communists in government, and in a sense he did. He rallied to a political banner a rag, tag and bob-tail of fundamentally apolitical citizens, and provided a prophetic voice, of sorts, for a sprinkling of disenchanted intellectuals, and a heroes' forum for an assortment of gumshoes and former Communists. But his essential lack of scrupulousness—in investigative method, in often uncritical reliance on circumstantial evidence, in accepting guilt by association and simple accusation, in disrespect for due process of law—perverted the awakening into a nightmare.

In the Republican National Convention of 1952, McCarthy played only a minor role. The choice of most of his followers, Robert A. Taft, was rejected. The Republicans needed a popular hero to lead their crusade against "the mess in Washington," and nominated General of the Army Dwight D. Eisenhower. After five successive Democratic administrations, he could not have been beaten. People liked Ike, including Democrats, anti-McCarthy Republicans and others who could not begin to stom-

---

[1] "The Pseudo-Conservative Revolt—1955," in *The Radical Right*, ed. Daniel Bell (New York: Doubleday, 1963), p. 80, note 8.

ach some of the General's fellow-partisans. Many reactionary Republicans who could not tolerate Ike, including some who were later to think and talk of him as a Communist dupe or agent, flocked to his banner simply because they were lusting for power after two decades of what threatened to become permanent minority status.

Much of the campaign was surprisingly bland. Television had become a major factor in politics and the Republicans dominated it with spot announcements. The brains that fashioned banalities to sell cereals to Mom through the kiddies now fashioned banalities to sell the Crusade to Mom through all her better instincts, if not through her intellect. The television commercial aspect of the campaign was dull simply because the output of the ad agencies was pitched to so common a denominator.

The visceral component of the Republican campaign appeared early as anti-intellectual opposition developed to the "egghead," Adlai Stevenson. Communism quickly became an issue, helped along by Joe McCarthy, who in one radio-TV address made a grinning reference to "Alger—I mean Adlai." Homosexuality became an underground issue, too, as eager anti-intellectuals snickered at the Illinois governor's elegance of phrase and courtliness of manner, seeing those qualities as a sure indicator of effeminacy.

It is ironic that in a widely discussed book of the year 1952, *Witness*, Whittaker Chambers, the nation's most celebrated recanted spy, noted that derision of intellectualism and imputation of homosexuality were two of the favorite defamatory techniques among Communists in factional battles during his early years with the Party.

The Democrats met the anti-intellectual outbursts head-on, and loudly bemoaned the lowbrow caliber of the Republican TV spot announcements. Initiating what was to become a national pastime for eight years, they fought back by ridiculing Eisenhower's lapses in syntax. They also were unrelenting in exploiting the more grossly over-simplified of the General's arguments. One which received particular attention went, "Every time you eat a boiled egg, unless you raise it yourself, you pay 100 taxes on that egg. One hundred taxes and then we wonder where the prices come from." The Democrats riposted that this was the saga of "The Egg and Ike," whereupon the Republican candidate simply played back the original homily and presumably won more votes. The Democrats may have been making the unpardonable political blunder of baptising the already-baptised, for apparently nobody was listening to them but the intellectuals. The Democrats even compiled an "Ike-lopedia" of nearly 600 pages, cross-indexing the General's utterances on every subject from "*Acheson, Dean* [see also *Secretary of State*]" to "*Yugoslavia.*"

Many Democratic partisans engaged in two largely spontaneous whispering campaigns, passing along the word that Mamie Eisenhower was a drunkard and that the General himself was a bit of a lad with the ladies. No effort was made to persuade anyone that these allegations, if true, were relevant to the office of the Presidency; the thrust was simply to deflate the General, to suggest that he was tainted and therefore scarcely qualified to lead a crusade. This line of attack, of course, was made inevitable by the Republican decision to label the campaign a crusade.

The Republicans, running one of the major military heroes of the era and of the whole world, accused the Democrats of being the war party, and trotted out the old anti-Roosevelt war-death statistics, updated with casualties from the Korean War.

When Eisenhower was chosen by the Republicans, Adlai Stevenson is said to have thought perhaps the General ought to win. But Stevenson warmed to the campaign, and made an impact on American politics that deserves the gratitude of coming generations. Two contributions that were largely overlooked in the eulogies attendant upon his death in 1965 were of the greatest significance. By the time of his death his rhetoric had come to be taken for granted; by this time also, the eloquent speeches of John Kennedy had been heard in the land. But Stevenson brought to American politics for the first time in recent history political argument that was not only brilliant and polished, like Wilson's; confident and persuasive, like Franklin Roosevelt's; but also lucid and moving, superbly written and beautifully cadenced. Here was a tongue that made the celebrated orators of American politics look vulgar and florid.

The second forgotten contribution was the remarkable effect Stevenson had upon the intellectual community in America. Democrats, and many Republicans, were moved not just to admiration, not just to support, but to political involvement and action because of Stevenson's logic and wit. "Volunteers for Stevenson" was more than a name; it was a fact of political 1952. Much of the Republican effort in that year was to persuade Americans who had abandoned faith in politicians to turn the rascals out in favor of a politically unsullied military leader. Yet much of the intellectual community was to rally to Stevenson and, more important, to work mundanely and argue passionately and immerse themselves in politics. Kennedy in 1960 did much the same thing, but the trail was blazed by Adlai Ewing Stevenson in a campaign only gallant men and fools believed he could win.

As is so often the case, the dirtiest campaigning in 1952 came from levels beneath the major candidates. The Communist issue was the most irritating to the Democrats, and the hardest to handle, partly because of the way it was presented and partly because of the facts that enabled it to be an issue. The campaign of the Republicans was keyed to the "where there's smoke, there's fire" approach. There was abundant smoke, in the form of accusations and implications and some facts. The McCarthy mania was at its crest. The Wisconsin Senator referred to "twenty years of treason," and the Republican Vice Presidential candidate, Richard M. Nixon, spoke of Truman, Stevenson, and Acheson as "traitors to the high principles" of the Democratic Party. To fancy that the phrase would be remembered intact, "high principles," Democratic Party and all, was naive, and to use it knowing it would be forgotten, with only "traitors" ringing in the memory, was dishonest.

The issue swelled and festered, apparently largely escaping the notice of the Republican candidate, whose respected friend and onetime patron, General George C. Marshall, was among the prominent victims of McCarthyism.[2] When Eisenhower deleted a defense of General Marshall from a campaign speech in Wisconsin, Republicans were dismayed. Not enough, however, to affect the predestined result. Eisenhower swamped Stevenson.

The 1956 election offered a replay of 1952, both as to principal candidates and Stevenson's chances. This time, of course, the Republicans could not work over the old "time for a change" material, and, by virtue of a small but growing assortment of Republican peccadilloes, they were unable to rerun Harry Truman's cronies and their freezers and mink coats. The resignation under fire of the administration's Secretary of the Air Force had taken the shine off Republican exploitation of the Democratic conflict-of-interest didoes of the Truman era.

The censure of McCarthy by the Senate at the end of 1954, and Eisenhower's incumbency, helped slow the pace of GOP exploitation of the Communist issue. Basking in the Korean armistice of 1953 and Eisenhower's unparalleled image as a warrior/man of peace, the Women's Division of the Republican National Committee did get considerable mileage out of the familiar war/death-toll dodge, counting casualties in all the "Democratic Wars," including Korea, and illustrating the point with rows of crosses on reams of flyers.

Democrats gleefully twisted 1952 Republican slogans dealing with the Mess in Washington and began to emulate the Republicans in their deft employment of advertising agencies and television techniques. Local enterprise went farther: in one Michigan area a handbill purporting to be a news flash was stuffed in mail boxes on election eve. It announced Eisenhower's death.

Republicans, particularly women, made much of Stevenson's recent divorce. In fact, one lady candidate for Congress from Florida, Mrs. Dorothy Smith, took oblique notice of the divorce in a seconding speech for Vice President Nixon. In delicately vicious tones, she spoke of candidates who "exemplify the highest

[2] The John Birch Society was half a dozen years ahead, and its leader, Robert Welch, had not yet envisioned Eisenhower as Marshall's Communist colleague, taking orders from the General's brother Milton.

in family relationships." "We know," she purred, "that a man who is devoted to the welfare and happiness of his wife and children will also protect the well-being of our children. We know that a happy and devoted family working together for the best interests of all members of the family is the best possible asset for a strong and prosperous America."

On the whole, smear at the Presidential level was modest in 1956. The year's crises were substantial, and magnificently timed for the Republicans. Hardly had Stevenson been re-nominated when Nasser seized the Suez Canal. The Hungarian revolt began two weeks before Election Day and was crushed two days before the polls opened. Eight days before the election, Israel invaded Egypt's Sinai Peninsula; the French and British demanded a cease-fire and when Egypt did not comply they landed troops on Sinai over a 48-hour period ending about the time the polls closed in the United States. Under circumstances like these, who needed a campaign? Certainly not Eisenhower, whom the voters returned in a near-landslide of 57.8 per cent of the two-party vote, compared with his 55.4 per cent of 1952.

Although by the end of the Eisenhower era an emerging radical right was beginning to question even the loyalty of the General-turned-President, a different test of loyalty dominated the consideration of a successor: Could a Roman Catholic run for President, and be elected or defeated on the basis of ability, not faith? Would a Catholic in the White House give his first loyalty to the Constitution, instead of the Vatican?

The questions had been asked once before, in 1928. The answer then was a thundering no.

When Alfred Emanuel Smith, New York's brilliant and humane Democratic governor, sought to defeat Herbert C. Hoover for the Presidency in 1928, Smith's Roman Catholicism was not the only cause of his defeat, although it remains the most celebrated.

A campaign question swept women's clubs: "My dear, can you imagine a President named Al?" Al was a pushy newcomer, an Irishman in the days when the epithet "donkey" was still heard in the middle west to describe the Irish railroad laborers of a generation before. When Al Smith's nasal, East Side New York voice bit out the word "raddio," patricians, Yankees, English-extracted middle westerners, Daughters and Sons of the American Revolution, and assorted snobs winced violently.

After a long wrangle, the framers of the Democratic platform had agreed that Prohibition was to be enforced; Al Smith had suggested instead that the law should be repealed. The slogan so inopportunely and vainly raised against Cleveland in 1884—Rum, Romanism and Rebellion—was revived among Americans who had learned to live with Prohibition and bootleggers. The *Demon Rum, Ten Nights in a Barroom, The Face on the Barroom Floor,* these were the images Al Smith conjured up among self-conscious, self-righteous Americans.

So much for Rum: now where did America stand on Romanism? "Members of the Romanish religion" were denied civil rights by all the early colonies except Maryland. It was not until 1876, when New Hampshire repealed a provision that its governor must be a Protestant, that the last civil disability of Catholics fell away legally.

As early as 1830, nativists were becoming alarmed at the influx of Irish, which did not reach its peak until after the Potato Famine of 1846. Samuel F. B. Morse, the inventor and painter, was an early and rabid Catholic-baiter. The story goes that Morse, on a visit to Rome, was watching a Papal procession. When he did not remove his hat, a Papal guard knocked it off. When Morse came home, he began fulminating, not against one lout in the Swiss Guard, but against the Pope and the whole infernal system.

Morse's hysteria, and that of other bigots, caught on, and soon an aroused population of anti-Catholics was ready for action. Inflammatory stories circulated about sinful and evil goings-on in nunneries. A Boston mob burned a local convent to the ground. Morse's rabid essays were published as "Foreign Conspiracy Against the Liberties of the United States." In 1836 a horror story of convent orgies and brutalities came from a demented Canadian girl named Maria Monk. Her "Awful Disclosures" [3] purported to be the autobiography of a nun, which Maria never was. However, aided by fervid Yankee divines, Maria, clad demurely in a nun's habit, made the most of her notoriety on the lecture circuit. All these activities metamorphosed into the Native American Party, whose platform offered a solution: increase the residency requirements for naturalization to 21 years.

Rampant anti-Catholicism found expression in school books which were outrageously and specifically anti-Catholic. Catholic children in the public schools of the Protestant Land of the Free had to recite Protestant prayers, sing Protestant hymns, and read the Protestant Bible. The Catholics introduced parochial schools, and sought relief from some of the taxes they continued to pay after their children had left the public schools. The proposal was rejected.

In 1844 nativist sentiment caused the formation of the American Republican Party, which ran Henry Clay as its candidate. His ensuing defeat was laid to "abolitionists and foreign Catholics." The party gave way to a secret order whose members were pledged to respond to questions about the order by saying, "I know nothing about it." Thus the "Grand Council of the Supreme Star Spangled Banner" passed into history as the Know-Nothings. By 1855 the Know-Nothings were riding the crest of a nationwide orgy of Catholic-hating. Their governors sat in seven states; their men controlled five state legislatures; their members and allies made up one-third of the Congress.

The madness began to pass as soon as the excesses became ludicrous, as when the Massachusetts legislature created a Nunnery Committee to ferret out of church and convent cellars the hidden arms cached there to arm the underground for the Pope's invasion. The Grand Council could not bear the weight of such fatuity; within a year the organization was dead, but the bigotry that had motivated it was not.

[3] Her book is still in print, an awful monument to the marriage of virtue and prurience.

In 1915, when the Ku Klux Klan was being revived, Georgia's Tom Watson found a happy combination of explosive issues when he appealed to the white Southerners' rape complex and anti-Catholicism with this plea: "Heavens above! Think of a Negro priest taking the vow of chastity and then being turned loose among women who have been taught that a priest cannot sin. It is a thing to make one shudder!"

Klan influence was substantial in the south, the midwest, and in the mountain and northwestern states. In Oregon the Klan managed to get through the legislature a law requiring all children to go to public schools. It succeeded in softening a denunciation of the Klan in the Democratic Platform of 1924 and helped beat back Al Smith's effort at that year's nomination. Its power reached a short-lived peak in 1925. In August of that year, 35,000 hooded and sheeted (but unmasked) Klansmen staged a march on Washington to demonstrate their potency. At the Washington Monument they stood reverently in the stifling heat and invoked God and General Washington. It began to drizzle as the host Kleagle, of the District of Columbia, addressed the multitude. The multitude began to dwindle. The Kleagle urged the Almighty not to let it rain, and the multitude to have faith. It rained harder and the multitude dwindled to a throng. The Kleagle turned the praying over to a specialist, a minister from Ohio. It rained harder. The clergyman bade the white-robed crowd, now flapping wetly in the gathering storm, to kneel. He prayed harder: "Oh God, I pray that the remainder of this service will be conducted without rain." The storm became a downpour. The exodus of the Klan continued, stragglers gathering up their sheets and fleeing like schoolgirls before a summer shower. An estimated thousand remained, sinking slowly into the turf as the heavens continued to pour down rain.

The rout was prophetic. The Ku Klux Klan was never the same again. Factionalism and occasional embezzlement within the Klan, plus growing resentment, criticism, and ridicule from the outside sped its dissolution. But before it gave up the ghost the Klan mustered its waning strength in 1928 for a massive effort to save the nation from Al Smith.

Klansmen swelled the pre-convention chorus of whispers against the Romanist candidate. Their journals, the *Kourier* and the *New Menace*, printed exposés and denunciations of Papal plots and Smith's fealty to Rome. They burned crosses and hanged Smith in effigy. They printed anti-Catholic tracts and circulated the output of other bigoted groups.

The Klan helped significantly to swell the distribution of one sensational forged document, the so-called "Knights of Columbus Oath." The piece had originally been created by an anonymous nineteenth-century author to attack the Jesuits. It purported to be a secret oath that priests of that order had to take. It pledged them to persecute Protestants in every imaginable way, to flay, lay waste, spoil, burn, poison, and so on.

At some point the ascription of the oath was shifted from the clerical order of the Jesuits to the lay Catholic order of the Knights of Columbus, and in 1912 a Pennsylvania Catholic who was a candidate for Congress found the spurious oath peddled widely in the campaign against him. A House of Representatives election committee investigated the campaign and exposed the vicious falsity of the "Oath." The "Oath" itself was reprinted and denounced in its entirety in the *Congressional Record* for February 15, 1913.

In 1928 Klansmen and other loyal white Anglo-Saxon Protestants dug the "Oath" out of the 1913 *Congressional Record,* citing its appearance there as proof of its veracity.

Bigotry was not confined to the Klan, nor were all of its expressions as crude as most. A joke, to be heard again in 1960, described a one-word cable Smith would send to the Pope after he lost the election: "Unpack."

Newspaper cartoons, speeches, leaflets, whispering and letter-writing campaigns, every device known to bigots and politicians, deluged the country to brand Al Smith the agent of Rome. The gullible were shown news photographs of work begun a year earlier on the Holland Tunnel under the Hudson River. This, they were assured, was the start of a tunnel to the Vatican that the New York governor had ordered.

Smith's selection of John J. Raskob, the head of General Motors and a leading Catholic layman, as chairman of the Democratic National Committee confirmed for the suspicious the candidate's determination to surrender to Rome. And the anti-Catholics left Al Smith no opportunity to deny any such determination. Preachers exhorted their parishioners about the danger from Rome, and often instructed them quite explicitly on how to vote. Much was made of what frightened Protestants saw as Catholic sanction of lies in the long-range interests of the Church. "What is a lie to the Vatican if it takes a lie to win?" The bigots possessed revealed truth.

Protestants innocent of bigotry were less certain, but most of them were also innocent of any knowledge of Catholic faith and practice. If they were not certain of Al Smith's potential disloyalty to the nation, they were not certain of his loyalty, either.

Women had had the franchise for eight years now, and good Protestant ladies turned out with a will to save the nation from the Vatican. Mabel Walker Willebrandt, Assistant Attorney General of the United States, went back and forth across the land speaking against Smith, including a plea to the Methodists to unite to keep him out of the White House.

Mrs. Willebrandt's prime concern was with the enforcement of the Volstead Act, but her excursions against Smith's Catholicism were entirely compatible. The Anti-Saloon League pulled its strongest support from fundamentalist Protestants, and these were the most apprehensive about the Democrat's religion.

Hoover won, beating Smith by six and a half-million votes.[4] Many citizens suppose that Al Smith's Catholicism was the only factor which cost him the Presidency. Of course it helped, but it

[4] Hoover beat Al Smith so badly that almost no one noticed Smith's improvement over the real Democratic debacles of 1920 and 1924. The Democrat Cox, opposing Harding in 1920, polled only 35 per cent of the two-party vote. In 1924, against Republican Coolidge and Progressive La-Follette, the Democrat Davis slumped to less than one-third—32 per cent—of the three-party vote. But Al Smith in 1928, for all the landslide of his Electoral College defeat, won back more than 39 per cent of the popular vote.

was far from the only reason for the punishing defeat that embittered him and helped turn him within a few years to a leading role in the Liberty League, that early precursor of the radical right.

The damage that anti-Catholic bigotry did in 1928 was not in defeating Al Smith but in rousing the beast in the American polity. As Smith himself had put it in a speech in 1924, "The Catholics of this country can stand [bigotry], the Jews can stand it, our citizens born under foreign skies can stand it, the Negro can stand it. But the United States of America cannot stand it."

The situation in 1960 could not have been more different from that of 1928. John Fitzgerald Kennedy was the precise image of style and grace. He was witty, handsome, beautifully educated, a splendid writer, a penetrating student of world and national affairs, and an authentic war hero. He was a campaign manager's dream of the letter-perfect candidate, with only one flaw: he was a Roman Catholic.

Thus, while bigotry had vied with snobbery, xenophonia and Prohibition for low-level attention in 1928, Catholicism stood in splendid isolation as the only obvious illegitimate issue for 1960.

In 1956 John Kennedy's aides, John Bailey and Ted Sorenson, had prepared a private memo to influence Democratic convention delegates. It pointed to Catholic voters the party had lost to Eisenhower in 1952 and suggested that only a promising Catholic—like Kennedy—on the ticket could stem further losses in 1956. Although Kennedy lost the Vice Presidential nomination narrowly to Estes Kefauver that year, the memo made more sense than ever in 1960. It was publicized repeatedly, and in 1960 worried Republicans saw its argument as an unfair switch on religious bigotry

Meanwhile, responsible and concerned Protestants, Jews, and atheists wanted answers to some questions about Catholic attitudes toward the state. The candidate had answered them repeatedly, but Protestants in particular were bothered that the huge monolith they saw as the Roman Church had never delivered an authoritative, monolithic answer, yes or no.

Catholics, they reasoned—much as their fathers had done in 1928—believe error has no right and truth has every right, and they have the truth. They believe the Church has precedence over the state. They believe the ideal state is a church-state with the church on top. What is the optimum treatment for heretics? See the Spanish Inquisition.

Here was a range of widely-held attitudes about Catholicism. Well, were they true or not? And if not, why, pray, had the Pope not answered them?

Many Protestant thinkers agonized about these questions and concluded that, however regrettable the fact that the Pope hadn't seen fit to answer them, the answer must be no. The evidence of Catholic practice in recent years was heavily on the side of a no answer. At this level the questioning was enlightened and honest and utterly without bigotry, and caused no real trouble in the 1960 campaign.

Richard Nixon merits hearty applause on this point. He was determined on, he insisted on, he would not permit any deviation from, a rigid and unexceptioned policy of leaving the religious issue out of his campaign.

On the Saturday following Kennedy's nomination at Los Angeles, as the Democratic convention was dissolving, his press chief, Pierre Salinger, asked me to brief him and his staff on the pitfalls ahead with regard to the "Catholic issue." Everyone in the room was deeply apprehensive that Nixon in fact would use every opportunity to say something like, "There is no religious issue in this campaign. It is of no importance that my opponent is a MEMBER OF THE ROMAN CATHOLIC CHURCH."

Considering, for instance, the role that a high government official, Mabel Walker Willebrandt, played in the Al Smith campaign to awaken and stir bigotry, it was small wonder that the Democrats were apprehensive. But Nixon did not stir, and would not permit his campaigners to stir, from his own resolve. First with impatience, then with irritation, then anger, Nixon rebuffed newsmen who sought to trick him into exploiting the Catholic issue. Invariably, he said simply and only, "There is no religious issue between me and my opponent."

Early in 1960, with the cooperation of the National Conference of Christians and Jews, the Fair Campaign Practices Committee brought together in Washington a distinguished group of religious leaders and laymen, Protestants, Catholics and Jews, fundamentalists and liberals, to study the "religious issue" in the campaign.

Charles P. Taft, chairman of the sponsoring Fair Campaign Practices Committee, presided, with the cooperation of NCCJ head Lewis Webster Jones. At the close of the two-day meeting, which had been planned for more than two years, Mr. Taft drew out of the discussions a brief set of principles for considering "the injection of religious issues into the 1960 campaign."

The statement condemned "stirring up, fostering or tolerating religious animosity, or injecting elements of a candidate's faith not relevant to the duties of the office he seeks." And it called for "intelligent, honest and temperate public discussion of the relation of religious faith to the public issues." [5]

The Taft proposals were widely printed in general newspapers, as well as in religious newspapers and periodicals. Without doubt, they were a substantial influence for calm and reason among thoughtful Americans.

However, millions of Americans were not disposed to be calm. They knew the history of Catholic perfidy as well as Samuel F. B. Morse or Maria Monk. They knew that Catholics had murdered Abraham Lincoln after he had warned against encroachments by the Pope. They knew that a Catholic had handed Franklin Roosevelt a poisoned drink shortly before his death. They knew that Catholics had concocted a nerve drug that immobilized Woodrow Wilson. They knew that Catholics had killed Harding with an injection to simulate a heart attack. They knew the harsh and medieval pronouncements of every harsh and medieval Pope, and they reprinted them all—without dates. They distributed the Knights of Columbus Oath in so many versions that different, individual, single-sheet samples occupy a folder

[5] See Appendix II for complete text.

57

half an inch thick in the Fair Campaign Committee library. Sex obsessed them. The harlot of Babylon, the whore of Baylon, a "nun's confession: My Convent Daze." Nunnery tales of priest-fathered babies dropped in wells to drown. Monastery tales of wild orgies with nuns. Virgins seduced in the confessional. Mystics and numerologists with allusions to the Book of Revelation and "the Mark of the Beast: 666." Pamphlets were illustrated with woodcuts from Foxe's *Book of Martyrs* showing priests breaking and branding heretics, and pouring scalding oil down their throats.

One anonymous pamphleteer wrote what purported to be an exhortation to Republican Catholics to kick over party traces and vote for Kennedy so "we Catholics" can have it all our way and to hell with the perfidious Protestants. A lay preacher of a schismatic Lutheran sect—identified only with initials—wrote another tract, ostensibly to Catholics: "Elect Kennedy so our Blessed Lady Ever-Virgin Mary will be the First Lady of our Land." Naturally, both documents went only to Protestants.

The circulation of the sick, and the vicious, and the lying pieces numbered untold millions of copies. Out of the unknown total of anti-Catholic tracts, the imperfect collecting mechanism of the Fair Campaign Practices Committee acquired more than 1,500 different editions of rabid and unfair anti-Catholic propaganda, 80 of them anonymous. One-third of this trash came from New York, California, Pennsylvania, Texas, and Illinois, in that order. Nine other states accounted for the next 25 per cent: Tennessee, Ohio, Indiana, New Jersey, Kentucky, Michigan, Minnesota, Missouri, and Wisconsin. The Bible Belt states, it was clear, were secondary factors.

The really vicious stuff of 1960 won few converts; it simply excited those who were already excited. There was a middle ground of deeply apprehensive Protestants who wrote against Catholics in the guise of seekers after truth, let the chips fall where they may. These won converts.

Early in 1959, an organization called Protestants and Other Americans United for Separation of Church and State took cognizance of "the possibility of a Presidential candidate of the Roman Catholic faith." It did so in a press release "made in connection with the approach of Brotherhood Week," warning against "increasing circulation of a so-called Knights of Columbus 'oath,'" which, the announcement said, was "fraudulent," and ought not to be published or distributed.

Accompanying the release was the full text of the spurious oath.

POAU, the statement said, had sent copies of the document to the Fair Campaign Practices Committee. The release continued: "Scarcely a day passes . . . in which we do not receive inquiries about this supposed 'oath' of the Knights of Columbus. We have noted a sharp rise in the inquiries recently . . . we are convinced that the 'oath' is being more widely circulated than ever.

"After careful research we are convinced that the 'oath' is fraudulent and should not be circulated by anyone," POAU said, circulating it. The release went on to give the history of the discrediting of the oath.

The Fair Campaign Committee received POAU's mimeographed version of the oath with a letter saying it had "recently made its appearance in connection with certain political campaigns." The Committee asked in which states and campaigns it had appeared, and whether it was in connection with a candidate or a ballot issue in each case.[6]

POAU never answered the letter, and never went on public record as to where the oath had appeared. The Fair Campaign Committee then asked political leaders in every region, along with Catholic journalists known to be particularly sensitive to any reports of its circulation, whether they knew of the appearance of the oath. Every answer was negative.

[6] The matter was of keenest interest because the Committee had been anticipating circulation of the oath against John F. Kennedy, and had alerted volunteer observers in many states to watch for it in particular. Even in a rabidly anti-Catholic campaign against a private school tax-exemption issue in California the preceding fall, it had not appeared. In the 1958 elections it was reported only from one judgeship contest in New England.

Perhaps the POAU staff leaders did think of their oath-deflating mission as beneficial and appropriate for Brotherhood Week. If so, the episode reveals a remarkable confidence that so poisonous a document, mailed, even with an accompanying release denouncing it, to papers including the most fundamentalist and anti-Catholic journals, would not be misused.

Before the campaign was over POAU revealed that its confidence in Catholics was more limited. The organization published and distributed in every state a long and impressive list of its publications of assorted sizes, thickness, shapes, and color combinations. Most of these were of a tone that was restrained but might be described as somewhat tense.

A random sampling of some of the calmer titles includes: "The Last Best Hope—Insurance Against Holocaust," "Captive Schools," and "Facing a Common Peril," all by C. Stanley Lowell, Associate Director of POAU. Others were "Ecclesiastical Justice in Spain," "The Ramparts We Watch," and "An Unholy Alliance —The Franco-Vatican Concordat," by authors including Executive Director Glenn L. Archer and POAU Counsel Paul Blanshard.

Among the less calm, three leaflets by the ubiquitous Dr. Lowell merit further comment. "The Roman Catholic Church and Democracy" was the heading of a flyer promoting a larger pamphlet of the same name. "*What do they want to change?*" the sheet asks. It answers: "It is the first Amendment, which guarantees freedom of religion and church-state separation. This law protects you from police interference in religious worship. Except for this guarantee it would be legal to take your taxes to support another man's religion." A note at the end of the principal message read, "In this crucial election year, *POAU urgently needs your support* . . ." The leaflet did not say where Dr. Lowell found out "they" were going to change the First Amendment, but a box at the bottom of the page said that P.S., if you act promptly (that is, send money) you will get "the booklet 'The Roman Catholic Church and Democracy,' which gives actual quotations from the teachings of Pope Leo XIII on church and state."

Dr. Lowell's scare-sheet offered no perspective on Leo XIII and his relevance to American politics in 1960. That Pope was born in 1810—while James Madison was in his second year as President of the United States—and acceded to the papal throne in 1876.

A lengthier Lowell POAU document unfolds into twelve pages, and is titled, *"If the U.S. Becomes 51% Catholic."* The final three paragraphs of this document are the most intense in the whole piece, but they are offered by Dr. Lowell as a last word in the pamphlet and for that reason are offered here as a summary: "The long tolerant tradition of the United States would likely modify the threat of anti-Protestant violence. There would probably be little or none of this so long as Protestants worshipped quietly in their own homes and churches, off the beaten path. But the full weight of official policy and promotion would be thrown against them; vast sums of money, much of it contributed by themselves, would be devoted to their reduction and eventual destruction. There is precedent for this in every land where the Roman church is strongly joined with the state.

"Protestants would be treated with snide amusement and official contempt. They would be reduced to second-class citizens and treated as damned souls. Their young would be cajoled and bribed to leave their traditional faith. They would be steadily, systematically whittled away. They would be left at length a devout but inconsequential minority, just as Protestants are in Spain today.

"After 50 per cent—*that!*"

Fortunately, more rational and honest non-Catholic writers and preachers brought most of their audience to conclude that no twentieth-century American Catholic, and certainly not John Fitzgerald Kennedy, posed any kind of threat to subordinate America to "Vatican Power."

Notwithstanding the Sorenson-Bailey memorandum on the pulling power of a Catholic candidate, the religious issue hurt Kennedy more than it helped him in 1960. But his opponent, Vice

President Richard M. Nixon, suffered more from the relatively few other really abrasive elements of the campaign.

In early 1950, some liberals and moderates were heard rejoicing, if temperately, that young Congressman Nixon's pursuit of the Hiss-Chambers case had been in sharp and honorable, and even useful, contrast to the reckless tactics of Joe McCarthy. But by 1960 McCarthy was dead and Nixon had replaced him in the demonology of most liberals. Many moderates retained a most unflattering picture of Nixon's checkered career through political morality. The remembered excesses of his campaigns against Jerry Voorhis and Helen Gahagan Douglas, and his stinging innuendoes about Democrats and treason, were reinforced by the murderous caricatures of Herblock and other cartoonists. Nixon got scant credit for maturing, for the scrupulous way he now was handling the religious question, for the decorum and rationality of his attacks on Kennedy, and least of all for his abstention from accusations of softness on Communism. The fact that Kennedy was not a very vulnerable target for the charge did not deter other practitioners of the art of the Commie Smear. The redoubtable "Cowboy Evangelist," Harvey Springer of Colorado, took a few minutes off from fighting Rome to point up Kennedy's "pro-Communist" record of supporting legislation the rightist saw as pro-Communist.

In 1960 Nixon and the Negro was a major topic north and south. In the north and west, minions of Adam Clayton Powell and others distributed, in at least a dozen different editions, handbills and posters reproducing excerpts from a real estate deed to a house the Republican candidate had bought in Washington in 1951. These flyers featured a restrictive covenant barring future sale of the property to any Negro, or, for good measure, "Armenians, Jews, Hebrews and Syrians."

The document obviously was peddled to paint Nixon as a bigot in general and anti-Negro in particular. Some versions of the piece carried as an over-printing in large, bold, red script the word "Shame!" at intervals down the page.

When Senator Nixon bought the house in question, restrictive covenants had been outlawed for three years by the Supreme Court,[7] and the Senator knew the deed's restrictive language had no force or effect. But in one of those curious bursts of artlessness which occur in his career, amid high-water marks of artfulness, he simply didn't go to the trouble to require deletion of the offending part of the deed. His record does not support the assumption that he would knowingly have been a party to a discriminatory deed or act.

Meanwhile, in the South, some bigoted Democrats played a wonderfully cynical counterpoint to the saga of the discriminatory deed. They peddled, never officially, but rather widely in white communities where the tactic would clearly pay off, a flyer displaying three photographs of Nixon in various poses of affection and affinity with Negroes. Some were Americans in business suits and some Africans in tribal regalia. The caption presented the devastating fact: Nixon had been a member of, and a contributor to, the NAACP for ten years.

While the low-road Democrats were having it both ways against Nixon, Kennedy and Johnson themselves were very much on the high road, pledging full equality of opportunity to the Negro. Kennedy intervened for a jailed Martin Luther King [8] and Johnson, himself a Southerner, spoke for equal rights in the Deep South. Peter Lisagor of the *Chicago Daily News* reported a revealing incident.[9] "When the perspiring Johnson, who had worked his [South Carolina] audience up to a frenzy with his shouting, slashing attack upon the GOP ticket, spoke of 'human rights' and the justice of treating everyone equally, regardless of race, religion or region, the farmers were whooping and applauding. So were the two Governors [of South Carolina and Georgia].

"Later, when a couple of reporters buttonholed one of the

[7] Shelley vs. Kraemer [334 U.S. 1, 1948].

[8] Nixon considered such a move but rejected it as demagogic.

[9] March 21, 1965. The story, recalling the 1960 campaign, also reveals Southern political rhetoric in action. Style is more important than content; for generations the goal of the Southern stump-speaker has been to leave his hearers limp, swooning with delight, if oblivious to the content of the message.

Governors and asked why he applauded so vigorously at the point of Johnson's demand for equality 'for colored and white babies,' the Governor seemed flustered, and said, 'Why . . . why, he didn't say anything like that.' His uncertainty suggested that he was so wrought up by Johnson's passionate oratory that he didn't really hear what the Senator was saying. And one had to conclude, sadly, that maybe the farmers hadn't heard rightly, either."

As Election Day drew near, John Kennedy's hour in the sun of distortion arrived. Since pre-Convention days assorted hand-bills had capitalized on the real and fancied faults and aberrations of Kennedy *père*, all implying or stating that John Kennedy was heir to the worst of them. In temperance country, Joseph P. Kennedy Sr. was portrayed endlessly as a whiskey baron: "Kennedy and his 100-proof whiskey damnocrats," one sheet had it. In Jewish terrain the old man's fancied one-time Nazi leanings were disinterred with morbid care and persuasive out-of-context "documentation."

By Election Day both members of each ticket were depicted to Jews as anti-Semites and to anti-Semites as Jew-lovers. The late Conde McGinley distributed a full-page newspaper-size sheet dominated by a photograph of John Kennedy standing with and somewhat in front of a group of Liberal Party leaders, including David Dubinsky, Alex Rose and Adolph Berle. A bold caption explained: "Behind Kennedy Stands the Jew."

A Washington newsletter called *Human Events*, a weekly bible to much of the right wing, published in July a sour examination of Kennedy's socialist economic leanings by a Catholic scholar, Rev. Juniper B. Carol, under the title "Kennedy for President? A Roman Catholic Priest Says No." The article was widely reprinted and circulated in most states, especially in areas with sizable Catholic populations. Many Democrats, acutely sensitive to anything smacking of religious bias, complained.

Such protests were based on having read the title but not the article; actually the point made by the Spanish-born priest had nothing to do with religion. He was simply writing a standard arch-conservative rejection of what the right wing sees as socialist economic policies. The interesting aspect of the affair was that *Human Events* had reprinted the article from a longer one in a far-right Catholic publication, the *Wanderer,* of St. Paul, Minnesota. In the original article, Father Carol had reviewed the economic policies of both Nixon and Kennedy and concluded that one was as bad as the other, both Keynesian to the core.

In New York a motivational researcher named Alan Marcus found himself so offended by the deceptions of the Nixon camp that he formed a paper, "Clean Campaign Committee," whose role was to help the voters "keep score of Nixon's fouls." A leaflet assisted voters in spotting smear techniques, all of which, by virtue of a delicate blend of fact, innuendo, out-of-context quotes and tricky footnotes, emerged as standard Nixon tactics. The folder said the "committee" *would* expose Kennedy "if he did the same thing. Senator Kennedy does not."

Republicans, in questioning the state of Kennedy's health, had probed into his adrenal insufficiency, which had become fairly well known. At the eleventh hour a California surgeon passed around a letter noting "that Kennedy takes cortisone to support his adrenal needs." The doctor went on to equate taking cortisone with addiction to marijuana, cocaine, and heroin. "Such an unreliable, sick man," he concluded, "should not be allowed to assume the responsibility of our national leadership."

As the campaign ended, many of the smears appeared to have canceled one another out. Kennedy clearly lost some states because of religion—notably Kentucky, Tennessee and Oklahoma. He gained in others from the issue, but mostly these were states he was sure to carry in any case. Yet his election did lay the ghost that Al Smith could not, and his conduct in office did much to put to rest the fears that still rankled POAU-type Americans. The trenchant wit of Monsignor Francis Lally, editor of the Boston Catholic paper, *The Pilot,* made the point during President Kennedy's opposition to legislative proposals for Federal aid to parochial schools. "If he keeps on at this rate," Lally said, "he'll have the Baptist vote in '64 and lose the Catholics."

Murder denied John Kennedy a chance at re-election, and it set the stage for the 1964 campaign.

Barry Goldwater, who admired and liked Kennedy, is said to have had no heart for a Presidential race after the assassination. But his supporters would not be put off. They had the heart for it, and the spleen. They set in motion a campaign of polarization the likes of which America had never seen.

Other elections have offered a choice between ruin and salvation. "Van Buren and ruin," said the Whigs in 1836, was the alternative to "Harrison and prosperity." The voters chose Van Buren. In 1924 Democrats urging the election of John W. Davis spelled out the alternative offered by the Republican Coolidge: "RepUblIcaN." The voters chose Coolidge. "FDR and Ruin" was a theme of Republican campaigners in 1932, 1936, and 1940. Roosevelt won every time.

The right-wingers in 1964 feared more than just general ruin. They also feared Communism and what they saw as the breakneck pace of integration. They identified one with the other, and Democrats and liberals—especially Lyndon Johnson—with both. And they prepared to split the country on *three* polarizations: left and right, good and evil, black and white.

Except for a few haters, there was no split along a line that might have been expected, between Jew and anti-Semite. The Arizona Senator's roots were too deep in the west and southwest for the anti-Semitic dodge to make much headway. Also, he was born and baptised into the Protestant Episcopal Church, a fact which led Harry Golden, the columnist and humorist, to observe wryly that he might have known the first Jew to have a chance at the White House would be an Episcopalian.[10]

---

[10] It is true that in some Southern areas where anti-Semites abound and there are few Jews, references to Goldwater's antecedents were made to reduce the defection of general-purpose bigots from the Democratic ticket. A year and a half before the 1964 elections, a Texas Congressman, a friend of John Kennedy, remarked to his constituents—and the press—in a routine newsletter that only in America could the grandsons of two immigrants aspire to the highest office in the land. The letter detailed briefly the careers of Kennedy's grandfather, Patrick Kennedy, and Goldwater's grandfather, Big Mike Goldwater, and noted that Big Mike Goldwater started out

Another reason for Goldwater's relative freedom from anti-Semitism in the campaign was probably his own sunny good humor about his background. He told of an apocryphal visit to a restricted Phoenix country club where he was turned away for being Jewish. "But I'm only half-Jewish," he quotes himself as saying. "Can't I play nine holes?"

Rightist causes have long attracted anti-Semites. The McCarthy era and the subsequent rise of today's radical right, beginning in about 1958, offered anti-Semites an alternative target for their loathing. So long as there were Jew-Communist Atom Spies like the Rosenbergs, one could have all the fun of baiting Jews without risking opprobrium; one merely concentrated on Communist identification, and soft-pedalled the Jew part. Of course, the rightist who is also an especially passionate Jew-hater has to choose his friends and foes on the basis of which set of hates is more important to him. The voter who hates socialism and Jewry equally can always stay home.

In 1963 and 1964, there were enough rightists willing to love Barry to provide formidable shock troops for the necessary preliminary battles. They were ready for Goldwater before he was ready to run.

These people were the Goldwater amateurs, who gave the professionals a lesson the latter will forget at their peril. Not all were extremists but a great many were—Birchers and adherents of lesser groups that believed America had been taken over from White House to PTA by the Communists. Their take-over of the machinery of the Republican Party, largely according to the rules, is discussed in Chapter 5.

The pre-Goldwater Goldwaterites were handicapped in the New Hampshire primary by the paucity of arch-conservative fanatics in a state more at home with a Nelson Rockefeller or a Henry Cabot Lodge. Their idol, however, turned to with a will and covered the appropriate rounds, showing old conservative

as an itinerant Jewish peddler. There was some outcry that the newsletter deliberately carried anti-Semitic overtones. It could have, but there is no evidence it was not simply an illustration of the American dream.

New Hampshiremen a neo-conservative in action.

The prospect chilled the New Englanders. The candidate's candor impressed them, and the nation, but negatively. His penchant for saying what to him was the right thing at what to everybody but his most dedicated zealots was the wrong time and place resulted in lost votes before the snow melted. Even Dean Burch, Goldwater's choice as Chairman of the Republican National Committee, was to confide later that the party and its nominee were "suffering from a New Hampshire hangover."

California was a different story only because the Arizonan was so widely—and wildly—revered in that perplexing, exotic, and rootless state. The excesses of his followers, especially in the south, led advisers of Nelson Rockefeller to prepare a campaign movie for television reporting some of the storm-trooper tactics of harassment, intimidation, and innuendo that Goldwaterites used to cozen and thwart Rockefeller supporters. The sound track of the film featured martial drumbeats and marching footsteps evocative of goose-stepping Nazis. It was never shown after the New York Governor's strategists fell into a bitter quarrel over the propriety and political utility of showing it.

After the California primary, it quickly became apparent that the hard-core Goldwater supporters viewed Johnson with at least as much fear and hostility as the Rockefeller troops had felt for the Arizona Senator. Before the Republican Convention ended, the GOP bitter-enders started circulating cards and flyers and newspaper ads stating that Johnson had the support of the Communists and implying that the only sensible anti-Communist course was to vote for Barry. "COMMUNIST PARTY USA SUPPORTS PRES. JOHNSON," read a banner headline on a typical example. This was a reprint of a two-page newspaper ad which adorned walls and shop windows in countless Citizens for Goldwater-Miller headquarters.

The Communists did support Johnson, by opposing Goldwater with hysteria and zeal. They considered the Republican nominee a fascist. They left off attacking Johnson at about the time of the Republican Convention, and did not resume until their *bête noir* was safely defeated.

One effort to use the President's words to depict him as a socialist was made by the right-wing magazine *Human Events*. The publication had, by 1964, dressed up its format and branched out into conducting schools of politics for conservatives. Now its role in the campaign for Goldwater extended beyond editorial support. It circulated vast quantities of little cards that quoted President Johnson as addressing a group of senior citizens as follows: "We are going to try to take all of that money that we think is unnecessarily being spent and take it from the 'haves' and give it to the 'have nots' that need it so much."

The words were accurate, but the use to which the cards were put was completely false. Goldwater people passed the cards around to document their contention that Johnson was a socialist, planning a redistribution of wealth.

Actually the President had been talking of Federal budget policy, and "have" and "have not" government agencies. The remark, it is true, was perfectly suited for distortion when quoted out of context. An honest presentation of what he said appeared in a bank's newsletter: [11] "To make room for [proposed tax] reductions, the spending restraint of the past year must be continued.

"A review of the fiscal '65 budget is useful in highlighting the Administration's basic approach. The President has combined overall spending restraint with a budget policy of taking all the money that we think is unnecessarily being spent . . . from the 'haves and [giving] it to the 'have nots' . . . shifting budgeted outlays from the 'haves' to the 'have nots' . . .'"

Many liberal Democrats were nearly as unreasoning in their attacks on Goldwater, counting him a Bircher and, in some cases, a fascist. He was supported by the radical right; *ergo,* he was a radical rightist. This tendency to identify the candidate with his most alarming supporters poses a grave threat to American politics. It is the approach that led some early Americans to describe

[11] Monthly Economic Letter of the First National City Bank of New York; December, 1964.

George Washington as a Tory-lover and a would-be king, Thomas Jefferson as a Jacobin, and Abraham Lincoln as a Southern agent. We see how absurd these accusations were then, but we continue them today: Roosevelt, Truman, Eisenhower, Kennedy and Johnson—Communists; Hoover—heartless and unconcerned; Goldwater—a fascist or a Bircher.

Glib over-simplifications in a slightly different vein brought about the second polarization of 1964: good versus evil. Goldwater supporters saw their candidate as a truly moral man and Johnson as the very essence of immorality. Their reasoning was simple: birds of a feather flock together. Who were Johnson's cronies? To hear the Republicans tell it in 1964, they were Bobby Baker, Billie Sol Estes, and Walter Jenkins.

Baker was precocious and brilliant, a shrewd, effective, and tireless Secretary to the Senate Majority when Lyndon Johnson was Majority Leader. The young South Carolinian's ability, energy, and grasp of complex legislation and the political facts of life was remarked by the most respected men in both parties in the Senate. Baker fell from grace when his financial involvements began to indicate he had been using his position to enrich himself. He resigned so it would not be necessary to dismiss him.

Before the fall, Johnson had observed on several occasions that Baker was an invaluable aide. Once in 1961 when Baker received an honorary degree, most of the powerful men in the Senate, Democrats and Republicans, lauded Bobby to the skies. Now the Republicans were quoting Johnson in praise of Baker, but ignoring, naturally, the even more fulsome GOP tributes uttered on the same occasion.

When Goldwater's supporters sought to blacken Johnson's name by linking it with Billie Sol Estes, they were on shakier ground: the only quotes they could cite were from Estes, a young Texas financial manipulator who had occasionally bragged about how easily he could get into the White House or reach President Johnson by phone. No witnesses were presented by the GOP to attest to Estes' self-proclaimed access to the President, but Billie Sol was quoted ad infinitum on the subject.[12]

[12] Actually, Johnson's Texas enemies spent untold man-hours probing the

Walter Jenkins had been close to the President and his family both professionally and personally. The tragic episode of Jenkins's collapse is commented on more fully in Chapter 6. Pro-Goldwater efforts to tar Johnson with the Jenkins affair were more covert than in the Baker and Estes matters, and the Republican candidate himself did not refer to it.

In all three connections, cards—about the size of a business card—were circulated, bearing a comment or question that linked the President with Baker, Estes, and Jenkins, sometimes separately, sometimes together. Occasionally Communists and civil rights leaders were thrown in for good measure.

More influential than the cards, and certainly equally ubiquitous, was a major phenomenon of the 1964 election, the "dirty books," which are discussed in Chapter 10. While one attacked Republican moderates and another all liberals, the last to appear, J. Evetts Haley's A Texan Looks at Lyndon, depicted the President as completely without scruples.

Republican television spots featured the immorality theme. A five-minute film dealt starkly with the violence that gripped the land in the "long hot summer" of racial tension in 1964. What the country needed, it implied, was a leader with the right moral fiber.

The Democrats played a different game, but scarcely a prettier one. They painted Barry Goldwater as a madman, a trigger-happy, totally irresponsible maniac, whose election would plunge the world into a deadly round of bomb tests, escalation, and catastrophe.[13]

Although the Democrats have been called the war party repeatedly, it is doubtful that the trigger-happy gambit has been used so extensively since 1848, when the Democratic Presidential

tangled Estes affair for evidence of any link between the entrepreneur and the President. Their silence speaks eloquently of the absence of pay dirt.

[13] A few months after the election, columnist Art Buchwald had some acid fun with the Democrats' campaign theme of "Barry the warmonger." He wrote of his gratitude that Goldwater had been defeated, and he listed most of the dread events that would have occurred if he had been elected. The list consisted of things that had gone wrong under Johnson since the election. Goldwater himself, with understandably less amusement, made the same points in a column at about the same time.

candidate was a hero of the War of 1812, General Lewis Cass of Michigan. This former Senator and Cabinet member was so harassed by the trigger-happy charge that he stopped making any reference to his substantial military distinction.[14]

In 1964 the Democrats had television to spread fear of Goldwater. Their imaginative and relentless use of it is discussed in Chapter 10.

Barry Goldwater initially won his way into the hearts of Republican pros by his tireless and effective performance as a speaker at party rallies and fund-raising events. As chairman of the Senate Republican Campaign Committee, he showed his mettle with the highly partisan oratory that is standard at such functions. Therefore he was on record with a great many hyperbolic statements, many of them controversial and many inflammatory. He had, in his Senate career, been on several sides of some important issues. The restraint that comes to serious candidates for so awesome an office as the Presidency of the United States came late to Goldwater, probably because it was not until well into 1964 that he realized that he actually was to have a chance at the White House.

Thus it was a simple matter for the Democrats to quote Goldwater on Goldwater, to select contradictory and damaging utterances, in full context and often of fairly recent date. A ready man with an opinion, he was a natural candidate for the "shoot from the hip" tag that rival Republicans—and finally the Democrats—affixed to him firmly.

However, once his candidacy was established, Goldwater had some claim to the right to be heard on the basis of what he was saying as a candidate, and not what he had said as a partisan crowd-pleaser a year or several years before.

Goldwater's off-the-cuff observations often blurred the image his campaign was trying to advance. These departures anguished his managers, and they made a major effort to get him to stick to

---

[14] Curiously, Cass's victorious opponent was General Zachary Taylor, who defeated General Winfield Scott for the Whig nomination. And Cass's running mate was General William O. Butler.

the text. By the time they prevailed on him, they found to their dismay that they had also inhibited their man's most attractive attributes, the candor and spontaneity that endeared him to audiences. They also found Goldwater unshakeable in his determination to say unpopular things that were important to him on principle. So in the TVA heartland he pointed out that he did not favor "selling TVA" as charged, but that he *did* favor transferring such activities as steam-operated power plants from the Authority to the hands of private enterprise. In the rest of the country this line was easy enough to take, but in Tennessee and Kentucky it was pure poison.

The final polarization of 1964 centered around the race problem. The Republican Party had at last been making some slow inroads into the Democratic South on conservatism free of racism. Now suddenly the party found itself with a jackpot of hard-line Southern segregationists ready to rally to Goldwater because he had voted against the Civil Rights Act of 1964 in the Senate and because his Northern support included many right-wingers who were coincidentally racists.

Most of the pro-Goldwater segregationists held sincere beliefs that "forced" integration was evil, unnatural, un-American, and Communist-inspired. This position was palatable to Goldwater only as long as the emphasis was on force. But the more implacable of his segregationist supporters saw any efforts at integration as force, and literally would not participate in any efforts toward equal opportunity for Negroes without being forced.[15]

Some cynical operators in the Goldwater campaign manipulated these Southern racists deftly, and some rabid segregationists themselves became important factors in state and local campaign organizations. The alliance between racism and pseudo-conservatism is a natural one, so bigots and radical rightists worked cheerfully together, alongside conservatives, arch-conservatives and reactionaries, to elect Barry Goldwater, who is neither a bigot nor

[15] See Chapter 6 for an amusing episode involving Goldwater's own creditable record on integration.

73

a radical rightist. The common output of literature was of a low order: cards, leaflets, mimeographed and photo-offset tracts with sentiments like "If you want a nigger for a neighbor, vote Democrat"; photographs of Negro men posed intimately with white women; and assorted material imputing Communism to civil rights leaders. Most of this trash was anonymous and thus a violation of Federal election law.[16]

Considering the unappetizing array of segregationist diehards supporting Goldwater with zeal, it is not surprising that millions of Negroes saw the Republican candidate as a racist. The Negro vote was monolithic, to a degree that startled even opinion research experts as all but beyond the laws of probability. Many Negro organizations and leaders were intemperate in their opposition. The usually rational NAACP, for example, published a flyer saying Goldwater endorsed the theory of white supremacy which led directly to the Mississippi murder of three civil rights workers in the summer of 1964.

Goldwater was also tagged as the candidate of the Ku Klux Klan, which was no more true or relevant than the charge that Johnson was the candidate of the Communist Party. In the case of Goldwater, however, the matter was complicated by his genial running mate, William E. Miller, an all-purpose political hatchet man who had been chairman of the Republican Congressional campaign committee and of the Republican National Committee. Various Grand Dragons and other leaders of the recrudescent hooded order offered to endorse Goldwater, and many Klan bodies and leaders worked diligently to elect him.

Newsmen questioned the Vice Presidential candidate about his Klan support, and Miller obediently began to defend the right of any American, including Klansmen, to vote and support anyone he chose. Within a day or two Goldwater denounced the Klan, a step that might not have been necessary had the Republican platform done so.

---

[16] 18 USC Section 612 prohibits unsigned literature in a campaign for Federal office. The Johnson Administration, in a spirit of *bonhomie,* has quietly discouraged prosecution of violators.

Republican campaigners in 1964 painted a nightmare scene for the voters: a totally corrupt and cynical Lyndon Johnson, surrounded by Communists and Negro rioters. The Democratic version of the same dream presented an irresponsible warmonger named Barry Goldwater. The Democratic version was more credible. By his seeming acceptance of support from even the most unsavory right-wing and racist quarters, Goldwater alienated the moderates. The contempt for moderation enunciated in his acceptance speech became the albatross to Goldwater's Ancient Mariner: "He killed the bird that made the breeze to blow." He offered a choice, not an echo. The people chose.

"In your heart you know he's right," ran the Republican slogan in 1964. Democrats had a ready answer which tickled many Republicans and unaligned voters. It was harsh, and unfair, but it was the verdict of a landslide majority: "In your head you know he's nuts."

CHAPTER 3

Calumniating Congress

WHAT with George Washington and Lyndon Johnson and the Presidents in between, the American people have elected a chief executive 45 times. These 45 Presidencies were won by 31 human beings. Historians have found it easy to keep track of the circumstances in which they were chosen.

In the same period, the people have elected members of the House of Representatives for a total of 26,680 two-year terms. Since the 17th Amendment, effective for the 1914 elections, causing all Senators of the United States to be chosen by popular vote within their states instead of by their legislatures, Senate seats have been filled 839 times. In toto, by the voters of the states, directly, there have been more than 27,500 Congressional elections.

If we had picked our members of Congress one at a time, as we have done our President, we would have chosen a Senator or Congressman every Monday, Wednesday and Friday since 1789.

Thus it is small wonder that not every schoolboy knows which Congressional candidate has been calumniated how badly and by whom as well as he knows who did what to which candidate for the Presidency. Because of the very inward focus of each House race upon a relatively small district, it is not even surprising that campaign headlines in California may never reach citi-

zens in New York. Only rare Congressional drives catch nationwide attention, and even those that do are not necessarily representative. Two in recent history are noteworthy.

The first, in 1946, demolished the political career of California Congressman Jerry Voorhis, a five-term Democratic liberal.
As was California practice, both candidates filed in both party
primaries and Voorhis won the Democratic nomination and
amassed a big minority in the Republican contest, which was won
by a newcomer, Richard M. Nixon. The ensuing campaign was
bitter. In the first of a series of debates, Voorhis protested a
Nixon newspaper ad: "A vote for Nixon is a vote against the
Communist-dominated PAC with its gigantic slush fund." The
Congressman pointed out that he had not been endorsed by the
CIO's regional Political Action Committee, and had not sought its
endorsement. Nixon read off a report of a Los Angeles unit of the
nationwide Political Action Committee recommending support of
Voorhis by the national labor-political group and handed the
document to his opponent with a flourish.

Voorhis responded later that he neither had nor desired the
support of the California CIO people, that at that time there was
a "grave question whether the Communist Party does not exercise
inordinate if not decisive influence" over California CIO bodies.
For the remainder of the campaign Voorhis was kept busy ex-
plaining the facts and denying that he was the PAC's man. Nixon
kept the spotlight on the twin questions of Red domination and
red-blooded Americanism, with thrusts about Administration and
other officials fronting for "un-American elements" by seeking
"increasing Federal controls over the lives of the people." No one
could prove that Nixon ever called Voorhis a "lip-service American," but many voters remember it that way. In fact, Nixon
tossed off general warnings against "lip-service Americans" without naming the Congressman he was trying to unseat. Then, with
classic last-minute timing, the Nixon forces released a blast at
"the insolence of Moscow in telling the American voter to elect
PAC candidates, such as Mr. Voorhis." It cited the Republican
version of the Voorhis record, one of "consistently voting the

Moscow-PAC-Henry Wallace line in Congress."

Voorhis lost.

He later observed that he probably would have lost even without the loyalty implications; the GOP legislature had gerrymandered his district ruthlessly a few years earlier and the district really was a conservative one. The Nixon campaign had a good deal going for it in other areas, and it was not a New Deal year. The winds of change blew Voorhis and a lot of fellow Democrats out, and the Republican 80th Congress, including Richard M. Nixon, in.

The second campaign ended the political career of liberal Democrat Helen Gahagan Douglas. Mrs. Douglas, a three-term Congresswoman from Los Angeles, announced her intent to unseat conservative, Democratic, two-term Senator Sheridan Downey [1] in the 1950 California primary. Promptly she belabored him for a record negligible except for its support of big business in general and the power interests in particular. The vigor of her campaign, and perhaps the awkwardness of opposing an aroused and articulate woman, celebrated as an actress, and entirely familiar with the ways of the Federal legislature, told on Downey. He pulled out of the contest several months before Primary Day, bowing to the heavy demands of the "personal and militant campaign against the vicious and unethical propaganda" he saw as emanating from Mrs. Douglas and her "extremist" friends.

Senator Downey was quickly succeeded in the race by Manchester Boddy, editor and publisher of the *Los Angeles Daily News*. He proved to be spoiling for this fight. Submerging chivalry beneath "Americanism," he swung obliquely at Mrs. Douglas, a vigorous anti-Communist but not his kind of anti-Communist, by directly assailing "a state-wide conspiracy" by a "subversive clique of red-hots to capture, through stealth and cunning, the nerve centers of our Democratic Party." He talked of "the red-hots' blueprint of subversive dictatorship."

Nixon had declared his candidacy for the seat back in No-

---

[1] Downey had taken the seat from William Gibbs McAdoo in the 1938 primary.

vember of 1949, with a statement only a little less intense than Boddy's fulminations. Nixon identified the enemy as "planned economy, the Fair Deal, or social welfare—but it is still the same old Socialist baloney, any way you slice it." Now he cross-filed in the Democratic primary.[2]

Meanwhile, Senator Downey took to the radio with what was to become the theme of the stop-Douglas efforts for the rest of the year. The Democratic solon, who was later to ignore a White House request that he endorse Mrs. Douglas in the sweet name of party harmony, linked her with New York's controversial American Labor Party Congressman, Vito Marcantonio. Despite his Republican origin and early service, Marcantonio leaned so far to the left that for all practical purposes he registered "tilt."

Mrs. Douglas, Senator Downey declared, not only gave aid and "comfort to the Soviet tyranny by voting against aid to Greece and Turkey," but she also "joined Representative Vito Marcantonio, an admitted friend of the Communist Party," in opposing an appropriation for the House Committee on Un-American Activities "to uncover treasonable communistic activities."

At this point the foil, Marcantonio, offered a surprising bit of friendly advice to his Republican colleague, Nixon.

Marcantonio, like other left and right extremists, had nothing but contempt for liberals, and he particularly despised Helen Douglas. When he read of the efforts of California Democrats to kill her off in the primary by linking her votes with his, Marcantonio, no stranger to demagoguery or deception, chuckled to a friend of his Republican colleague, candidate Nixon, "Tell Nicky to get on this thing, because it is a good idea." [3]

---

[2] This was standard California practice until it was outlawed a decade later. Major candidates tried to get the nominations of both parties, and strenuous efforts were made to avoid partisan identification. Nixon angered many Democrats when he titled his first primary leaflet "As one Democrat to another." The unofficial ground rules were a bit sophistic: it was proper to hide one's own party label, so people might think of a Republican as a Democrat; but it was morally wrong to come right out with a false statement about partisanship. Nixon's trick here was a false implication.

[3] Earl Mazo tells the story in *Richard Nixon* (New York: Harper, 1959), p. 81n.

Nicky did. In both primary and general election campaigns, Democrats and Republicans rang the changes on the Marcantonio ploy. Almost every anti-Douglas statement tied her to:

"the notorious radical, Vito Marcantonio;" or
"the notorious New York radical, Vito Marcantonio;" or
"Representative Vito Marcantonio, an admitted friend
  of the Communist Party;" or
"notorious Communist party-liner, Vito Marcantonio of
  New York;" or
"notorious party-liner, Congressman Vito Marcantonio
  of New York."

Late in July Mrs. Douglas decided that any number could play the game, and had a fling at it herself. She taxed Nixon with voting like the much-aligned Congressman [4] against aid to Korea and to halve European aid.

For Nixon's part, the direction of the campaign had been clear since he won the Republican nomination. His campaign chairman said that Mrs. Douglas' record revealed "the truth about her soft attitude toward Communism." His supporters began to taunt the Congresswoman as "the Pink Lady." Then the famous pink sheets appeared. They remain the most remembered aspect of the campaign.

These flyers on pink paper, 550,000 of them, were headed "Douglas-Marcantonio Voting Record." The remarkable facts were that "Helen Douglas and the notorious party-liner" had cast 354 identical votes in the House of Representatives. The votes were identified with dates and convoluted references whose very awesome detail persuaded laymen of their accuracy and significance. What was not mentioned was that most of the measures were eminently mundane and that on a great many of them Marcantonio's vote had also been identical with that of certified anti-Communists like Nixon, Un-American Activities Committee Chairman Francis Walter and other non-party-liners.

This was a dirty campaign in a dirty year. When it was over

[4] Mazo's phrase.

Mrs. Douglas had been beaten by 680,000 votes and she carried into political retirement scars she will always bear. Nixon was scarred, too, and most unfairly, many of his supporters insist. They point out that he did not originate the ridiculous oversimplification, the constant implication that beneath ill-advised votes and actions lay treason, the linking technique by which it is argued that identical votes are cast from identical motives. It is true that he himself later argued against unrestrained Redbaiting. He himself became so sensitive to the hostile interpretation of his public record by others—Herblock, for example—that he would not subscribe to the *Washington Post* in order to shield his daughters from the vengeful Nixon caricatures of that cartoonist.

The controversy that goes on to this day between the admirers and the haters of Richard Nixon is silly, and so obtuse as to be dishonest. The contention of the hero-worshippers that Nixon was not to blame for traducing Mrs. Douglas because Democrats did it first merits contempt. It might be noted that Nixon stated the issue as Socialism from the very first; although the Boddy crowd raised the red flag over her, the Nixon campaign made it her shroud. And all this was done coolly and without rancor. Marcantonio, not Nixon, was the one who hated Mrs. Douglas. Nixon and his backers had no personal animus toward her. Nixon wanted the Senate seat and this kind of campaign appeared necessary to win it. It was a wholly unemotional blend of patriotism and cynicism, all executed, as Mazo has noted, with surgical precision. The Nixon cuts were deft, exactly and only where and when they were needed. The Douglas responses were flailing and inept, possibly, Nixon's biographer suggests, because Mrs. Douglas and her liberal friends were not at ease with the studied application of hyperbole and innuendo.

The Nixon-haters refuse flatly to acknowledge that a man— at least this man—can change, can mature, can learn and grow from his own mistakes and offenses. Neither interpretation of Nixon, as perfect hero or utter villain, can survive the light of reason.

While American liberals are still bitter about Nixon's defeat of Helen Douglas, the California Senate contest was far from unique in the bloody election year of 1950. All around the country the theme was Communism. Alger Hiss had been convicted of perjury in denying complicity in a Washington spy ring; Joe McCarthy was in high gear. The Republicans had been out of office for eighteen years. The Korean War was at its peak. For political exploitation of anti-Communism it was a red banner year.

In Ohio, Robert A. Taft, elder son of the 27th President and ninth Chief Justice, himself already known as "Mr. Republican," was seeking re-election to the Senate, opposed by the Democratic state auditor, Joseph "Jumping Joe" Ferguson. The labor movement had confidently, even arrogantly, put Taft down for extinction, and marshalled tremendous resources of money and talent to beat him.

The Taft people set out to attack labor on what they believed to be its most vulnerable flank, Communist influence. At every turn the Senator and his supporters tagged the "get Taft" effort as Communist inspired. Taft himself declared that the campaign against him had been "blueprinted" by Communist leader Gus Hall in the Red magazine, *Political Affairs*.

Earlier in 1950 the CIO had expelled thirteen unions it found to be Communist-dominated, amid indignant cries of "purge" and "Red-baiting" by the radical left, so naturally the labor leaders who had managed the expulsions were angered at the Taft strategy.

Taft was undeterred. He said of the CIO's Political Action Committee: "The PAC was conceived in communism, had communist midwives assisting in its birth, and was carefully nurtured in its formative period by communist teachers." Most of his active supporters were even less restrained, and the Gus Hall blueprint theme dominated the entire campaign. Indeed, Taft's campaign manager later noted bitterly to a Senate elections subcommittee investigating the campaign that "A desperate attempt has been made [by Democrats and labor] to disassociate the notorious convicted Communist Gus Hall from the campaign. Yet it is impossible to deny his public statement which appears as exhibit 12 of Senator Taft's testimony, and a reprint of Hall's article in *Political Affairs*, exhibit 14, from the *Daily Worker* dated January 1950, entitled "The Target is Taft—the Year is 1950.' Senator Taft referred to this as a blueprint for the campaign. It should be noted with interest that while these statements of Mr. Hall were made early in 1950, there is no disavowal of it [by Democrats and labor] until this late date." [5] And the Republican campaign ignored the fact that Gus Hall had castigated the CIO and PAC leaders in another passage of the very *Political Affairs* article from which the Republicans were quoting. The Communist leader said, "To win a struggle means placing reliance on certain decisive factors and to bring them into full play. The Boyles, the Krolls, the Greens, the Murrays [all anti-Communist labor leaders opposing Taft, and instrumental in throwing the Communists out of the CIO] and Trumans are not elements spelling success for the people. They represent double dealing and disaster." [6]

The Democrats struck back in kind. They linked Taft's voting record with that of Vito Marcantonio. Citizens for Ferguson published a campaign tabloid in Taft's home city of Cincinnati. Page three was headed "Taft and Marcantonio," and it demonstrated that the conservative Ohio Senator and the left-wing New York Congressman had opposed a number of the same measures and supported others.

The Democratic candidate obtained a photograph of Taft and one-time Communist leader Earl Browder, from a feature article on Taft published in *Look* Magazine. Ferguson carried the picture, made in 1936, "all over the state of Ohio." He showed it to large and small audiences, challenging Taft, as a Portsmouth newspaper quoted him on one such occasion, to "Tell the people of his meeting with Earl Browder, the Red leader. Maybe Taft's

[5] Testimony of Willis D. Gradison, campaign manager for Robert A. Taft, 1950; Hearings, Subcommittee on Privileges & Elections, U.S. Senate, Investigation into the 1950 Ohio Senatorial Campaign, 82nd Congress. Committee on Rules & Administration, Washington, p. 330.

[6] *Ibid.*, interrogation by Senator Monroney, p. 359. Note that Hall's point is a more restrained phrasing of Taft's.

Communist connections are stronger than others."

Taft supporters prepared and distributed a small cartoon leaflet to show the sinister forces arrayed against him. One panel showed a pair of conspirators, obviously Communists. On the following page the first panel was reproduced and beside it appeared another drawing of a Union Racketeer, greedy arms encircling a tableful of money. Next appeared malevolent Union Dictators, and finally a hand bearing a whip lashing the puppet-like and pitiful figures of The Workers.

Now labor introduced a full-size comic book, which was one of the most widely condemned artifacts of the campaign against Taft. It egregiously distorted the Senator's position on such key issues as housing, minimum wages, and wartime benefits for Armed Forces personnel. A million copies of the piece were distributed in the state by a variety of labor groups of both CIO and AFL affiliations. The Taft people were outraged, and the vast circulation given the booklet, coupled with the wide newspaper coverage given Taft's indignation, probably caused its net effect to be a severe backfire.[7]

The Democrats made much of the fact that whenever Taft visited a factory, which was often, he would be received cordially by Republican-oriented management, and he would be shown through the plant, a privilege denied his Democratic rival Jumping Joe Ferguson in most Ohio factories. Taft was able to retort, for his part, that labor had threatened to close down establishments he wanted to visit. He proved his point in at least one instance by producing a typically florid letter from John L. Lewis to the president of the Ohio Coal Operators Association:

[7] It is conceivable that the fervent application of graphic arts in the Ohio campaign of 1950 stemmed from a pair of photographs printed in the *CIO News* of October 14, 1946. A one-column photograph portrayed Senator Taft. Beside it, separated from the Taft shot by an eighth of an inch of white space, was a much wider shot of Nazi leaders Hjalmer Schacht and Hans Fritzche. A single caption ran beneath the pair of pictures: "ROBERT A. TAFT AND 'FRIENDS'." Taft described it to the Senate elections subcommittee as "the grand-daddy of all composite photographs." Labor spokesmen denied, Scout's honor, any intent to imply that Senator Taft was pro-Nazi or that he was *really* a friend of Mr. Fritzche and Mr. Schacht.

Dear Mr. Eireland:

Taft's secret political handlers propose to have him enter coal mines to cozen the men underground. This will be bad from the standpoint of coal production.

Taft was born encased in velvet pants, and has lived to rivet an iron collar around the necks of millions of Americans. He is the relentless, albeit witless, tool of the oppressors of labor.

You should refuse him entry into mines where Americans toil. The underground workings are necessarily confined, and the air therein is easily contaminated. The effluvia of the oppressor is ever disagreeable and could enrage the men to a point of evacuation of the mine. This we would both deplore.

Yours truly,
John L. Lewis [8]

A year before the campaign for Taft's seat, AFL President William Green had declared, "The defeat of Taft is the number one point on our legislative program." This was the attitude of virtually every labor leader in or out of the AFL. The proclamation alerted Taft's friends and labor's foes, as well as the "labor vote" that was to destroy the author of the Taft-Hartley Act. Through the medium of the AFL's Labor's League for Political Education and the CIO Political Action Committee, union money could be spent in the campaign, although only voluntary contributions to these political education agencies, and not income from union dues, could be spent politically. Business had no such device open to it, and had to resort to indirection so far as spending corporate funds went, for state and Federal laws prohibit business contributions to election campaigns.

An enterprising free-lance advertising salesman and copy writer had discovered, some years before, a way in which corporations could make political points without running afoul of the law. The device was institutional advertising lauding home and mother and coming out against evil, Communism, and the like. It had been successful in Ohio and other industrial capitals in 1942, 1944, 1946 and 1948. Now in 1950, working through the *Colum-*

[8] Hearings, Subcommittee on Privileges & Elections, *op. cit.*, p. 40.

bus Dispatch, the entrepreneur, Arthur L. Conner of Cleveland, mapped out a series of ten full-page ads to run in thirteen major Ohio daily papers. The import of the series was viewed differently by the people it affected. Democrats saw the ads as thinly veiled attacks on the Democratic Party and exhortations to vote for Taft to save all that was left of the American way of life. Businessmen who gave money for the series saw the ads pretty much as salesman Conner put it to them: "a strong and stirring message against communism . . . [and for] Free Enterprise, Taxes, the Four Pillars of Democracy, the Preservation of the Church, the Home, the School, the usual—". Mr. Conner saw them as "pages on Americanism, on postwar plans, on economy, against communism, the usual bromides." In lieu of signatures, the ads carried the modest line, "This is one of a series of important messages brought to the public's attention by public-spirited individuals and organizations." The "organizations" were 157 Ohio corporations, and the "individuals" were eleven businessmen who paid by company check—and one whom Mr. Conner called "overly cautious" for paying his share by personal check.[9]

Another 1950 Senate campaign in which fears of Communism were skillfully exploited ended the public career of Millard Tydings, the aristocratic, conservative Democratic Senator from Maryland. Too conservative for Franklin Roosevelt, who sought to purge him in 1938, Tydings had served in the Senate 24 years when he sought re-election in 1950; only Senators George of Georgia and McKellar of Tennessee ranked him in seniority; he was chairman of the Senate Armed Services Committee and in the spring of 1950 he headed a special subcommittee of the Senate Foreign Relations Committee to investigate Senator McCarthy's charges of Communist infiltration of the State Department.

The Tydings investigation of McCarthy's charges proceeded on a tack that puzzled some observers, irritated others, and infuriated McCarthy's partisans. It became more of an investigation of McCarthy than a sedulous and searching look at what facts, if

[9] *Ibid.,* pp. 420, 422, 423–25.

any, underlay the Wisconsin Senator's remarkable contentions and disclosures.

One of the most provocative charges was that a Johns Hopkins professor named Owen Lattimore, a State Department adviser on Far Eastern affairs, was the "architect" of the State Department policy that "surrendered" China to the Reds. One witness before the Tydings Committee was Earl Browder, the American Communist leader. In the course of his testimony, Browder said he would not identify as Communists any actual Communists who were still in the employ of the State Department. Tydings persisted in his questioning, and elicited from Browder a statement that Owen Lattimore and another man were not Communists. The information was useless, of course: either they were Communists and Browder knew it and lied; or they were not Communists, and Browder was telling the truth. But after the Communist leader's testimony that he would not identify Communists still connected with the State Department, he could not be believed. So the question and response clarified nothing. Worse, it gave partisans of every hue a plausible basis for attack or defense.

When he was finished examining Browder, Tydings ended the interview with a courteous "Oh, thank you sir." Apart from the perplexing elements of Tydings' conduct of the hearings, there were some disingenuous aspects. McCarthy had said his charges would be proved by FBI data in 81 security files the Tydings Committee was examining. In the course of the hearings, McCarthy charged that these files had been tampered with, and this assertion raised its own sensation.

During his campaign for re-election, Tydings put out a campaign piece which said, "The committee stated it had not found evidence in the files to support Senator McCarthy's charges. Senator McCarthy then said that the files were raped, rifled or incomplete.

"The investigating committee asked the FBI to run down this new Senator McCarthy charge. So if you hear that the files and records examined by the investigating committee were raped, rifled or incomplete, tell them the FBI says 'No'."

McCarthy then produced a letter from J. Edgar Hoover stating that the FBI had "made no such examination and therefore is not in a position to make any statement concerning the completeness or incompleteness of the State Department Files."

Like so much of the goings-on in the McCarthy era, the charges were oblique, the responses tangential, and the confrontation forensic rather than substantial and direct. It later developed that the FBI had checked the files in the hands of the Tydings Committee—at Tydings' request to the Attorney General —to ascertain whether the *FBI* data therein was intact, but had not examined them as to whether the State Department files themselves were intact, so far as non-FBI data was concerned. There was a gap between the Tydings and McCarthy positions, on this and many other elements of the controversy. The absence of complete and direct answers to damaging questions left ample room for doubt about Tydings' judgment, motives, and, conceivably, his loyalty

McCarthy's allies descended on Maryland in force, with money, talent, and legmen. Mrs. Ruth McCormick Miller, a granddaughter of Ohio's Mark Hanna, had just acquired control of the Washington *Times-Herald,* the last voice of hard-nosed conservatism in the capital. Mrs. Miller, "Bazy" to her friends, imported a Chicago public relations man named Jon Jonkel to run the Senate campaign of Tydings' Republican opponent, John Marshall Butler. A bitter Democratic primary set a low tone for the campaign. Tydings had several opponents, and one, Hugh J. Monoghan, said the Tydings Committee report had "given the green light to Stalin's agents in this country to gnaw at the foundation of our national security." [10] McCarthy's people wanted to push the "green light for red spies" line but Jonkel calmed their ardor and directed it into more productive channels.

"Our slant on the Tydings' hearing was not this frontal approach at all," Jonkel told a Senate elections subcommittee hear-

[10] Maryland Senatorial Election of 1950; Report of the Committee on Rules & Administration, U.S. Senate, 82nd Congress First Session; p. 44.

ing the following year. "We worked with the fact that a very, very big doubt existed in the minds of the people of Maryland, and in my original survey we found many doubts. There were 70 per cent of the people who did not know if he [Owen Lattimore] had or had not been whitewashed. We worked in the white-washed area. All we wanted to prove was that the people did not know, and we worked in that area. That is the only area where we worked it. It would have taken, I don't know how many, but literally thousands of pages of words of testimony to try to prove a point . . . I said, 'Let's not get into the business of proving whether or not it was a whitewash, let's stay in the business that a doubt does exist.'" [11]

The exploitation of that doubt was accomplished deftly and on a broad front. The best remembered expression of it was a composite photograph in a campaign tabloid called "From the Record," nominally sponsored by "Young Democrats for Butler." The picture showed Tydings gazing attentively and respectfully at a benign Earl Browder, who looked back, soulfully and benignly, at the Senator. Between the figures of the two men was a fine white line, readily detectable by a suspicious person with 20-20 vision. Beneath the picture was the following legend:

> Communist leader Earl Browder, shown at left, in this composite picture, was a star witness at the Tydings committee hearings, and was cajoled into saying Owen Lattimore and others accused of disloyalty were not Communists. Tydings (right) answered: "Oh, thank you, sir." Browder testified in the best interests of those accused, naturally.

The "Oh, thank you, sir" ending Tydings' interrogation of Browder had of course appeared in the transcript of the hearings, and McCarthy's allies had combed the record. One of these allies was Frank Smith, chief editorial writer for the *Times-Herald*, who worked hard on the tabloid and the Butler campaign, and later became Butler's administrative assistant. The "thank you" phrase had caught his eye. He showed it to Garvin Tankersley,

[11] *Ibid.*, p. 272.

assistant managing editor of the *Times-Herald,* previously its picture editor.

Tankersley ordered all available pictures of Tydings and Browder separately and together, and at length came up with two shots that nearly filled the bill. Unhappily, both men were facing the same way. The Browder photograph, made on April 17, 1950, was reversed, so that the Communist, who was facing right when the picture was taken, came up facing left on the print. It was also reduced in size so that Browder and Tydings would appear in the same proportion. The Tydings picture had been made twelve years earlier, under circumstances which explained the Senator's attentive expression: he was listening to the election returns in 1938, the year he survived Roosevelt's purge.

Responsible observers do not contend that the picture or the tabloid made *the* difference in the campaign. In fact, the Butler people believe only part of the half-million press run was distributed. But no one denies that whatever quantity did reach the voters—200,000 or 300,000—the photograph influenced at least some of the 43,000 voters who made the difference and elected John M. Butler, the first Maryland Republican to win a seat in the Senate since 1928.

Frank Smith a few years later wrote a critique on the coverage of the campaign by the press, in which he pointed out that the Butler tabloid was not the only piece of photo fakery in Maryland in 1950. Smith wrote bitterly—and accurately—that the Tydings people themselves had played fast and loose with the facts in a campaign ad which portrayed their Senator on the cover of *Time* Magazine. *Time* had cited Tydings as one of the ten most effective members of the Senate in a March 3 story. Under the tender ministrations of his campaign aides, the gentleman from Maryland appeared in the ad on the *cover* of that issue of *Time,* and therefore, presumably, was the most illustrious of the most effective ten. Actually the March 3 issue of the news magazine carried on its cover not Tydings but the monarch of Siam, Phumiphon.

Now, to be sure, the prospect of Tydings cheating in a modest way is less offensive than the McCarthy crowd's effort to encourage people to think that Tydings *might* be a traitor, but it takes the edge off some of the indignation that otherwise could go unreservedly to the Butler campaigners.[12]

In the Butler-Tydings campaign, Jonkel was meticulous in not trying to prove that Tydings was disloyal; he settled for exploiting doubt. The effort had a certain gloss, as it should have had, for Jonkel was a professional public relations man.

The professional smear artist uses the same ingredients in a cruder manner. An illustration is the fate, in 1946, of Montana's one-time wild man, Senator Burton K. Wheeler. The Senator was an ardent and prickly advocate of the common man against "the interests," and his political career was long and varied. He was an early beneficiary of the political support of the Non-Partisan League when it spread beyond North Dakota. The League was a plains states phenomenon of the era centered on the end of World War I. Originally it was an effort to get for the farmer some of the profits made by middlemen in grain shipments. The movement spread into neighboring states and became a political factor ranging from appreciable to overwhelming in the area north of Colorado and from Minnesota to Idaho.

When Wheeler, in 1920, sought the governorship of Montana as the nominee of the Non-Partisan League, he was described by opponents as "Bolshevik Burt." As a United States Attorney in Montana he had been startled and angered by the depth of World War I anti-German feeling in the state and was outspoken in opposition to "patriotism" of this stripe. His political hegira took him from Republican to Progressive [13] to Democrat, but on the eve of World War II he found himself solidly in the isolationist camp, and he was described as a Fascist and Nazi. In 1946 the accumulated resentments from the two wars were harnessed to

[12] Butler served a lackluster two terms in the Senate, to retire voluntarily in 1962. He was replaced by Tydings' step-son, Joseph D. Tydings, who won his nomination after another bitter Democratic primary in which both sides generated more heat than light.

[13] He was the elder Robert LaFollette's Vice Presidential candidate in 1924 on the Progressive ticket.

beat him.

One of the political hatchet men who brought him down was Walter E. Quigley, an early organizer for the Non-Partisan League who defected from it and began a half-century career as a self-styled "political dynamiter." Quigley, who was memorialized in a study by the Utah political scientist Frank Jonas, played a significant role in numerous hot campaigns in the northern and western states. His "dynamiting" technique was to find a single issue or area in which the candidate was or could be made to appear vulnerable, and then to devote a special campaign "newspaper" to the issue, selecting bits and pieces out of context to "make the most respected individual appear a downright scallawag, but there never is anything upon which a libel pleading can be based." [14]

Quigley built such an issue out of what he had come to see as Wheeler's fascist bias, using comments and quotes lifted from a variety of contexts to make Wheeler's isolationism appear thoroughly un-American. "I was happy to help defeat Wheeler for what I believe was his aid to fascism and Hitler," Quigley observed a few years later. [15]

Quigley's ability to avoid entanglement with the law is shared by most competent professional smear artists. However, these cynical artisans are few in number, and most of the volume of unfair campaign literature originates with over-zealous amateurs. The amateurs, generally, are unaware of legal restrictions against anonymous literature, and therefore are more apt to find themselves afoul of the law. The individual citizen who feels passionately for or against one of the candidates may not even have the political sophistication necessary to know that what he is doing violates the rules of the game as well as the law of the land.

Such a situation, compounded by maladroitness, led to what may be the most incredible boner of modern politics. Barry Gold-

[14] Jonas, "The Art of Political Dynamiting," *Western Political Quarterly*, Vol. X, No. 2 (June, 1957) p. 388n.

[15] *Ibid.*, p. 388n.

water was seeking his second Senate term in 1958, opposed by the man he had beaten six years before, veteran Senator Ernest McFarland. The Phoenix newspaper, the *Arizona Republic,* had given outrageously one-sided coverage to Goldwater. One day the paper ran a banner headline across page one: "GOLDWATER HONEST, SINCERE, MINERS SAY." The small print revealed that a mine union chief didn't like Goldwater but believed that he was honest and sincere enough so you always knew where he stood.

The "miners" reference was to the Mine, Mill and Smelter Workers Union, important in the state because mining is a major economic factor there. The union had been thrown out of the CIO for Communist domination, and had not been readmitted. The newspaper had been attacking responsible labor leaders on page one, among them anti-Communist enemies of the Mine, Mill leadership.

One Arizona trade unionist, an aircraft worker named Frank Goldberg who belonged to the International Association of Machinists, was infuriated by the *Republic's* use of a Mine, Mill leader's words—and a distortion at that—to push Goldwater, when the paper had been traducing anti-Communist unions.

Goldberg recalled a recent Machinists' union journal containing a cartoon of Joseph Stalin, grinning and winking and suggesting that good union members support "right to work" laws, which hamper union power in a number of American states and in all Communist countries. The aircraft worker arranged with a friend employed by the Machinists' union to have the cartoon reproduced on a sheet with the "Honest, Sincere" headline across the top. In the new version, Stalin would be saying, "Why not vote for Goldwater?" At the bottom of the page would be a comment about the newspaper's use of the Miners' "endorsement" to support Goldwater, noting that "politics makes strange bedfellows."

Shortly before Election Day, the job was ready and the sheet was distributed in Phoenix and a few other areas. It was immediately interpreted as suggesting that Barry Goldwater had Communist support.

It had never occurred to Goldberg that Federal law required

him to put his name on the document, so it was illegal.

Goldwater was furious, and assumed that McFarland had sponsored the smear. The latter assumed that Goldwater had created the piece as a reverse smear, to discredit the McFarland campaign, and he was furious. Goldwater summoned the FBI and McFarland the Senate elections subcommittee. A committee investigator arrived and could only find copies of the sheet in the hands of newspaper men to whom Goldwater had sent them to prove McFarland's smear tactics; in doing so Goldwater also had broken the law by distributing anonymous campaign literature.

The FBI quickly found Goldberg and his ally, Earl Anderson, the Machinists' union employee. They were indicted, tried and convicted of violating the Federal statute. A final irony remained. Anderson had the printing done by a Los Angeles firm he dealt with on union business, and through error the International Association of Machinists had been billed—and had paid for the smear sheet. The moral was clear: if you don't know your way around the legal pitfalls when you are tempted to enter a campaign, don't make a move without your lawyer.

The trouble Frank Goldberg got himself and his friend into by remaining anonymous was avoided by a vengeful Minnesotan in the same year. A Democrat named Joseph Robbie was running against the veteran Republican Congressman Walter Judd. A Twin Cities man named Earl Joseph Seymour French was persuaded, for whatever personal reasons, that Robbie's election would be a major misfortune. He trotted off to a neighborhood print shop and ordered a quantity of handbills which he then set out to distribute.

Jos. Robbie
Not a State Man — from S. Dak.
Ran for all sorts of offices in So. Dak.
Claims he is a Lawyer.

Earl Joseph Seymour French, in compliance with Minnesota and Federal law, signed his name and address to the sheet and peddled his papers wherever it seemed they would embarrass

Robbie. Robbie assumed, naturally enough, that this was the work of a Judd henchman and challenged Judd to repudiate the tactic. The Republican Congressman, who, like Robbie, had accepted the Code of Fair Campaign Practices, reviewed the Code's plank on repudiating unfair tactics. It committed a candidate to repudiate unfair tactics used *on his behalf*. Judd reflected on the fact that he had never met French or even heard of him, and the fact that the handbill did not so much as mention Judd, and declined to repudiate it.

It developed that French was not especially eager to see Judd returned to the Congress; he simply didn't like Robbie and found this an effective time to say so. Judd won. As an aftermath, Judd's decision not to repudiate the handbill led the Fair Campaign Practices Committee to amend the Code for the first time since its adoption in 1954. Candidates are now committed to repudiate unfair tactics used for them *or* against their opponents.

On occasion dirty tactics will be carefully and skillfully carried out by a regular political organization with full knowledge of the legal ins and outs and elaborate efforts to cover all tracks (except when giving an occasional false lead). Such was the case in 1958 when the Republican Congressional Committee moved against a threat by West Virginia's Robert H. Mollohan to retire Republican Congressman Arch Moore.

When the "United Miners Journal" appeared in a four-page special edition devoted to devastating assertions about Mollohan, people assumed that the mine union had abandoned the Democrat and endorsed the Republican incumbent. Talk of scandal was rife in the district, West Virginia's First, which embraces the panhandle country between Pennsylvania and Ohio.

The importance of the United Mine Workers in West Virginia elections is obvious. Miners' endorsement could make a vast difference, particularly if custom were breached and the union backed a Republican.

The special edition was so special that its masthead, *United Miners Journal*, had been cut and pasted up from a copy of the bona fide *United Mine Workers Journal* in the offices of the Republican Congressional Committee in Washington. The phony publication had then been reproduced by photo-offset and peddled widely in the district. On this occasion angered Democrats invoked the rarely-enforced Federal prohibition of anonymous literature, and Congressman Moore's former staff member, Keith Jaques, was indicted and tried. He was acquitted, on the reasonable ground that he had no real complicity in the plot beyond following orders and carrying material back and forth between the district and the Republican Congressional Committee in Washington. The real culprits never came to trial.

The same Committee was involved in an unsuccessful effort to unseat a downstate Illinois Democratic Congressman, Melvin Price, in 1964. A multi-colored folder attacked him, urging the electorate to "get rid of the Democommies." The effort was recognized as sheer invective, and backfired.

The Republican Congressional Committee involvement came to light in a curious way. Through error, the printer of the piece billed it to Democratic Congressman Price, with a curt note pointing out that the bill was long overdue. Taken aback, Price set the printer straight, and was bemused to learn that the typesetting had been ordered by a staff member of the GOP House campaign committee. It is unlikely that the campaign committee prepared the copy, for its staff members usually are too sophisticated to lean so heavily on invective and innuendo; it is more likely that a staff man gave layout and similar help to the candidate or an over-eager aide.

Another candidate himself claimed full responsibility for a leaflet that introduced an appeal to anti-Semitism into a California House campaign in 1958. Long Beach is the principal city of what was the Golden State's 18th Congressional District. A Jewish businessman who had been educated for the rabbinate got the Democratic nomination to oppose Congressman Craig Hosmer, a handsome, wavy-haired former naval officer and a Republican. Hosmer, playing the comparative biography game that California pioneered, set forth all his claims to big-league Americanism in one column and next to it ranked Jewish and Jewish-sounding affiliations for his opponent. He cited as a prime source for his own background *Who's Who in America,* and for his opponent, *Who's Who in World Jewry.* A listing in *Who's Who in World Jewry* which read "President, Metal Products Corp., South Bend, Indiana" was changed in the Hosmer leaflet to "Scrap Metal Business."

Hosmer insisted he was not anti-Semitic, and explained that he was simply indignant at the fact that his opponent's background, particularly his religious education, had been so esoteric by contrast with the incumbent's all-American-boy-rising-young-lawyer career. Politicians were puzzled as to why Hosmer did it. One observed that the district was so anti-Semitic that the Virgin Mary's Jewish background would have been too much for the electorate. Whether it cost Hosmer votes or increased the margin by which he won is hard to guess. But it proved a tactical blunder in at least one way: the Democrats secured such quantities of the leaflet as they could and used it as a fund-raising appeal in Jewish communities nearby. Acquisition of the leaflet became difficult for the Democrats, for Hosmer destroyed half of his print order of 100,000 when the storm of protest arose.

A few years later another Congressional campaign resounded with smear charges stemming from a candidate's actions, but in this case the candidate appears to have acted wholly out of a naive unfamiliarity with the facts of life in the office he sought. A New York City Congressman, Republican Seymour Halpern, was already a veteran legislator when he ran for re-election in 1962. His young Democratic opponent built a campaign around Halpern's "do-nothing" record in the 87th Congress. Democratic Congressional Campaign Committee sources had provided the inexperienced opponent, Leonard Finz, with a detailed record indicating that, aside from a handful of so-called private bills for the relief of constituents who had suffered hardship through the fault of some government agency, Halpern had not had a single bill enacted into law. He had introduced more than 300 bills in his two terms in the House. This was enough for Finz, and he had no one to tell him the facts of life in the House of Representatives. Those facts are shrouded beneath a cloak of ancient lore, procedure, custom, and House Rules. Under the rules, Representatives may not co-sponsor legislation, a common and well-known practice in what Congressmen are pleased to disdain as "the other body," the Senate. Halpern was a minority of a minority. He was one of three or four Republicans in the New York City Congressional delegation, and beyond that a Republican in the heavily Democratic House. Thus he had little chance to put his imprint on any substantive legislation, and no chance whatever to hitch his name to that of a Democratic colleague as a co-sponsor.

The House has a practical way around the ban on co-sponsorship. All members who agree on the details of a bill they want to push may put identical bills into the hopper. Halpern had done this on numerous occasions, and had helped materially in shepherding such legislation—often Administration requests—through the tangles of minority politics in the House of Representatives. The Finz campaign, therefore, angered him. Worse, the 87th Congress wound up its business perilously close to Election Day in 1962, and Halpern, conscientiously at work on his constituents' business, and the nation's, got a late and ill-prepared start into the campaign.

Frustrated and perplexed, the Congressman went to the Fair Campaign Practices Committee with his problem, bringing the artifacts of the campaign against him, and proof of his own record. Questioning by Committee staff people revealed that President Kennedy had given the legislator pens he had used in signing bills into law on six occasions, as a token of gratitude for Halpern's help in getting them supported by Republican Congressmen. There was the answer; Halpern had been too close to the problem. He returned to the campaign, summoned a press conference, told the story and brandished the six pens from the Democratic President—and won the election by a substantially greater margin than his election in 1960.

Certainly, misinterpretation of the facts, or at least of a candidate's behavior, may explain a number of smear charges. In 1964, Republican Representative Glenn Cunningham, who serves eastern Nebraska in Congress, suffered from a disease that affected his balance. The Democratic chairman of his county jumped to the assumption that Cunningham, who does not drink, had to be helped to various speaking platforms because he was drunk. He then launched a puritanical attack at the conservative Republican, himself somewhat puritanical of mien and deportment. The county party chairman may have been unaware of the true facts regarding Cunningham. On the other hand, there is always the possibility that the initiator of such a smear could have been appealing to a suggestible electorate.

Confidence in the ignorance and the gullibility of the electorate has been demonstrated in some bizarre episodes in American politics, and occasionally it seems abundantly justified. In one campaign against Oklahoma Senator Josh Lee there were not one but two opponents, both named Josh Lee. In election after election during the life of John F. Kennedy another John F. Kennedy got himself elected to a constitutional office in the Commonwealth of Massachusetts.

Robert R. Reynolds played upon the gullibility of rural voters when he sought successfully to beat Senator Cameron Morrison in the 1932 Democratic primary in Depression-weary North Carolina. Reynolds would flourish a jar of caviar before rustic audiences and say of Senator Morrison, "Cam eats fish eggs, and Red Russian fish eggs at that, and they cost two dollars. Do you want a Senator who ain't too high and mighty to eat good old North Carolina hen eggs, or don't you?"

They did.

Rural voters, especially in the South, have often been courted in ways that do not flatter their intelligence. Such an effort, with some sinister overtones, was employed in a Florida Democratic primary campaign that unseated U.S. Senator Claude Pepper in 1950.[16] Pepper, whose seat dated from 1936, was known as one of the most eloquent orators in that body of orators.

An ardent New Dealer, he became the target of accusations of pro-Communism, and in the 1950 primary he succumbed to a

[16] Pepper was elected to the House in 1962 and re-elected in 1964.

hard combination of opponents: a handsome, youthful Marine Corps veteran and two-term Congressman from Miami, George A. Smathers; a widely-circulated leaflet detailing real and imagined left leanings under the title of "Red Pepper"; and a slick and funny back-country gossip campaign which suggestively spelled out Pepper's secret vices. He practiced nepotism. He had a sister who was a thespian and a brother who was a practicing homo sapiens. He went to college, where, horror of horrors, he matriculated.

When the gullibility of the electorate is compounded by hysteria, startling things happen in the political system. In North Dakota, in the early days of the John Birch Society there, it took a regional coordinator months to calm down the Birch addicts. They were militating against the genuinely conservative Republican Senator Milton Young as a crypto-Communist who ought to be retired at once. Young was equated with Lenin because there were numerous aspects of the twentieth century which the Senator had not moved to repeal. At length the patriots were prevailed upon to realize that if they did beat Young he might well be succeeded by an even more dangerous, even more liberal type. The agitation began in the summer of 1960 and was aimed at Young's re-election bid for 1962, but it began to subside in 1961. The death that year of Senator William Langer, the venerable maverick Republican, opened up a real threat to the radicals when an intelligent liberal Democrat, Quentin Burdick, filed for his seat in the special election. He won in the face of a determined effort by the rightists to expose him as a dangerous Red, and won again for a full term in 1964. Fortunately, if enough non-doctrinaire citizens go to the polls, they can turn back any threat from the remote right.

It is a combination of frustration and hysteria that leads unsophisticated conservative citizens to turn on their own kind as traitors. Frustration at a world where the old verities seem not to be eternal joins with hysterical apprehensions about the devilish cunning of the Communist Foe. Political literature tends to deal only in black and white, and spoken political argument degenerates into accusation.

Political invective, by and large, has fallen on evil days of late. Gone are the days when a John Randolph could tell the whole House of Representatives that an Edward Livingston was "a man of splendid abilities but utterly corrupt. He shines and stinks like rotten mackerel by moonlight." No longer is there a Clay to harpoon a long-winded speaker addressing "posterity" with the comment that the speaker is determined to await the arrival of his audience. Gone, too, is James Michael Curley, who could vilify a man simply by reporting him as eating a steak at a formal dinner. The perfect squelch appears, alas, to be down the political drain, revealing on the bottom of the tub the pattern of things present and to come: pedestrian epithets like McCarthy's "mental midget" for his brilliant adversary William Benton. Dull-witted hammerings like "blueprint of subversive dictatorship." Mean and vicious tactics like imputation of treason as the only rational explanation of differing views.

The electorate can hardly exert a direct and immediate influence on political style. But it can look sharply at the truth and relevance of campaign argument; it can demand proof and refuse to settle for glibness. And, most important of all, it can present a readiness to believe the worst, not about a public figure, but about the traducer of a public figure.

CHAPTER 4

Other Victims

I AM NOT A POLITICIAN, AND MY OTHER HABITS ARE GOOD.

—*Artemus Ward*

THE DANGEROUS doctrine that politics is a dirty business, practiced mainly by knaves and thieves, wins many adherents at the level of state politics. In part this traces to the ancient democratic mistrust of government. Jefferson it was who said "that government is best which governs least." State constitutions frequently limit a governor to one term of office and the basis is the assumption that if in power too long a governor may find ways to usurp power he does not need or deserve. So we make the governorship of many of our states a two- or four-year interlude in a political career rather than a goal toward which many honorable men would strive for a lifetime. Second, the growing Federal power in America has been accompanied by a diminishing state power, so that governors today wield less influence than they did in the old days.

These circumstances help explain the secondary status many citizens accord to the governorships of their states. When the youthful Senator Edward Kennedy paid a courtesy call on the venerable Senator Russell of Georgia, he noted that Russell, too, had come to the Senate at the minimum constitutional age of 35. Russell dryly observed that before *he* came to the Senate, youthful as he was, he already had been the governor of his state.

There are exceptional states, of course, where the governorship is sought above any other prize by able and conscientious men, and there are exceptional men who approach the job as a civic responsibility, having faint heart for it but willing to seek the office and discharge it selflessly. However, as a nation we tend not to expect much of our governors—when we think of them at all—and to regard them with suspicion and hostility somewhat greater than what we reserve for members of Congress.

Candidates for governor thus come in for a rich variety of abuse when they seek election. Imputing immorality to a candidate is a favorite means of attack.

In New Hampshire, in 1956, a Democrat lost the governorship in part because of a whispering campaign that he was a drunkard. John Shaw was the candidate, and New Hampshire voters appeared to be flirting with the unfamiliar prospect of electing a Democrat. It happened that Shaw was a total abstainer from alcohol. Yet the rumor spread in Protestant church circles: "Would you believe it? That John Shaw the Democrats are running for governor—they say he's a terrible drinker, positively a drunkard. And he hides it so. Such a pity, what a nice man he *seems* to be."

Ironically enough, in Wisconsin in the same year, a moderate drinker nearly lost the governorship because of a rumor that he was a temperance worker.

The Republican candidate for governor, Vernon Thompson, happened to reside in Richland Center, a town which was dry under local option. The resort business is of huge importance to many sections of the state, particularly the various wooded and hilly areas easily accessible from Chicago, Milwaukee and Minneapolis-St. Paul. Through these resort belts in the fall of 1956 rumors spread about the future of the resorts, which, obviously, rely heavily on bar trade. Two men, or perhaps several pairs of men, would appear at a resort bar, a few minutes apart, and strike up a conversation which, though friendly, grew loud enough to attract the attention of the bartender and nearby patrons. The conversation would go something like this:

"You know this fellow Thompson the Republicans are running for governor?"

"Yeah, seems to be a nice guy."

"Yep, he's a good man. Looks like he'll get elected. Too bad, though."

"How you mean, 'too bad'?"

"Oh, he's a dry, you know. Lives in Richland Center, quite a power there. They're dry, you know."

"No kidding?"

"That's right. If he wins, he's gonna dry up the state. Good man, but it sure will raise hell with places like this."

Thompson won, but with a margin sharply below what had been forecast.

In both the Thompson and Shaw affairs, there was no effort to produce evidence that the allegations were true. They were passed along by word of mouth. A defense against this tactic is difficult because by the time the rumor reaches the candidate there is no certain way of knowing how widespread the story is and where it is circulating at the moment of discovery.

Sometimes a smear that seems to be documented may be even more difficult to counteract, especially if the documentation is accurate and the background is complex. Such a smear helped materially to deny Democratic Congressman Samuel Stratton his party's nomination for Governor of New York in 1962.

On a college holiday in 1936, young Stratton had visited Germany on a bicycle tour. The Olympic games were being held there, and in deference to the sensibilities of international tourists the Nazis had soft-pedaled their Jew-baiting. When he went home, Stratton commented in an article for his college paper on the visible material improvements that had been made by the Hitler administration. He noted that if the anti-Semitism of the German people could not be tolerated, at least one could understand the various bases for it.

Stratton finished college, entered politics and became the mayor of Schenectady. While mayor, he protested against the practice by the Mayors' Conference of New York of holding its meetings at an Adirondack Mountain resort that discriminated against Jews. In various other ways he won the respect and trust of assorted local and national Jewish organizations, and was even named man of the year by one of them.

Now, in 1962, 26 years after the college article, Stratton found it disinterred and interpreted so as to make him look like an anti-Semite. The impact on the New York Democratic Convention was substantial, and observers believe it was the dominant factor in denying him the nomination.

False attribution of religious and ethnic prejudice is a favorite gambit of dirty campaigners. Equally favored is the practice of rallying the bigots by appealing to their prejudices against a candidate's faith or background. When Huey Long's brother Earl was ending his term as Governor of Louisiana a big field materialized for the 1951 Democratic primary. The constitution forbids a governor to succeed himself. One of the hopefuls was a young New Orleans Congressman named Hale Boggs. Boggs was an old friend and Congressional colleague of Louisiana's junior Senator, Russell Long, Earl Long's nephew. Russell Long endorsed Boggs and campaigned diligently for him and with him up and down the state.

Uncle Earl had other ideas. He was backing Carlos Spaht and he zeroed in on Boggs to nullify his appeal and the magic of Russell's name. Midway in the primary, Earl persuaded the Louisiana Register of Lands, Lucille Mae Grace, herself a candidate and the first woman to seek the governorship in the Pelican State, to test the eligibility of Congressman Boggs in the courts. Her grounds: Hale's "socialistic and left-wing tendencies" when he, some two decades before, was a student at Tulane. The hearing generated statewide publicity. The finding, that the charge was without substance, got little mileage outside of Boggs' home territory of New Orleans.

Now the preliminaries were over, and in the Bible Belt of

north Louisiana, Uncle Earl got down to business. He stumped vigorously for his candidate, Spaht.

"You-all've heard that ol' Hale is a Communist," he would say. "Shucks, ol' Hale's no Communist! Why he's one of the finest *Roman Catholics* in the state (and you-all know Roman Catholics aren't *allowed* to be Communists. Not only that—Hale's brother is one of the finest *Jesuit priests* in Louisiana.)"

Ol' Earl was not content to leave it at that. He referred to the young Representative and his friend, the young Senator, as "the gold dust twins, down from Washington." They were plucked too green, he said.

Boggs on occasion would be mistaken for Senator Long, and he would modestly reply, "No, that's Huey Long's son over there —the handsome one."

This suited Earl. He would take a few mincing steps and say to his audience, "Those gold dust twins go around the state telling each other how pretty they are."

Boggs lost, but so did Earl Long's stand-in.

Earl Long was willing to use the bigotry of some of his constituents to advance a political cause, but the Longs were not bigots or Ku Klux Klan supporters. Huey despised the Klan for its bigotry and violence. Once when the Imperial Wizard of the Klan offered to come to Louisiana to campaign for him, Long rejected the offer. "Quote me as saying that that imperial bastard will never set foot in Louisiana, and that when I call him a son of a bitch I am not using profanity but am referring to the circumstances of his birth."

The popular northern liberal conception of all Southern politicians as racists and Negro-baiters does not stand up under investigation. Save for the wild excesses of a few of the more flamboyant demagogues, the Negro was not even a political issue in the South between the end of the Reconstruction and the recent succession of Supreme Court decisions and civil rights bills.

There have been few politicians in the South who would spew the venomous cant of a Cole Blease, who, when he was Governor of South Carolina, made political capital out of the

Southern rape complex. He defended the lynching of Negroes, to the screaming, hysterical approval of his audience: "Whenever the Constitution comes between me and the virtue of the white women of the South, I say to hell with the Constitution!"

Exploitation of the Negro through the manipulation of anti-Negro bias has been much more common. Even so, imaginative exploitation is rarely in evidence today. One of the last great practitioners of this art was Georgia's Gene Talmadge. When he was seeking the governorship in 1946 he was opposed in the Democratic primary by one James V. Carmichael. There is no evidence that Carmichael harbored any integrationist leanings. Nevertheless, the resourceful Talmadge ran across a man who was a dead ringer for Carmichael. The double's job was to drive around Georgia accompanied by two Negroes. At every stop, the hired Carmichael would leave the impression that he was Talmadge's bona fide rival, while the Negroes would loll arrogantly in the car, puffing great clouds of smoke from big cigars.

Imaginative chicanery in exploiting Negroes has been visible in the North as well as the South. A shabby but effective effort to intimidate Negroes into staying away from the polls came to light in Detroit in 1962. In that city, Negro families frequently move to new residences within the city. They also tend to vote heavily Democratic.

In the 1962 campaign for governor, Republicans set up a bi-partisan committee "to fight election abuses," raised some money for it, and hired the Honest Ballot Association to send its chief investigator there as counsel. All this preparation was the framework for a letter to Negro voters warning them of the danger of committing election fraud if they voted from an address from which they were not registered.

What the warning letter's stern tone did not convey was that (1) Negroes when they move in Detroit usually move within their election district, and (2) under those circumstances—moving within the district—one may vote unhampered.

The whole affair was conducted without the knowledge of the man who was supposed to be its chief beneficiary, George

Romney. The plan was detected by the Democrats and exposed in time to dampen most of its effect, but it offers considerable support to the political truism that a man can take care of his enemies, but his friends may do him in.

A friendly, if dishonest, gesture helped to beat a Republican gubernatorial candidate in Maine in 1956, where Edmund Muskie, a Democrat who had done the impossible and been elected governor, was seeking a second term.

Substantial aid was given Muskie's opponent by Republican strategists in Washington. One of the men who became involved was a hard-boiled political pro on the Republican National Committee staff. He recalled seeing a recent newspaper photograph of Governor Muskie which would lend itself admirably to cropping. The photo had shown the Governor mediating a labor dispute between the head of a textile industry group and the state CIO leader, Dennis Blais.

The Republicans had been making a major issue of their contention that the CIO and its Political Action Committee were really pulling the strings that made Muskie dance. There was a story that he had accepted an exorbitantly large gift of $2,000 for his campaign from the CIO, as well as advice and even instructions.

The National Committee pro took the picture to the Republican candidate, Willis A. Trafton, and pointed out that by simply eliminating the industry representative from the photo there would be persuasive evidence of Muskie's intimacy with the labor boss; after all, people know photographs don't lie. Trafton, to his credit, refused to use the picture, recognizing it as a patent and wholly unfair distortion.

The pro was not so squeamish. The photograph was cropped and put into the hands of a friendly newspaperman. Shortly before Election Day the picture appeared in the *Boston Herald*, which circulates extensively in Maine. It illustrated a round-up story on the gubernatorial campaign. Muskie sat beside the CIO chieftain; the other man was missing, and in his absence Muskie appeared to be listening attentively and respectfully to what the labor leader was saying. The caption identified Blais as the CIO-PAC boss, and, for good measure, as the "POWER IN MUSKIE CAMPAIGN."

The story does not end there. Both Muskie and his opponent had endorsed the Code of Fair Campaign Practices. The Democratic governor took to television before Election Day with enlargements of the cropped photo, the original, and a copy of the Code. He pointed to the last item in the Code, committing candidates to repudiate unfair support. The voters were persuaded, and Muskie won a second term, after which he went to the U. S. Senate.

A different means of using the press to deceive victimized another Democratic candidate for governor in the same year. Herschel Loveless of Iowa saw circulated against his candidacy a photo-offset reproduction of part of a page from the Ottumwa (Iowa) *Courier* of April 24, 1934. "Ottumwa Man Accused of Cash Theft," the headline read. The story told how H. C. Loveless had been jailed on a charge of embezzling some $450 from an oil company for which he worked. The story jarred supporters in far parts of the state and stirred a storm of righteous indignation among Republicans, until all the facts emerged. The clipping had been used years before when Loveless was running for a lesser office, and on that occasion a GOP leader, outraged at the deception involved, had denounced its use. In the 1934 episode Loveless had indeed been accused of the embezzlement, but was cleared within hours when the real thief was found. Naturally, the 1956 sponsors of the 1934 clipping did not include with it the subsequent story of his exoneration. The smear backfired and Loveless was elected.

The disinterment of another legal matter of ancient vintage helped elect Republican Mark Hatfield Governor of Oregon in 1958. Young Hatfield was Secretary of State in Oregon, and he was an able and ambitious politician. He had set his sights on the governorship while he was still in junior high school, and now he was ready to claim the prize.

Twenty years earlier, when Hatfield was seventeen, a car he

was driving had struck and killed a little girl. Hatfield's mother owned the car, and the parents of the child filed a negligence suit against her. In court, the youth testified that he had not seen the little girl dart out from behind a parked car just before he struck her.

In the 1958 campaign, shortly before Election Day, Democratic Senator Wayne Morse recalled the auto accident and observed that the jury had found young Hatfield guilty of negligence, therefore refusing to accept his word. This, Morse suggested, added up to perjury. The Senator went further: "Hatfield is thoroughly, intellectually dishonest. Hatfield cannot be relied on. This is an old mental pattern of Hatfield's." Newspaper headlines proclaimed: "Morse calls Hatfield Liar." Voters rebelled at the assertion. At age 37, Hatfield fulfilled his junior high school ambition to sit in the Governor's mansion.

Six years later Hatfield had become a major national Republican figure and he keynoted the GOP National Convention with a speech that angered the substantial right wing delegations there. Curiously enough, one of his principal allies against the rightist delegates, William W. Scranton, had won the governorship of his own state in a campaign that included standard right-wing tactics.

In 1962 Scranton was a Pennsylvania Congressman seeking the governorship in a heated campaign against Democrat J. Richardson Dilworth. Both candidates were articulate, colorful, and artists at invective. Scranton's running mate, seeking the U.S. Senate seat held by Democrat Joseph W. Clark, was Congressman James Van Zandt, the only non-patrician among the top four candidates. Van Zandt breathed fire on the Communist issue: "First and last, Jimmie Van Zandt is a patriot," he shouted. "My opponent is the voice of appeasement and conciliation of Communism." He portrayed Senator Clark as representing the "left-wing ADA" instead of Pennsylvania.

Clark tagged Van Zandt as a dirty campaigner whose record in the House was not only reactionary but insubstantial; he reminded voters that Dwight Eisenhower, a Pennsylvania voter, was cool to the Altoona Congressman's Senatorial ambitions.

Van Zandt maintained his shrill pitch: the Senator was "just as soft on Red Cuba as he is on Red China." Scranton (although he was far to the left of Van Zandt) noted that the "Communist Party of Eastern Pennsylvania" supported the top Democrats, while offering no such help to Scranton and Van Zandt.

Cries of rage emanated from the Democrats and much of the press. Scranton told a radio interviewer in Lancaster, "I see no necessity for apologizing." He went on to repeat the assertion, attributing its source to radio commentator Fulton Lewis, Jr., and noted again the Communist statement that they would not help the Republican candidates. "And I agreed with them," he said. "We were not the type of candidates which were going to be helpful to the Communist Party." Scranton did observe that he knew Clark and Dilworth weren't Communists themselves, a concession his running mate was not willing to make. "Color him red, white and blue," said a GOP tract of Mr. Van Zandt.

Scranton won the governor's mansion, and Clark was re-elected to the Senate. Van Zandt's fate might be regarded as a step in the political education of Scranton. At the Republican Convention two years later the Pennsylvania Governor became the focus of a last-minute stop Goldwater effort. He was dismayed to find himself the target of Red innuendoes no more substantial than those he had helped to shower on his 1962 opponent.

The Scranton and Van Zandt campaigns against Clark and Dilworth may have been Pennsylvania's first substantial taste of electioneering by fighting Communism, as some newspapers said. But elsewhere the approach was as old as worry about Bolsheviks.

In California, where campaign innuendo about pro-Communism evolved from a crude tactic to an art form, former Vice President Richard Nixon in 1962 challenged the incumbent Democratic Governor, Edmund G. ("Pat") Brown.

Conservative California Democrats began to receive in the

mail an oversized postcard, with a return card attached. It purported to come from a "Committee to Preserve the Democratic Party in California." The return address was a San Francisco Post Office box. A request for funds for the committee lent authenticity. Among other things, the questionnaire asked Golden State Democrats whether they approved of admitting Red China to the United Nations and "allowing subversives the freedom of college campuses." A yes answer, it was made plain, was "the CDC leadership viewpoint."

The CDC is the California Democratic Council which, since its founding after the Second World War, quickly became the largest volunteer political movement in the nation. Its impact on Democratic politics is great but not dominant. The CDC is solidly and ardently liberal, and a major California political pastime among Republicans is splitting off the conservative Democrats from their dedicated liberal brethren. This the postcard poll set out to do.

Having demonstrated the far-out left wing stance it attributed to the CDC, the questionnaire then blandly asked, "Can California afford to have a governor indebted to the CDC?"

For anyone whose anger and shock did not suggest a course of action, the postcard offered some possibilities: (1) demand that Democrats repudiate the CDC; (2) refuse to support Democratic candidates who fail to denounce it; (3) support "a Republican candidate rather than sell out the Party and the State Government to CDC Objectives."

When the poll appeared the Democrats got a temporary court order restraining its continued circulation and freezing the bank account of the sponsoring organization, the Committee to Preserve the Democratic Party. The action was made possible by the postcard's pitch for money; California law forbids seeking funds in the name of a party organization without proof that it really is a party organization.

After Election Day, and an eminently satisfying win for Governor Brown, the Democrats eschewed the victor's customary post-election magnanimity and refused to drop the legal action begun with the temporary injunction. Months later, at a cocktail party, Leona Baxter, [1] the Republican mother superior of political public relations, ran into Roger Kent, vice chairman of the Democratic State Central Committee. She expressed curiosity as to why the Democrats had not abandoned this legal action along with others that had been initiated during the campaign for purely tactical considerations. Kent suggested that the Democrats wanted to find out who was responsible. The conversation revealed that both Democratic leader Kent and Republican publicist Baxter had an idea that the trail from the postcard poll just might lead to the door of Richard M. Nixon, the defeated gubernatorial candidate.

"Do you want to destroy Nixon completely?" Miss Baxter gasped. Mr. Kent replied, "It might be a useful by-product."

In 1964 a California court confirmed the Kent suspicion and the Baxter apprehension. Superior Court Judge Byron Arnold found the poll to be "instigated, financed, prepared, implemented, supervised and executed by the Nixon for Governor Campaign Committee and the Nixon for Governor Finance Committee." He found that Nixon felt it would help, "since it reflected his own position concerning the relationship of Democrats to the CDC."

Judge Arnold also found that "This postcard poll was reviewed, amended and finally approved by Mr. Nixon personally," and that the list of objectives attributed to the CDC in the questionnaire "were substantially the same as charges made repeatedly by Mr. Nixon in his campaign speeches."

Perhaps the final blow was the judge's finding that while the polling company billed the Nixon campaign for a "statewide mailing to 900,000 *conservative* Democrats," the returns were publicized by the Nixon people as the "voice of the *rank and file* Democrat." (Emphasis added.)

Roger Kent had hoped all along that the bank balance established for the "Committee for the Preservation of the Demo-

---

[1] Of the campaign management firm of Whitaker & Baxter, "Campaigns, Incorporated."

cratic Party" at its inception would be awarded as damages to the Democratic complainants. Some $9,000 was in the account when the action was brought, and had come directly from the Nixon campaign organization. "What a way to finance the Democratic Party," Kent mused. However, the judge awarded only the total of contributions raised by the poll—$368.50—to the Democrats, as damages and costs.

Although Nixon had control of the postcard poll maneuver, he, like all politicians, has been the beneficiary of unwanted "help" that could not be controlled. One such volunteer in 1962 was one of those professional former counterspies for the FBI who appear to thrive in California. Karl Prussion devotes himself to warning the American people about the Communist menace through the usual newsletters, lectures, articles, and occasional pamphlets. In one of the pamphlets, whose point was underlined by its shiny red cover, he used an acrostic to locate the menace in the California Democratic Council, or CDC. The title was:

C alifornia
D ynasty of
C ommunism

This work portrayed the CDC as conceived in and dedicated to Communist goals, and Pat Brown as the eager slave of the CDC. Inside the pamphlet was a photograph of Pat Brown bowing deferentially toward a picture, on the facing page, of Nikita Khrushchev, looking truculent and demanding. The Governor's hands were clasped in front of him as though in prayer. His expression clearly indicated affection and humility and eagerness to please. However, when the photo was made Brown was bowing not to Khrushchev, but to a young Laotian minstrel girl visiting Los Angeles under the sponsorship of the Department of State. At the end of the visit, the Governor had asked something to this effect: "And how do you say good-bye in your country, little girl?"

The Laotian lass smiled, clasped her hands, inclined her

head graciously, and bowed. The governor smiled, clasped his hands, inclined his head graciously, and bowed. "So?" he asked. "So," said the girl. And that is how Pat Brown came to bow down to the Red boss.

Brown was able to locate the original photograph, and he supplied it to the press with copies of the Prussion pamphlet. The Republican state chairman, Casper W. ("Cap") Weinberger, had already sought to stop circulation of the Prussion booklet in Republican headquarters around the state. Greatly embarrassed at the insistence with which some southern California right-wing Republicans continued to peddle it, he repudiated it publicly and angrily. The intractables continued to entertain each other with the red pamphlet, but for thinking Californians the magic was gone.

Smoking out Communists is, of course, a way of life in much of the Golden State, and it seldom matters whether there are real Communists available or not. The sportsman hunts for the joy of the chase and the majesty of the forest, not for meat.

Brown has been called a Communist off and on for years, as has any prominent California Democrat or moderate-to-liberal Republican. But the Golden State's distinction in conducting dirty campaigns is not at all limited to shouting red. The state's politics has been complex ever since the railroads lost their total grip on California, and a variety of reasons (discussed in the next chapter) conspire to make California elections often the dirtiest in the nation. Against this background, there is wide agreement that the campaign of 1958, when Pat Brown first sought the governorship, was one of the most tangled and one of the dirtiest in what then was the 108-year history of the state.

The Democratic Party had been moribund in California ever since the Progressive era; Hiram Johnson's reforms had stripped away patronage from the parties, and patronage is the glue that holds political organizations together. The Republicans had outsmarted and out-manipulated the Democrats at every turn. The practice of cross-filing often gave Republican candidates the Democratic nomination as well as their own. Shortly after World

War II some fresh new faces had become active in Democratic politics and set about the tedious business of building a party out of the driftwood available. Among these newcomers were Alan Cranston, who founded the CDC; Roger Kent, dean of northern California Democrats and often state chairman; Libby Smith, now Libby Gatov, who became John Kennedy's first Treasurer of the United States; Stanley Mosk, later Attorney General; and Pierre Salinger, who was Kennedy's Press Secretary. They organized patiently and by 1958 in Attorney General Pat Brown, the only Democrat holding statewide office, they had an attractive candidate as well as a laboriously built political organization.

So in 1958 many strains of California politics came together. The resurrecting Democratic Party was seeking to undo the mischief of a generation of wily Republican exploitation of the complaisant Democratic majority; the practice of cross-filing was under attack and soon to be abolished. Earl Warren's successor as the permanent Republican Governor of California, Goodwin Knight, was being shunted off the track by conservative Oakland publisher William F. Knowland, Minority Leader of the U. S. Senate. Knight, with the politician's sensitivity to vacuums, was moving into the GOP designation for the Knowland Senate seat.

An extra complication was the long list of initiative measures on the absurd California ballot, by which, in the sweet name of reform, the people do much of the work of the legislature. Two of these propositions for 1958 were pure dynamite. Proposition 18, the so-called right-to-work proposition, would outlaw the union shop in California. Labor fought it with total dedication and with a sophistication new even to the movement's veteran political pros.

The other initiative proposition with catastrophic potential was number 16, which would repeal a fairly recent removal of private and parochial schools from the tax rolls. This provided California's abundant crop of anti-Catholics with a splendid rehearsal for the big one coming up in 1960, when a Catholic would pretend to the Presidency.

The political landscape, then, was a minefield, with instant destruction at hand for the unwary and the unlucky. Most California candidates all but broke arms and legs in the scramble to get clear of any involvement with the parochial school tax proposition, but Brown was involved willy-nilly. He was a Catholic, and as Attorney General he had enforced the state law against Bible reading in the public schools. Thus he was a particularly inviting target to California's Bible Belt.

In the case of the "right-to-work" proposition 18, here, too, scores of politicians sustained wounds in the rush to get clear of involvement. Senator Knowland, however, serenely and majestically embraced the proposition.

Knowland shared the popular vision of himself as the Republican nominee for President in 1960. He decided he needed broader experience than his Senate minority leadership would afford, and so shoved Goodie Knight out of the governor's race. Knowland gave short shrift to dominant state issues such as water, old-age assistance and education, and concentrated on blaming Brown for increases in narcotics addiction, pornography, and crime—Brown, the Democratic Attorney General in the Republican Goodwin Knight administration. Naturally, Knight as well as Brown was implicated to some degree, and Knight fired back from time to time in self-defense; these shots hit Knowland and helped Brown.

The Knowland campaign linked Brown with corruption by documenting at tedious length the fact that a Chicago law firm in which one of Brown's advisers, Democratic National Committeeman Paul Ziffren, had worked years previously, had at one time represented certain business interests of Capone-era gangsters. It depicted him also as a complete stooge of Walter Reuther and the labor movement.

The Senator's wife, Helen Knowland, was particularly alarmed at the threat of Reuther. She shrilly attacked "big labor," and in a memorable seven-page letter to Republican leaders denounced California unions for abandoning "macaroni-spine" Goodie Knight in favor of the Democratic candidate, and enunciated the goal of her husband's campaign: to keep California free from becoming "another satellite of Walter Reuther's labor-political empire."

Mrs. Knowland found a new tool. Longtime reactionary and sometime anti-Semite pamphleteer Joseph P. Kamp had prepared a lengthy tract which blamed Walter Reuther for virtually every ill but the common cold. It was titled "Meet the Man Who Plans to Rule America," and it described the abstemious Reuther, who neither drinks, smokes, nor rides first-class planes when coach seats are available, in horrifying terms. Mrs. Knowland acquired and circulated 500 copies of the tract and ordered thousands more. Labor, already fighting Proposition 18 and Knowland, worked a little harder for Brown. There was an outcry about the pamphlet, in which the chairman of the Republican National Committee, Connecticut's Meade Alcorn, joined. The Kamp record was simply too unsavory for sensitive Republican stomachs. Goodie Knight muttered about un-Republican tactics. One Republican paper ran a biting editorial denouncing Knowland for using his wife as a hatchet-woman. Knowland growled that he didn't think he was "called upon to answer every piece of mail that comes into my office." Helen Knowland conceded that she had stopped her first distribution, not because of the outcry, but, surprisingly, because the document didn't have a union "bug," the label of a union printer.

The campaign got dirtier and dirtier. California voters, long used to sorting out the slander from the campaign arguments, were overworked. The confusing reversal of roles between Knowland and Knight took its toll. As one woman put it plaintively, "But I liked things just the way they were, with Mr. Knowland in Washington and Mr. Knight in Sacramento."

Precedent was shattered when the *San Francisco Chronicle* pulled out of its once inviolate political liaison with Knowland's *Oakland Tribune* and the *Los Angeles Times*. A few days before the election, the *Chronicle* listed its previous endorsements in editorial form on page one. There was one exception, and a separate box on the front page explained it. The *Chronicle* had withdrawn its support of Knowland because "we have been unfavorably impressed with his subsequent campaign." [2]

The *Chronicle* reflected the mood of California accurately. Brown won handily, and the nature of California politics had been changed; there was a two-party system, and Democratic majorities elected Democratic officials.

The misleading, and the downright dishonest, campaign tactics reviewed in this chapter have been tailored to the credulity and the biases of the electorates at which they were directed. When the tactics have not been exposed, and when they have not simply "gone too far," they have succeeded.

Discovered, however, and properly exploited by the intended victim, these smears have exploded, backfiring on their intended beneficiaries. In this fact is the most consistently effective antidote to unfair campaigning.

Another encouraging aspect is reflected in the experience of Governor Scranton: being the victim of a smear attack alters one's entire perspective about unfair campaigning, and sharpens one's perceptiveness about unfair devices that may appear easy and effective and even foolproof.

Finally, the case of the *San Francisco Chronicle* in the Knowland-Brown campaign offers a useful example to the press at large, which has not always been willing to abandon familiar partisans when the choice is between silent acquiescence and integrity.

[2] There were reports about this time that *Los Angeles Times* publisher Norman Chandler noted sourly that Knowland was being "too damn wishy-washy." The *Oakland Tribune*, Mr. Knowland's paper, remained calm.

CHAPTER 5

Political Order: Sweet Disarray

IF I COULD NOT GO TO HEAVEN BUT WITH A PARTY I WOULD
NOT GO THERE AT ALL.

—*Thomas Jefferson, 1789*

JEFFERSON, in this characteristic early American view of political parties, was of course thinking of narrow, fixed-focus parties, and the American political landscape is littered with their bones. The Federalists, the Whigs, the Anti-Masons, Abolitionists, Secessionists, Free Soilers, Greenbackers, Populists, LaFollette Progressives, Wallace Progressives, Dixiecrats, a welter of leftist parties and more—all these were to greater or lesser degree one-idea, ideologically-based parties, and they have not thrived in the American climate.

The first viable American party emerged as a loose consensus group reacting to the narrow focus of the first party, the Federalists. By the time the republican anti-Federalist party had become the Democratic-Republican Party it had broadened its base, and before it became simply the Democratic Party it had to solidify its strength as well as widen its appeal.

It was not until the eve of the Civil War that another coalition of interests arrived at party status with an appeal broad enough to pre-empt some of the national consensus that the Democrats had monopolized and that now was contorted by slavery and the economic issues dividing North and South.

Narrowly focused parties necessitate coalition government. If in today's world the Democratic Party, for example, were to be supplanted by a roster of splinter parties, *some* of the parties it would take to fill the void are: Northern Negro; Labor (at least one—probably two or three); White Integrationist; White Segregationist; Eastern Industrial and Financial; Midwestern Industrial and Financial; Eastern and Southern Farmers; Midwestern Farmers; Western Growers; Western Grazers; Utilities and Railroads; Petroleum and Solid Minerals; Negotiate with Red China; Bomb Red China; Live with Castro; Annihilate Castro; and so on. Political parties would proliferate like Protestant sects in the 18th and 19th centuries. The ensuing maelstrom, in which a coalition of interests would have to be forged to constitute a government and operate a Congress, would be incredible.

Americans coalesce in their parties instead of their government. Thanks to the party system they have four years between conventions to re-align and re-weigh different party factions. In the absence of a coalition party system, such juggling of interests would have to take place between election and inauguration, and the complications would be fearful and wonderful to behold.

Indeed, the party system is at its weakest when temptations toward ideological party organization and focus are strongest. And when the urge to focus on a narrow set of issues is strongest, the likelihood of dirty campaigning is at its peak.

For smear is the handmaiden of political parochialism. The all-important single goal becomes so essential that it must be won at any cost. When the Republican Party is being pulled toward exclusive concern with anti-Communism, campaigns like those of 1950 and 1954 result. When the Democratic Party is engaged chiefly in fighting the radical right, personified (falsely, to be sure) by Goldwater, and when simultaneously the Republican

Party is focused mainly on fighting immorality personified in Johnson (however falsely), then we are doomed to a campaign like that of 1964. Debate on real issues is impossible, because real issues don't fit the focus.

The standard animal symbols for the two parties are deformed by newspaper editorial cartoonists in such times of stress to present a two-headed elephant or a two-headed donkey—usually with the extra head on the rear end trying to guide the party into the past or to fight the direction taken by the presumed leader. Often enough the internal party rumblings and pullings and haulings would justify five or six heads, all steering in different directions.

Thus in 1954 President Eisenhower assured the nation that fear of Communists in government would not be a campaign issue. Vice President Nixon, meanwhile, spoke of Democrats who were guilty of treason—to the high principles of the Democratic Party. The Republican National Committee prepared material recalling Congressional investigations and reports of Communist efforts at infiltration, successful and unsuccessful. The Women's Division of the National Committee and the Women's Federation of Republican Clubs emphasized the war issue—the son you save may be your own. The Republican Senatorial Campaign Committee pitched in with blatant innuendo: a pamphlet showed the head of veteran Senator James E. Murray of Montana on the body of a spider stamped with the hammer and sickle: "SENATOR MURRAY and the RED WEB OVER CONGRESS." And the Republican Congressional campaign committee ran a classic radio spot announcement suggesting that the Kremlin ordered the Republicans defeated. (See Chapter 10 for details.)

It would be naive to suppose that all these handsomely interlocking pieces just happened to occur independently of one another. Eisenhower surely meant what he said, but the staffs of the various Republican committees—and indeed of a number of government agencies—were manned with people who knew that Ike was simply a babe in the woods in these matters; let him stick to the high road. The National Committee, closely enough identified with the President and the White House, would stick to facts and records, however carefully edited and presented. Nobody could stop the women from expressing concern over the slaughter of their sons. And as for the House and Senate campaign committees—well, the President had no control over them. For that matter, both committees are large enough in membership so it is difficult for any member to know precisely what is going on at any point. In the case of the Republican House campaign group, its staff is so large that an offended moderate GOP Congressman could inquire for weeks without finding who was responsible for what piece of legerdemain about the loyalty of some Democratic incumbent or challenger.

There is one way to amend the practice of such a body, and that is for it to lose enough elections so the favorite theme will be abandoned or at least dealt with accurately, relevantly, and factually. This of course has been happening. The Republicans lost their fleeting control of the Congress in the 1954 elections; they had a ten-vote margin in the 84th Congress, elected in 1952 with Eisenhower; the 85th Congress, in which they had hoped to offset traditional off-year losses with the big Red gambit was controlled by the Democrats with a cushion of 29 votes. Democratic control has increased year by year since. The Senate picture is similar.

Yet the Republican Congressional Committee continues to ply the old trade. After the historic House losses of 1964, the committee entered 1965 singling out for special attention Democrats who had voted the "wrong" way on issues the Republican craftsmen saw as suitably anti-Communist. Press releases went to the local papers of each of these Democrats: "Unfortunately [the Democratic Congressman's] vote has lined him up with every subversive organization in the country . . ."

Nostalgia may explain the persistence of the practice. After all, the Communist issue did help the Republicans win control of the House in 1946, and it did not prevent them from cashing in on the Eisenhower wave of 1952. On the other hand, it helped them lose the House in 1948, 1954, 1956, 1958, 1960, 1962, 1964.

How long can one argue with unsuccess?

Although Republicans, especially in the House campaign committee, have virtually monopolized the Red issue in terms of unfair and dishonest exploitation, the Party has no monopoly on other electioneering sins.

The basic problem is that the political party in America has no real disciplinary power over its branches and sub-branches. Often—particularly at the state level—the party chairman doesn't know what his women's division, or nationalities division, or veterans division is doing and thus loses control through poor communications alone. The problem is compounded by volunteers of various degrees of wit, activity, and influence. In 1962 a Democratic opportunist in New York State thought to harness the topic of Republican Governor Rockefeller's then recent divorce and rumors of his impending remarriage. So the Women's Division of the State Committee came to be the sponsors of a large-space newspaper ad to be run in cities around the state late in the campaign. The headline declared, "Women Don't Want a Part-time Governor Any More Than They Want a Part-time Husband." The ad then went on to say that Governor Rockefeller was too busy "Romancing the White House" to worry about state problems. Near the bottom of the page was a snapshot of Democratic candidate Bob Morgenthau with his family. And where will you find Bob Morgenthau? the ad asked. Why, at home, worrying about the same problems *you* worry about.

A reform Democrat of high integrity saw the layout for the Rockefeller Romancing Ad. Practical as well as scrupulous, he saw boomerang as well as dirty trick. He was unable to persuade the instigator of the ad against using it on either ground. Dismayed, he then contacted the Fair Campaign Practices Committee, described the ad and asked for a professional estimate of its backfire potential. He was told it was not only high but practically certain. A short time later a colleague on the campaign staff made a similar inquiry and was assured that the Republicans would protest furiously if the ad were run, that it would be impossible to prevent a backfire reaction that could swamp Morgenthau. The ad never appeared. Morgenthau lost, but he did not carry with him into defeat the stigma of losing because of failure to control the cynicism and irrelevance of some of his campaign tacticians.

On paper it is possible to separate the campaign organization from the regular party committee, state or national. But in practice there is a large area where one merges into the other. Furthermore, it is difficult for the layman to separate bona fide volunteer or citizen committees from the carefully contrived fronts with which modern campaigns abound. Consider the impressive list of fairly large-scale committees that raised money for the 1960 Presidential campaign. It does not include front organizations created to beguile voters but not to raise money.

For the Republicans there was, of course, the Republican National Committee—plus the National Federation of Republican Women, the Women's National Republican Campaign Committee, the Young Republicans National Federation, and assorted Republican Finance Committees. There were also Citizens for Nixon-Lodge, for the Real Nixon, and for Eisenhower and Nixon in 1958. There were both Floridians and *Conservative* Floridians for Nixon-Lodge. There were Builders, Friends, Vote-Getters, and Volunteers for Nixon-Lodge. Nixon-Lodge Unlimited, and Nixon-Lodge Clubs. Independent Television Committee, and Television Committee for Republicans. Campaign Dinners—plus Restaurant Voters—for Nixon and, front of fronts, National Recount and Fair Elections Committee.

The Democrats were outdone in numbers but hardly in variety. The party name was borne only by the National Committee and the Young Democrats. There was a National Committee of the Arts, Letters and Sciences for Kennedy, and another of Business and Professional Men and Women for Kennedy-Johnson. There was Citizens for Kennedy, and for Kennedy-Johnson, and for Johnson for Vice President. Florida Headquarters for Kennedy-Johnson, Home Builders for Kennedy-Johnson and Independents for Kennedy. There were Kennedy Conferences and Clubs; and a Kennedy Campaign Committee, a Kennedy For

President Committee and a Kennedy Television Funds Committee. Apart from existing labor supporters there was a Labor Committee for Kennedy-Johnson, and Women for Kennedy.

Each group needs a letterhead composed of suitable names to impress the audience it purports to represent but really exists to convert. At the local level it is harder to be creative, because the audiences are smaller, and usually the most effective group is a committee of Republicans for a Democratic candidate or vice versa. Most political pros have a large or small stable of tame registered members of the opposite party who can be persuaded, or sometimes simply told, to join such a letterhead committee.

This tack was carried to an extreme in the 1950's by a New York City Congressman, Republican Frederic R. Coudert, who then represented the city's silk-stocking district. In a campaign newspaper the Coudert people published testimonials to the vision, diligence, and wisdom of their man, illustrating each plug with a photograph and accompanying it with a name. The testimonials proved to be manufactured by the campaign organization, the photographs were of professional models, and the names turned out to have been picked more or less at random from telephone directories. Some of the "supporters" actually held political sentiments sharply at odds with those attributed to them. The whole affair grew sticky and Coudert barely won his sixth—and last—term. District Republicans picked John Lindsay to succeed him the next time around.

In California, where everything is larger than life, it is possible to out-do the national pattern in political legerdemain. There, in 1962, an unsuccessful *Democratic* primary candidate for the gubernatorial nomination filed suit against a public relations firm representing part of the *Republican* ticket. He said the Republican agent promised him several thousand dollars to run and siphon off some primary votes from the incumbent Governor, Pat Brown. He sued because he said the Republicans didn't deliver.

It was in California that the political public relations firm came to its first and fullest flowering. The rootlessness of much of the state's population aggravates the general political apathy of the population at large. And the perennially over-burdened California ballot puts to the voters a score or more of initiative propositions. Thus the hapless voter must exercise wisdom about his governor, lieutenant governor, other state officers, legislators, Congressmen, and superintendent of public instruction; and he must make fundamental decisions about water, medicine, oil, taxes, housing, beach erosion, loyalty, and the like.

Perhaps 5,000 people in the state understand why they think even half of these proposals should be adopted or rejected. Of the remaining 16 million or so, probably ten million do not even have a firm, personal conviction about *one* issue on the ballot. Given the monstrosity of unbridled ballot initiative, and the floating character of the voter's foundations in his community, something has to be done to get the populace to mark its ballots by any method other than the pin and blindfold.

Thus a special interest group promoting, let us say, the adoption of a "right to work" law, as in 1958, hires a professional campaign organization to agitate for a yes vote on Proposition 18. In this case it is essential, for there is no real grass roots organization to do the job; the protagonists of "right-to-work" legislation who have a large personal economic stake in its adoption would hardly fill the Hollywood Bowl. Meantime, a special-interest group (labor, in this case) hires a campaign firm to augment its own troops in the battle against Proposition 18. True, the grass roots support exists in the labor movement, but its people are workers in hundreds of occupations other than politics; labor leaders can deliver the bodies, but even with the high degree of political expertise available among the professional staffs of the labor movement, they still are short of the sheer volume of brains and specialized skills needed for a statewide campaign.

With the virtual necessity that campaign management talent be available to handle the initiative measures in California, these special skills evolved in the state. Candidates began to use them, as well as proponents of various ballot propositions. Today there is not a major campaign for public office waged in the state without help from one of the expert firms.[1]

The practice began to spread beyond California, and it now has taken root here and there in the Midwest and the East. More often than not, the expertise is lodged in a public relations firm or, less frequently, an advertising agency.

Any politician should have a public relations adviser somewhere in his retinue while he is in office, and in an important position in planning and running his campaigns. There is, however, a significant difference between the counsel of a legitimate public relations practitioner and that of a professional winner of elections. The public relations adviser will accept the basic position and goals of the candidate, and will counsel him on presenting that position and those goals most effectively. But the professional campaign manager, whether an individual or part of a firm, tends to be more than an adviser, advocate, or spokesman. He is in the business of *winning* campaigns. He *must* win to stay in business. He comes to politics in the role of hired killer. What needs to be done, he will do. If the candidate's "image" needs to be changed, he will propose, even fight, to change it. If the opponent's record can be distorted effectively to present him in a false and damaging light, the professional will undertake to do so.

One factor that inhibits a candidate from going to any lengths to win is the knowledge that he and his family must continue to live in the community after the election is won or lost. The professional, brought in to win the election, not just to run a good race, is not similarly inhibited. Often he does not live in the candidate's community. Even if he does, he operates behind a professional anonymity that shields him from censure by angry voters; they take out their resentment of a dirty campaign on the candidate.

Thus the operative question ceases to be "how can I present my position and record most effectively?" and becomes "what do

[1] The best candid look at the practice and malpractice of public relations exclusively in the political realm is that of Stanley Kelley, Jr., Professor of Politics at Princeton University, in his *Professional Public Relations and Political Power*, published in 1956 by Johns Hopkins.

"*I have never stooped, my friends, nor will I now stoop, to the kind of vicious falsehoods, mud-slinging, and personal vilification indulged in by my opponent and his Commie pals.*"

Drawing by Whitney Darrow, Jr.;

Copyright © 1956 The New Yorker Magazine, Inc.

Treason, among other vices, was imputed to President Buchanan by Republican and Union Democrat antagonists (circa 1860). *Smithsonian Institution, Ralph E. Becker Collection of Political Americana*

JAMES BUCHANAN.

JUDAS.

(Opposite) James G. Blaine's adherents referred to him as "The Plume Knight," but in the election of 1884 the Democrats capitalized on rumors corruption. *Smithsonian Institution, Becker Collection*

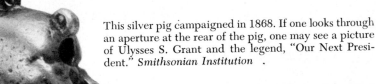

This silver pig campaigned in 1868. If one looks through an aperture at the rear of the pig, one may see a picture of Ulysses S. Grant and the legend, "Our Next President." *Smithsonian Institution* .

Republicans in 1884 taunted Grover Cleveland about a presumed illegitimate son, shown here en route to vote against his father. *Smithsonian Institution, Becker Collection*

HOW BLAINE GREW RICH IN OFFICE.

BLAINE'S HOUSE IN AUGUSTA, 1862.

BLAINE'S MANSION IN WASHINGTON.
(See the Other Side.)

A lapel pin graphically depicting Theodore Roosevelt as a braggart. The jaw was articulated to open and close the mouth. *Smithsonian Institution, Becker Collection*

Another lapel device was used in 1920 to deride Warren G. Harding. A lever behind the hat, when pushed down, became the Devil's tail, while the right hand thumbed the nose. *Smithsonian Institution*

Franklin Roosevelt and his family came in for a variety of abuse. These anti-Roosevelt buttons were circulated during the 1940 campaign. *Smithsonian Institution, Becker Collection*

ELEANOR START PACKING THE WILLKIES ARE COMING

THIRD INTERNATIONAL THIRD REICH THIRD TERM ???

NO FRANKLIN THE FIRST

NO MAN IS GOOD THREE TIMES

WE DON'T WANT ELEANOR EITHER!

(*Above*) This "coin" presented the Nation's alternatives in 1952: honesty and integrity with Ike; minks, deep freezes, and tax scandals with Truman's heir, Stevenson. *Smithsonian Institution, Becker Collection*

The false "Knights of Columbus Oath" has appeared in dozens of versions. One appears here. The "Oath" was used in 1928 against Al Smith and in 1960 against John Kennedy. Note *Congressional Record* "credit line." *Fair Campaign Practices Committee*

3216 CONGRESSIONAL RECORD—HOUSE

ove) In this classic
mposite photograph which
ped defeat Democrat
ard Tydings (right) in
0, photo trickery was used
osition Tydings with
Communist chief Earl
wder. The fine white line
tially separating the men
used as a defense against
rges of deliberate
eption.

ht) This 1958 cartoon
ned to imply that Barry
lwater had Communist
port in his race for
ection to the
Senate from
ona.

**Union Lauds Goldwater
"Honest, Sincere," Miners Sa**

Why Not Vote
For Goldwater?

*Campaign
tices Committee*

WASHINGTON . . . HARLEM . . . AFRICA

Vice President Richard M. Nixon shakes hands with the Rev. Martin Luther King, Negro boycott leader and organizer from Alabama, in Washington in June 1957.

Vice President and Mrs. Nixon in Harlem, meeting with presidential campaign workers in the Hotel Theresa in 1952.

Vice President Nixon hugs Paramount Chief Nana Osae Dyan in March 19.. in Aburi, Ghana, in Africa.

VICE PRESIDENT RICHARD M. NIXON HAS BEEN AN NAACP MEMBER FOR OVER 10 YEARS!

Order and circulate copies of this tract:

25 for $1.00   50 for $2.00   100 for $3.50

THE VIRGINIAN
310 - 53rd Street
Newport News, Virginia

While northern Democrats were implying that Richard Nixon was a segregationist, southerners circulated this photographic layout in 1956 and 1960.

In 1960, some zealots contrasted Nixon's poverty with Kennedy's wealth.

(AMERICAN)

HIS FATHER DIDN'T BUY HIM THE PRESIDENCY

Vote for NIXON and LODG

Fair Campaign Practices Committee

INVISIBLE GOVERNMENT PROMOTES HIM — WILL RULE HIM

BEHIND KENNEDY STANDS THE JEW

ants have been taken
ised plan by which
nedy has been por-
s an earnest, sincere,
n Catholic of presi-
only by anti-Catholic

has relied on the
experts and on the
l polls conducted to
of various segments
nedy's Catholic back-
litical image, etc.

edy ever entered a
his brand of Cathol-
a tremendous asset
ed his religion as a
al beliefs, to divert
from his political re-
self as an underdog
igotry.

this country and to
nd other Christians
resident?

will become the new
nting the decayed

nkfurter-David Niles-
destroy America —
ars ago — will come

ricans for Democratic
is will take over the
onage reins and es-
m reeking with evil.

nation League-Ameri-
tee-American Jewish
al bloc — so beloved
e given carte blanche
hey can proceed with-
rance in their plan to
to debauch the youth
to their own level of

Senator Kennedy chats with Liberal Party leaders (l. to r.) David Dubinsky, Al Rose, Adolf Berle at Hotel Astor, New York City, June 23rd. The Liberal Party conditions its members for communism.

Here is proof such a plan exists:

(1) From the first moment that **Joseph P. Kennedy**, the Senator's father, first appeared on the political horizon of America prior to World War I. when he started clawing

the market prior to the crash. He had fleeced the wolves on the Street, the public and anyone that got in his way until the signal for the crash was given. He was one of the tiny handful of men who had ad-

Anti-Semite Conde McGinley, in his paper *Common Sense,* showed Kennedy as a pawn of the Jews in 1960.

At the same time, bigots were horrified at the prospect of Kennedy's fealty to the Pope.

(AMERICAN)

OUR CANDIDATE?

eep Church and State SEPARATE!

Fair Campaign Practices Committee

REMINDER

Here is The Record on..
WAR OR PEACE

in this century

The War Death Toll Game has never been played more effectively than in this 1964 GOP tract. Below the battlefield scene, six Republican twentieth-century Presidents were listed, with their total of war dead: zero. Then followed four Democrats and their war dead: over half a million.

Fair Campaign Practices Committee

Fake money has been a perennial campaign device. A particularly vicious example appears here. It was used in 1964 against Lyndon B. Johnson.

we need to do to win?" And even the matter of straightforward presentation of facts is complicated by the relative character of truth in a political context. Many political truths are flexible, rarely rigid or black-and-white. Facts modify other facts.

To the candidate, the prize is the opportunity to demonstrate what he can do in office. To the campaign management professional the prize is a demonstration of how he can win elections, and to him the relative character of truth becomes even more relative. Equations develop apace. The opposition voted against the bill, even though he did so because he wanted to strengthen it in another version. Still he voted against it. Facts are facts. Who else wanted it defeated? Why, the Communists, or the oil companies, or the Catholics, or some other handy scapegoat group. The opposition voted with the scapegoat group to kill the bill. The oil companies ordered the bill defeated. The opponent took orders from the oil companies to kill the bill.

Usually this professional winner cannot fool the voter with a candidate who is absolutely mediocre. The real danger lies in warping the channels of political communication; in confusing the real differences between men; in twisting facts so that the voters give up in dismay and vote blindly or stay home. The danger, finally, is alienation of the electorate from the political system.

Fortunately, any professional campaign manager nourishes a self-protective desire not to be caught smearing the opposition. For to be *caught* smearing makes virtually certain a backfire effect that can defeat the candidate. Enough such blots on a campaign manager's record will destroy the luster of his name and, ultimately, his own employability by respectable causes or candidates.

The candidate may, of course, select—if he can find one—a campaign management firm run by a person of high integrity who understands the political system and respects it deeply There are a few such. One example is the veteran Democratic pro Sam Brightman. In 1965 he set up shop alone after nearly two decades on the staff of the Democratic National Committee, most of the time as Deputy Chairman for Public Affairs.

At best, however, protections against potential excesses by the professional campaign manager are seldom foolproof. The manager will know at any time from sample polls exactly where his candidate stands in vote potential. But especially in a state-wide campaign, neither the candidate nor the manager can keep a continuing check on the ethical level of the campaign in every area. The political horizon becomes obscured by crises and opportunities, provocations and temptations that loom at various stages of the campaign. As tension increases and the election nears, an unethical tactic begins to look like a mean but useful possibility, and finally becomes an unpleasant necessity.

The stresses on an individual political pro working within his own party are somewhat different. Consistency of involvement with one party leads to respect for the party system and in turn for the entire political system.[2] The party pro knows that dirty work by him invites dirty work against him at the first opportunity. He comes to know that a reputation as a smear artist is easy to win and hard to shake, and will limit not only his success, personal reputation, and access to power, but also his very survival in his job.

The old-time smear artist is disappearing slowly, as the electorate becomes more literate, and as the news media expose chicanery more fully and rapidly. He is being replaced by a different phenomenon, and a more frightening one. This is a new wave of amoral political technicians, who are clever, indefatigable, poisonous, and brilliant. Their calling is as old as Machiavelli's, but the scale on which they are emerging from graduate schools into the political structure is new.

These men do not make their livings running campaigns. They have come to work for members of Congress and the legislatures, and for governors and mayors, and in the numberless warrens of federal, state, and local bureaucracies. They are aides, counsels, executive and administrative and legislative assistants.

---

[2] Consistent involvement with one party, his own by preference, also affects the outside professional manager in this way. This is how the superior firms in the field usually operate.

They have brought, along with their scrubbed and innocent appearance, doctorates in law, political science, public administration, and economics—and an emotionless neutrality toward moral considerations in politics. They are human political computers.

Day to day they help make government go, applying their expertise to analyzing and untangling existing laws and prospective ones. And every two or four or six years, when their imperturbable intellect is brought to bear on election campaigns, they approach the hustings as they would any routine problem. Given: a candidate and an opponent, in a district or state. Find: election. Moral concerns are the worry of the opposition, or at most of their own candidate. The modern Machiavelli sees his role as telling his prince what he needs to do to win—what will work, always in terms of votes—what he can get away with and what he can't.

Machiavelli was dealing with realities. So are his latter-day disciples. But they miss a crucial distinction between truth as it applies to winning elections and truth as it applies to the responsibilities of high office.

The Machiavellian dictum makes some sense in national affairs. Once a national administration is constituted it must concern itself first with national survival. Truth is and must remain relative. That shrewd observer and adviser of presidents, Richard E. Neustadt, has put it that "I was the servant of the state before I was the servant of truth." There are situations in which the cause of truth may be best served in the long run by a white lie, or a gray one, or conceivably a black one.

But the process of constituting a government in our tradition requires truth and relevance in campaigns for office. The voter feels safer in relying on Morley than on Machiavelli: "Those who would treat politics and morality apart will never understand the one or the other."

If today's new crop of amoral political manipulators were to have its way, winning elections would be unabashed gamesmanship, in which manipulation of the voter would be the norm, and victory, whatever its cost, the only goal.

Politicians as well as voters will do well to beware of these cool, slick, and able men. They are a virulent minority in the government, but there are a few more of them every year. They are indifferent to the mark of their progress: the political corpses of honest men who committed the ultimate indiscretion of being in the way.

There is one way to redeem at least some of these political automatons, whose presence is being felt in both parties. That is to awaken in them a sense of moral outrage, an element in their personalities that their education either submerged or did not stir. I know one of these men whose candidate was smeared viciously and effectively, in such circumstances that the adviser's skill could not avail. The experience gave him a new perspective, and brought a new ethical dimension to his political career. It converted his value to the political system from negative to positive.

There is hope in the fact that maturity brings occasional reverses to any man, and with them new perspectives and new dimensions. In the meantime, a candidate aware of the dangers implicit in using amoral strategists can, with effort and firmness, accept the useful and honest advice and reject the unscrupulous.

In theory, the candidate should create a campaign organization that will free him of everything but policy review and scrutiny of what is said in his name. If the candidate trusts his organization, he should not have to worry that it will commit excesses. In practice, such confidence may be dangerous. In the Butler-Tydings campaign in Maryland in 1950, John Marshall Butler never saw the tabloid, "From the Record," and never knew of the notorious composite photograph. What is confidence, or even naivete, in one candidate may be sheer pliancy in another. Theodore White in *The Making of the President, 1960* refers to a pro who called his governor "the boob." Some candidates are operated with the wires and strings that this expression of contempt implies.

Other candidates find it difficult to perceive the fine line between too little and too much control. In 1960 Richard Nixon—as he has done in most of his campaigns—exerted final influence on practically every substantial effort by the party and campaign organizations. In one case master strategist Leonard W. Hall, frustrated repeatedly by Nixon's vetoes of proposed practical moves to which he saw no ethical objection, is reported to have responded to a new campaign idea by saying to its author, "I don't know. You'll just have to ask Sir Richard." Here the candidate shackled his experts, quite possibly to the detriment of his campaign.

In quite another situation in the same campaign, a Southern Protestant leader came to the Republican National Committee with an intriguing offer. His co-religionists gravely feared the prospect of a Catholic in the White House, and would go to great lengths to prevent it. The minister was intelligent enough to know that too much public hue and cry by Southern Protestants would backfire and create sympathy in other areas for Kennedy. So he proposed to turn over what amounted to several statewide organizations to the Republicans, in states where they counted dedicated and intelligent workers in mere handfuls. These people would do anything, the clergyman said—ring doorbells, lick stamps, carry messages. They were available for the taking, and the direction would come from Republican pros. They would not so much as mention the "religious issue." They would simply create a fully-staffed volunteer organization to do purely political work where no organization existed.

The staff pro at the National Committee was elated. The plan would not only solve the problem of manning organizations in the states in question, but would also eliminate the impossible problem of trying to synthesize an organization through purely Republican channels. Nixon vetoed the idea out of hand, on the ground that whether or not the workers uttered a syllable about the religious antagonism they felt for Kennedy, the very use of such a task force would be taking advantage of the religious issue. Nixon was determined not to do this. In recounting that episode later, the pro commented bitterly, "They say Nixon was honorable about the religion thing. I think he was a damn fool."

The dirtywork in general elections is often pale by contrast with the primaries, and here the party organization's proper role is limited to the purely mechanical and housekeeping functions of providing personnel for the polling places. The major role of the primaries, so far as the organization is concerned, is to renew the organization itself, for in the primaries are chosen the district and state committee members who will comprise the organization.

In primary selection of candidates for public office, it is legendary that one side may commit such mayhem on its own that the opposition party has only to replay the sordid tape of the primary to win the general election. The California Democratic primary of 1950 saw Sheridan Downey, and later Manchester Boddy, tearing and cannibalizing Helen Douglas. The 1960 West Virginia primary saw Franklin D. Roosevelt Jr. hang the draft-dodger tag on Hubert Humphrey to cement John Kennedy's victory in that state. So when Humphrey lost the Presidential nomination and ran again for the Senate in his own state, Minnesota Republicans had only to quote FDR Junior on Humphrey's service record to deprecate the Senator. No matter that the allegations were untrue. The Republicans didn't need to prove them; they only had to quote another Democrat about the particular Democrat they were fighting.

Certainly the blood let by Republicans among themselves in the Presidential preference primaries of 1964 helped to weaken Goldwater, and, for that matter, Rockefeller. Because of the political anemia that results from endless primary fights, an unengaged dark horse always has a chance of emerging the victor from a party convention: the odds are that in any hotly contested fight the principal figures, themselves or through agents, will have so maimed one another that neither can measure up to what the convention sees as the minimum to have a chance of election.

Primary elections to nominate candidates for public office—as distinct from those to select the party leadership—were conceived as a wholesome way to get politics out of the control of the corrupt politicians and into the hands of the whole electorate. It was a noble experiment, as well motivated as Prohibition, and as impossible to make come true.

If the day comes when the Presidential candidates are literally nominated by primary elections in the states, an era of unbelievable mischief will be at hand. For the electorate at large, capable as it is of distinguishing the gem from the fake, usually does not confront so stark a choice. Expertise is more valuable than unqualified and unsophisticated good judgment. The party system distills out of the electorate those who understand and enjoy politics and lumps them together into two party organizations. Here is where the screening should and must be done. Here are people knowledgeable enough of political ins and outs and facts of life to choose the party nominee wisely.

If the nation is faced with Republican and Democratic nominees who are able and honest men, and if the electorate then chooses one because of his television personality, we may have chosen a leader on a silly basis but at least we have wound up with a leader, thanks to the pre-selection at the party level. But to open the door to equally invalid reasons for choice at the *nominating* stage is to place more faith in luck than reason can support.

The path to reform is not through the preferential primary route, as a national candidate-selecting device, but through strengthening and improving the party nominating process, the convention. The convention process is open to abuse and chicanery and unethical pressure. But these weaknesses and others can be corrected, and the first step in their correction is for the high-minded above-the-battle types to get into politics.

This is a lesson the right wing of the Republican Party learned in preparation for 1964. Many of the pre-convention Goldwater supporters were only nominal Republicans until they were galvanized into action by the draft-Goldwater movement. They tended to view their party with huge disgust because of the degree to which it had "sold out" to the Eastern internationalists. They might or might not vote in primaries, usually against the "establishment," and they might well sit out general elections where they saw the choice as between Tweedledum and Tweedledee. These people stopped grumbling to themselves about the liberals and left-wingers, got into the political system, worked, ran, won, and controlled the 1964 Republican convention. There was nothing underhanded about their triumph. They simply found that complaining was futile unless it was accompanied by action through the proper channels. The surprise factor was that no one thought they *would* get out of the sidelines and into politics in such numbers so quickly.

Doris Fleeson told the story of a state Republican functionary who after years in power found himself ousted by a Goldwaterite. She asked him to describe his successor. Dazed, he replied, "I've never met the gentleman." "The gentleman," tired of never having his political opinion sought by the powers that *were*, set out to become one of the powers that *would be*. Hosts of these new winners in the party system had sat around for years muttering about dirty politics never giving honest men a chance. Now in state after state they took over state organizations and convention delegations and gave themselves a chance to advance their kind of honest man.

The rigging of conventions is commonly cited as the reason why they should be replaced with some superior means of choosing candidates. Conventions are rigged on occasion. The Harding choice is pinned down to the celebrated smoke-filled room in a Chicago hotel. Tom Storke, the venerable Santa Barbara newsman, tells in his autobiography [3] of the pre-election of Harding long before Chicago. He quotes the late Samuel Untermeyer as having assured Storke that Harding was picked and financed by a cabal meeting in a room on the 18th floor of New York's Biltmore Hotel six months before the convention. Storke also recounts a similar story about the Democratic selection of John W. Davis as their nominee four years later in 1924. Ten or twelve men, representing "the interests," met in a Wall Street office to decide on Davis and raised a quarter of a million dollars to assure his nomination in preference to Al Smith or California's Senator William Gibbs McAdoo because, so the story went, the plotters knew Davis would lose and Coolidge could be trusted. Smith or Mc-

[3] *California Editor* (Los Angeles: Westernlore Press, 1958).

Adoo, went the theory, might win and were wild men who couldn't be controlled.

Whether Tom Storke's informants were speaking from prescience, knowledge, or shrewd political speculation is not important. The fact is that rigging of the sort and scale described here is more than rare. But stories of this variety lend substance to the popular notion that "they" do it all in politics, and that "you" or "I" are powerless. The notorious or fabled rigging jobs make sinister the normal and proper prearrangement that occurs at any convention.

A state delegation committed by primary election or state convention to a candidate must know at what point it is prepared to switch to another if its man is obviously lost. The delegation must know which other state representations are leaning which way. And the delegation can't be in on every conversation, thirty or forty men strong. It has to have leaders and representatives whom it can trust but whose judgment it must respect and be prepared to endorse when the chips are down. Negotiation is the soul of politics. Those who argue that compromise is immoral would, if entrusted with the reins of government, be dictators by their own definition.

The open nominating convention, when it was developed by the Anti-Mason Party in 1831,[4] improved the party system, as the party system itself improved the political system. The convention is not a mere political appendix left over from an era when it filled some now unfamiliar purpose.

To be sure, there is room for improvement in conventions, conceivably by shortening them. But they cannot be so truncated as to convene today, nominate tomorrow and adjourn. There needs to be time for debate, for persuasion, for political contact and exchange, for rubbing elbows and noses and swapping tales and problems. The political convention is more than just a forum for picking Presidential candidates. Its importance as a quadren-

[4] The original practice was to pick the nominee in caucus of the party's Congressional delegation. In 1808 and 1812, the waning Federalists had less power in Congress than in the states, and the party held what amounted to secret nominating conventions instead of using the caucus.

nial meeting and re-constitution and get-together and clambake needs emphasizing. The cocktail parties and breakfasts and smoke-filled rooms and night-life are fully as important to political activists as they are to political scientists, or Legionnaires, or auto dealers, or secretaries, or insurance underwriters, all of whom convene without being denounced for it.

The convention is also a property of the nation, in that it is a stage on which will be dramatized the results of the political struggles of the last four years at the grass roots. It is a hall where masters at legerdemain occasionally baffle the crowd and an off-beat nightclub where political satirists harpoon their audience. It is a mass thirsting for a flash of charisma to set it roaring.

Sometimes the roar is frightening; at such moments, as in the Republican Convention of 1964, the convention is an oracle, portending the future and revealing the shape and meaning of the recent past. The 1964 Convention spoke prophetically to the nation of the new breed of Republican that now dominated the Grand Old Party.

If the California primary campaign of 1964 forecast what was ahead for the general election, the Convention certified and underwrote the forecast. After the ritualistic search of the news media—and the pathetic search of the moderate Republicans—for someone to stop Barry, or at least give him a contest, the one victory Goldwater's supporters knew he had won, the nomination, was in hand.

Again and again in the pre-convention period the Arizona Senator had been labeled an extremist, or the extremists' candidate. Now, in his acceptance speech to the strange mass of devotees at his convention, Barry Goldwater, of the moderate mien and the fire-eating phrase, did it again. With the help of his rightist speech writer, Karl Hess, but with his own specific approval and clearance, the candidate accepted the nomination and cheered his troops.

The acceptance speech was mimeographed for the press on eight legal-size pages, double-spaced. A moment's diversion for a word-and-numbers game is instructive.

In the eight pages, 27 single words were underlined once each; such words as *true, peace, courageously* and *humane;* and such words as *these, their, our* and *or.* Underlined twice each were these single words: *shall, balanced, that, will, whole* and *all.* *Democratic,* as in Party, was underlined three times. *Can* and *freedom* were underlined four times each. *Not* was underlined five times.

Five phrases were underlined one time each. The first four were *here and now, only then, can be,* and *must renew.*

The fifth phrase was what the faithful were waiting for. It was: *Extremism in the defense of liberty is no vice. Moderation in the pursuit of justice is no virtue.*[5]

Reactions were instantaneous and varied. Right-wingers were exultant; all they had said about Barry was true! Moderate Republicans withered, and were stunned; all they had heard about Barry was true! Democratic pros reacted like the two flies in Nabokov's *Lolita* that lit on the brow of a man who had just been shot through the head: they were "beside themselves with a dawning sense of incredible luck." All they were preparing to say about Goldwater was true!

Barry Goldwater was aware that some of his followers were really quite wild. In his acceptance speech he had urged that the powers of government be concentrated at levels closest to the citizen, including local government, *regional compacts,* and state government. Regional compacts is the stuff on which right wing cats sharpen their claws. They see it and fear it in many guises: super-government; regional planning; the demon Metro, right wing shorthand for consolidated government of a whole metropolitan county. This is a cause Goldwater has championed for years, and he mentioned it again in an interview with publisher John S. Knight the day after the Convention ended: "Goldwater referred to metropolitan government in the Miami area as the ultimate solution if local politicians would only give it a chance to work.

"He remarked with a wry smile that some of the 'kooks' sup-

---

[5] Between the sentences he ad-libbed, "And may I remind you that . . ."

porting him are convinced that the concept of metropolitan government is the handiwork of the Communist Party."

The candidate exhibited other moderate aspects at the Convention; he was taken aback at the vindictive roar that went up when Dwight Eisenhower referred in passing to "sensation-seeking columnists and commentators." Yet he found himself catering to the extremists, who set the tone of the Convention, and extremism was in vogue.

The drama of 1964 was in the icy resoluteness of the Goldwaterites and their refusal to tolerate moderation, but the chilling performance does not detract from the convention's role as the political focal point of each of the nation's parties.

The dramatic highlight of 1940 was the Philadelphia convention, at which a demonstration rigged with loving care took life, and stole the Republican nomination for Wendell Willkie. In terms of pure convention mechanics it was a blend of caprice and contrivance, yet it worked well for the Republicans and for the American people.

When the Republicans wrangled in 1952 over the seating of rival Taft and Eisenhower delegates, they were fighting out in the proper arena, a national convention, a dispute they had not been able to resolve over the course the party should steer. And when a young Wisconsin-born lawyer, Don Eastvold from the State of Washington, took on Everett McKinley Dirksen in debate, it made exciting watching, listening, or reading, as the stripling, deftly using what he later admitted was the country-boy approach, out-fenced the grand national champion.

Even dullness does not invalidate the convention as the party's great national forum and council. The Republicans, in 1956, tried desperately to pump some diversion into the evangelical rally that had assembled to hail the second coming of Ike. But the unplanned diversions took hold; the delegate from Puerto Rico demanded a poll of his delegation and the nation laughed. Terry Carpenter [6] from Nebraska offered an alternative nominee

---

[6] Carpenter was a Democratic Senate candidate from Nebraska in 1936. Franklin Roosevelt abandoned him in favor of the veteran Progressive, George W. Norris.

in his mythical Joe Smith. The counterpoint to the coronation was irreverent, and it gave pause for reflection, and sprinkled a little irony over the proceedings.

The 1960 demonstration for Adlai Stevenson at the Democratic Convention was arranged as deliberately as any other, yet it got out of hand as a mass of partisans, spectators and delegates found themselves stirred, not just exhorted, by Eugene McCarthy's soaring rhetoric, and by the remembered service—on the altar—of valiant Adlai Stevenson. The demonstration failed to do what its planners hoped it would—add up to another Willkie stampede. But in the strangely sensitive, responsive way of the party convention, the demonstration did something else that needed to be done: it bade hail and farewell to a two-time loser who had brought the party distinction and grace.

These moments are not extraneous to our political system. They are not merely the performance of carefully orchestrated scores. Such moments, and the tedious hours and days in which they are set, provide the ignition and fuel for the party machinery as well as inspiration, excitement, amusement, and instruction for the electorate. Refine? Yes. Abolish? By no means.

CHAPTER 6

Spies
and Stratagems

EVERY sophisticated politician acknowledges that an effective
intelligence and counter-espionage program is essential to a successful campaign. It is of the greatest importance to be able to
know accurately what the opposition is about to do. Sometimes,
given early and accurate warning, a damaging blow can be fore-
stalled completely. Sometimes it can be twisted to the rival's complete disadvantage.

Political espionage can be funny, diverting, and revealing, or
quite shabby and disgusting, depending in large measure on who
is doing it, and from what point of view. A seasoned practical
joker can be a valuable aide, provided he will accept restraint
when it is required. For there always is a danger that harassment
intended to be amusing may become vicious. And there is equal
danger that too flip an approach to political problems will detract
from the essential seriousness of the campaign.

Like paramilitary operations, the parapolitical world of espionage and harassment—guerrilla politics—revolves around
much that is mundane and utterly boring. Endless reading of
clippings, pamphlets, speeches, and press releases is one part of
the job. Usually it is filled by the campaign organization's re-

search staff. But this staff must have a sharp eye for what may prove to be a useful lead. To facilitate the routine surveillance of each other's basic material, the two national party committees for years have exchanged news releases. Each knows the other will acquire each new handout shortly, and each benefits by saving the time and effort necessary to pick up copies from friendly newsmen and other sources.

This practical relationship is strained from time to time, as it was in 1964 when Democrats discovered what apparently was a serious effort on the part of the Republican National Committee to infiltrate Democratic headquarters with a paid agent, or more properly to suborn the secret services of a Democratic National Committee employee in a strategic position. The prospective spy was one Louis Flax, a teletype operator for Reuters, the British news service, in its Washington Bureau. Mr. Flax was moonlighting at the Democratic committee, and his job was to teletype each day's secret schedules, other important details, and plans to the Democrats' network around the country.

Late one night Flax received a telephone call from someone obviously familiar with the nature of his job. The caller inquired whether Flax was generally alone in the office when he started transmitting his secret data at four a.m. Then the telephone voice put the proposition: "Get some friends of mine certain information and keep them up to date on any prospective campaign plans that you might come in contact with."

Flax demurred. The caller then delicately referred to "certain things" in Flax's background which might jeopardize his employment if the information fell into the wrong hands. The implication dealt with a term the teletypist had spent in the Maryland House of Correction on a bad check charge.

"Wouldn't you consider this something on the order of black-mail?" Flax asked.

The caller was grieved: "Let's not use nasty words." Flax was then urged to call a certain telephone number and ask for the head of security, identifying himself as Mr. Lewis. The telephone number turned out to be that of the Republican National Committee and an appointment was made for "Mr. Lewis" to come in.

Mr. Flax informed his superiors who, as will be seen, had been using spies, if not seducing them, for years. Flax's boss was the Democrats' communications chief, Wayne Phillips, and he heard Flax out with rising interest and appreciation. He suggested that the loyal teletypist seem to play along.

Flax made the date at GOP headquarters and was, his affidavit relates, received in the office of the temporarily absent chairman by Committee Executive Director John Grenier. The plan was cemented and two days later Double Agent Flax-Lewis delivered the first shipment of The Papers—a sheaf of carbons of secret messages already carefully screened by Wayne Phillips. In the Republican office Flax-Lewis was given a glimpse of a functionary who muttered that the agent would see him again. As Flax walked out of the building into the rain-drenched Washington afternoon, the man encountered him under a canopy, and shook hands with him so cordially that when the Flax palm was disengaged the agent found it to be crossed with $1,000 in bills. The teletypist continued his double life, which lasted another two weeks.

Then Phillips decided he was ready for the kill. Alerting the press, he arranged to have reporters and photographers secreted where they could watch the next payoff meeting. Nobody showed, except Flax, living up to his half of the date. When Grenier was accosted by newsmen and asked about the elaborate plot, he responded insouciantly that he knew no one named Flax. So the episode petered out.

At about the time that Flax was being asked to betray his trust, a more lighthearted secret agent caper was getting under way. The plot was created by Dick Tuck, an energetic Californian, a graduate in public administration from the University of California, and the world titleholder among political practical jokers. Since the 1950's, Tuck has been the Democrats' secret weapon, to the chagrin of harassed Republicans.

During the 1964 campaign, the Republican candidate was

scheduled to leave the capital on a campaign train headed west. The Goldwater Special would be packed with newsmen, and Tuck developed a scheme to poke fun at the GOP nominee on board his own train. Leaders of the Democratic National Committee debated at length over the propriety of the plan, and finally concluded that it would pass muster and was unlikely to backfire when exposed.

A pretty, 23-year-old girl named Moira O'Connor, a writer of fashion advertising copy from Chicago, was working in Washington as a volunteer at the Democratic National Committee. She volunteered for Tuck's undercover assignment, and covertly obtained credentials as a free-lance magazine writer, so that she could ride the Goldwater Special.

Not long after the train left Washington, bemused reporters found under their compartment doors copies of an en-route publication, "The Whistle Stop," dedicated to keeping them "advised, informed, protected, and, with considerable help from the senator himself [Goldwater], amused." A bulletin happily reassured the reporters that fluoride, that *bête-noir* of the right wing, had not been added to the train's water supply. A second edition was promised for delivery "at breakfast tomorrow."

Assistant press secretary Vic Gold began to prowl the corridors at five a.m., well before dawn, in search of the culprit. Instead he found copies of a second edition, with a scoop on how the Republican nominee had arranged to avoid confusion as the train rolled westward into the Central time zone: "The senator has decided to use Washington time. George Washington, that is."

Gold and his colleague, press secretary Paul Wagner, had been doing their homework, ticking off familiar faces in a process of elimination, and now they checked certain vacant compartments including one which held luggage full of future "Whistle-Stop" editions. This at least confirmed that no one had smuggled a mimeograph machine with a silencer on board the Special.

The two Goldwater aides located Miss O'Connor at her breakfast. "This is your last delivery, dear," said Gold. With Wagner, he escorted Miss O'Connor to her lair, room seven in car twelve, which she was properly aghast to discover had been entered in her absence. She protested that someone had gone through her luggage. The press secretary noted tartly that someone had been passing out "these joke sheets," and that she thought she was pretty funny.

Gold advised Miss O'Connor to get packed, as she was to be put off the train in five minutes.

What with one thing and another, including nervous tension, high tempers, righteous indignation, relief at having found the enemy agent, and possible embarrassment, voices in this *rondo capriccioso* were raised sufficiently to attract witnesses, who, worse luck, were reporters.

One of the newsmen observed that Gold was beginning to sound like Humphrey Bogart. Wagner spotted the reporters, and told his associate to pipe down. Gold pointed out that it was a good story. Wagner agreed, and suggested that they not make it any better.

The youthful Mata Hari was put off the train at Parkersburg, West Virginia. She returned to Washington, where she lived happily ever after until Johnson was elected and she went back to the real world of fashion copy.

Dick Tuck, the author of this magnificent nonsense, was no stranger to the world of trains in 1964. Two years earlier, when Richard Nixon was seeking the governorship of California, Tuck donned a trainman's cap and signaled the engineer of a Nixon Special to pull away from the station at San Luis Obispo. The engineer did, just as Nixon, standing on the rear platform of the train, was beginning a whistle-stop speech.

Tuck has made a major avocation of harassing Republican candidates. Because of the frequent availability of Richard Nixon in that role, Tuck has bedeviled the former Vice President in a variety of ways. Once he switched the signs identifying a pair of waiting buses during a Nixon campaign tour. One, labeled "Nixon," was ready to rush the candidate to a live television appearance. The other, labeled "VIP's," was standing by to take celebrities to a hotel.

One of Tuck's funniest schemes—depending, of course, on one's point of view—resulted in a photograph of an ebullient Nixon, beaming beneath a sign in the Chinatown of Los Angeles. "Welcome Nixon," the sign declared in English. Accompanying Chinese characters added color. "What about the HUGHES LOAN?" they accused in Chinese. The reference was to a massively-publicized Democratic campaign allegation that Nixon had abused his office for fiscal aid to his family.

A couple of generations before the Tuck era, a wily Republican agent, also from California, brought off a classic bit of political entrapment. The year was 1888, and the GOP had named Benjamin Harrison to oppose President Grover Cleveland. Cleveland had beaten Blaine in 1884, with the help of a last-minute shift of Irish-American votes. Now the California counterspy, George A. Osgoodby, set out to prevent a repetition of the Irish defection.

The Republican trickster, under the pseudonym of Charles F. Murchison, wrote a letter to the British ambassador, Sir Lionel Sackville-West. "Murchison" posed as a naturalized American of British birth, and asked the ambassador's advice on how an affectionate son of England ought to vote as between Harrison and the Democratic incumbent President.

Sackville-West was completely taken in. The Anglophobic adventures, in America as well as the British Isles, of Ireland's Fenian Society, predecessor movement to the Sinn Fein, had long irked the ambassador. He seized the opportunity to steer a vote away from Harrison, strongly preferred by many Irish-Americans. On September 13, Sir Lionel answered Osgoodby, or "Murchison," writing that Cleveland's return to the White House would serve British interests well.

The Republicans kept the letter secret until October 24, two weeks before Election Day, and then trumpeted the incident far and wide. President Cleveland, shocked at the ambassador's intervention in American politics, handed Sackville-West his passport the same day the story broke, but the damage was irreparable. New York's big Irish vote swung heavily against Cleveland, and Harrison nosed him out of the White House.

On occasion, Republican parapolitical operatives have contrived harassments as funny and imaginative as anything Dick Tuck does for today's Democrats. An epic ploy that generated a lot of heat, no light, and a hearty laugh for all except the Democrats, was pulled off by some forgotten Republican master in Louisville, Kentucky, in 1928.

Al Smith was coming to town to address the local Democrats and anyone else who would attend. The meeting was held in a municipal auditorium. When the Democratic candidate arrived, the hall was packed with people, and uncomfortably hot. The heat seemed to increase, and when Smith was introduced, it was hotter than ever.

The nation's irreverencer-in-residence, H. L. Mencken, was on the campaign train and at the meeting. He wrote later that before Al was "half way through his speech he was sweating so copiously that he seemed half drowned. The dignitaries on the platform sweated, too, and so did the vulgar on the floor and in the galleries. Minute by minute the temperature seemed to increase, until finally it became almost unbearable. When Al shut down at last, with his collar a rag and his shirt and pants sticking to his hide, the thermometer must have stood at 100 degrees at least, and there were plenty who guessed that it stood at 110." When the entourage returned to the train someone learned what had gone wrong: the Republican city administration, in Mencken's phrase, "had had its goons fire up the boilers under the hall, deliberately and with malice prepense."

For all the shrewd trickery of the GOP mousetrap play on Sackville-West, and the happy-go-lucky deviltry of Al Smith's overheated hall, recent Republican parapolitical ventures have sometimes become vicious. Occasionally they appear to be neurotic, or worse.

A significant example is the almost obsessive concern with sexual aberrations that crops out periodically in GOP headquarters. One staff member of the national committee, who somehow escaped the post-convention purge by Goldwater's lieutenants in 1964, complained to a purged colleague that there was no time for developing legitimate political issues, so concerned was the Republican research operation with probing for sexual anomalies in the Johnson administration.

The prurient thirst for evidences of perversion is a long-time phenomenon, particularly in the politics of the right. One recalls the equation in the McCarthy era of homosexuality with treason: "89 Communists and perverts . . ." The situation has changed little. The conservative writer Noel Parmentel notes the current concern of Ku Klux Klan types in the South over the "Jew-Communist pre-verts."

The subject of security and homosexuality requires thoughtful study. The reported incidence of homosexuals among defectors to the Soviet, the ready general assumption that sexual aberrations are a prime basis for blackmail, the occasional scholarly dissent from that view, the conscious efforts among homosexuals today to portray their inversion as a perfectly proper diversion, the public relations program of homosexuals to bring their practice up from underground to the status of a sect or faction— all these are persuasive arguments for careful, dispassionate, but not vengeful, study. However, the constant harping on the one note of sexual perversion that characterizes many leading far-right political efforts amounts to a perversion in itself, a bizarre, lustful drive to ferret out the homosexuals from the federal structure whether they are there or not.

There is no question that homosexuals have worked for many years in most government departments. From time to time they are reported, on the rumor circuit, to be members of the House and Senate. They reside in the District of Columbia and adjacent bedroom communities as they do in Chicago, Los Angeles, New York, or any other city.

Security agencies are keenly concerned about homosexuals as blackmail targets, and Washington, with the best reasons in the world, is an unusually security-conscious town. For years the District Police have guarded the populace against being overrun by sex deviates.

Understandably, this diligence has sometimes led to embarrassment. Comfort stations in the nation's capital are few and far between. Many a government employee, homebound after a night's drinking, has stopped his car alongside a darkened curb and begun to relieve himself behind a tree, only to be interrupted by a member of the District Police. At the police station he finds himself entered on the blotter not for "committing a nuisance" or some such standard formulation, but for indecent exposure.

Then there is the legendary incident in which two rival police forces collided in their relentless search for perverts. Lafayette Park, in front of the Capitol, like most other urban greenswards, largely unlit and sparsely populated at night, has been known for years as a rendezvous for men bent on homosexual encounters.

Since Washington is the Federal City, its public parks are protected by a police agency of the National Park Service. Its streets and other areas are policed by the metropolitan, or District, police. Both have been known to assign younger recruits to decoy duty in suitably dark places. So it happened one night that a youthful member of the District police, on such an assignment, chanced to pick up, or be picked up by, a beardless recruit of the Park police on a similar assignment. Each decoy sought to arrest the other. Each, not only embarrassed but outraged, resisted arrest. Whistles pierced the night. Reinforcements arrived. One thing led to another. A melee ensued, of policemen, by policemen, for the virtue of policemen. No one remembers the tally in wounded. There were no deaths. There were two compromises and abundant hard feelings.

This is reported not to criticize or ridicule the law enforcement agencies for discouraging homosexual loiterers in public places, but to explain how it was not only possible but logical for many District citizens to assume in late 1964 that Walter Jenkins had been entrapped by police when his distinguished public career came to its end in the men's washroom of the YMCA across the corner from Lafayette Park. It also explains how Jenkins happened to be collared by two officers stationed at peepholes behind a wall in the men's room.

The arrest occurred on the night of October 7, 1964. The blotter entry was "disorderly conduct (indecent gestures)." A day or two went by and the story did not appear. "Anonymous tipsters" telephoned local newspapers and suggested that an interesting entry might be beheld on the police morals squad blotter for October 7.

Reporters ambled into action. Queries reached Jenkins, who called prominent Washington lawyers, both friends and Democrats. The President was out of town campaigning. The lawyers, Abe Fortas and Clark Clifford, asked the newspapers to hold the story temporarily, which they agreed to do—temporarily. When it did not appear in the evening papers, Dean Burch, the Republican chairman, released a statement citing the "report sweeping Washington that the White House is desperately trying to suppress a major news story affecting the national security." The Burch statement pried the story loose and United Press International put it on the wire at 8:09 p.m.

By now the unfortunate Jenkins, overworked for a decade or more, was put into a hospital by his physician for nervous exhaustion. The President accepted his resignation with regret. Goldwater greeted the news with restraint and decorum, which lasted for several days. Bill Miller, the Republican Vice Presidential candidate, greeted it with righteous indignation. Dean Burch maintained silence. Goldwaterites in California fashioned a bumper sticker, "Johnson is King and Jenkins is Queen." In Louisiana at a Goldwater dinner, segregationist Leander Perez passed out three-dollar bills good for "three bucks at Jenkins House" and bearing a photo of the President and a drawing of the White House under the legend "BAKER & JENKINS HOUSE."

Meanwhile in New York rumors began to penetrate political and news circles that the real coup was under way; the last-minute bomb long talked of as a Republican blast was at hand; revelation upon revelation would enumerate the sexual peccadilloes of prominent Democrats. The predictions never were borne out.

As the 1964 campaign neared its end, another nasty strain of political underground activity emerged. One week before Election Day, a Negro who left the inference that he was an official of the Republican National Committee, walked into the office of an Atlantic City printing firm, Brooks & Idler, and handed over a rush order for 1,400,000 copies of a simulated telegram, along with billing instructions. Before the job was completed an unnamed man visited the printer and paid $2,500 in cash for it.

The "telegram," via "Western Unity," urged Negroes to write in on their ballots the name of Martin Luther King for President. It was signed "Committee for Negroes in Government, Louisville, Kentucky."

Democrats discovered the plot, and a Negro official of the Republican National Committee named Clay Claiborne, a resident of Atlantic City who had some political connections in Louisville, was indicted by a New Jersey grand jury. The charge was violation of the state's prohibition of campaign literature which does not carry the name and address of the person responsible. Claiborne insisted that he was innocent, and a trial jury acquitted him twenty months later.

At about the same time, Oliver Miles of Louisville, an employee in the Sanitation Department of that city, appeared in Chicago at the advertising agency of Bozell and Jacobs. Miles met with agency president Nathan Jacobs, and ordered a spot announcement to be carried on radio stations with large Negro audiences in eleven cities. The spot made the same point as the "telegram," and was sponsored by the same Louisville "Committee for Negroes in Government." Miles said he was secretary of the "committee," and that its chairman was Thomas H. Frazier, who is an employee of Louisville's City Works Department. Then and there, Miles paid Bozell $10,000 in cash for the spot announcements.

Kentucky law, unlike that of New Jersey, does not outlaw unsigned campaign literature. Still, the New Jersey statute has no way of requiring the culprit to reveal to the court where the money came from. The comparable Federal statute (18 USC Section 612) requires identification of the actual source of campaign literature, and offers grounds for Federal action against all concerned with the shabby affair. However, the Johnson Administration, apparently determined not to disturb sleeping dogs or consensus, has discouraged any effort to prosecute.

These maneuvers were obviously beyond Goldwater's knowledge or control, but *somebody* in the hierarchy knew what was happening, coordinated the efforts and paid the bills. Federal investigation could do much to purify the political system. Harmony prevails instead.

Of course, Southern Democrats have been playing fast and loose with the race issue for 100 years. Thus, when Lyndon Johnson of Texas ran for President on a civil rights platform, Democrats in the unquenchable segregationist areas were dismayed and perplexed. Should they support the national ticket; indeed, *could* they? How to pull the teeth of the potent appeal exerted on the red-necks by Goldwater's refusal to say anything to offend the white supremacists?

One Republican gave them what seemed to be an answer. He was Carl Shipley, chairman of the District of Columbia Republican Central Committee, and most of his constituents were Negroes, since the population of the District has been predominantly colored for years.

Shipley knew the details of Goldwater's consistent efforts to advance the lot of the Negro—his role in desegregating the Arizona National Guard and a variety of other pro-integration acts and statements. He ordered printed for distribution in Negro areas of the District a leaflet revealing Goldwater as a consistent benefactor of the Negro.

As soon as distribution began newspapers reported it, for here *was* a story indeed. In the South the Goldwaterites were acting as though their Senator had voted against the Emancipation Proclamation. Now in a Northern city, Republicans were draping him in Lincoln's mantle.

Many Republicans immediately recognized the unbridled hell-raising potential if Democrats should distribute to Southern whites this Goldwater-for-the-Negro pitch from the North. And Democrats, meanwhile, were determined to find and reprint the leaflet for the widest possible circulation among defecting anti-integrationists.

There ensued a frantic scramble for copies. For hours it appeared that the Republicans had recovered them all. (To this day, when one expresses interest in seeing a copy of the original document, one probably will not succeed—even though there may be from 50 to 100 in the possession of individual archivists. Great care and zeal and promise of anonymity may get one a look at a photocopy; no one who has an original will trust it in hands other than his own.)

Somehow the Democrats managed to acquire one copy. Printed mainly in light blue ink, it was difficult to reproduce effectively by photo-offset. So, substituting a photograph for the drawing of a smiling Goldwater that adorned the front fold, and matching the type and paper as carefully as time would permit, the Democrats printed untold thousands of their version of the leaflet—identical with the original in content and page-to-page layout, except for a new credit line on the back fold. Beneath the intact Republican identification, there was a statement that the leaflet had been reprinted, as a public service, by the Democrats. One version went principally to Klan types in South Carolina and Georgia; another to similar audiences in Alabama and Mississippi.

Parapolitical warfare between the parties is occasionally carried on at the convention level. The object may be to gain intelligence on a sure or probable nominee for use later, in the campaign proper, or it may be to embarrass the presumed winner. On occasion, however, other motives predominate. So it was that in the summer of 1952 the Taft convention forces found their ranks swelled by a suave and handsome gray-haired Irishman from New York City, William R. Peer. Bill Peer was a lifelong Democrat, a veteran newsman, and a resourceful and astute public relations practitioner. He understood politics and political in-fighting, and what is done and what isn't, as a fish understands that flies are hatching. He was an aficionado and supporter of the Irish Republican Army, and his store of lore and legend of that guerrilla way of life merged with his comprehension of politics.

Once I asked Peer why he, a Democrat's Democrat, had gone to the wars for Bob Taft, Mr. Republican. He looked up in surprise at the question and explained with the patience reserved for silly children: "Why, we figured he would be easier to beat."

Guerrilla warfare has its place in the parapolitical world, along with intelligence and the effort to get misleading intelligence to the opposition. Embarrassment and exposure, harassment and counter-harassment, diversionary tactics and defense tactics, all can be important to political maneuvering in campaigns and occasionally outside them.[1]

While these strategic infiltrations and tactical forays are necessary, and often can be done either soberly or with high merriment, they seem to have special appeal to a vicious disposition. It is as true of domestic politics as it is of the international variety that a spy or counterspy must have a highly specialized personality.

Too much of the practical joker can be a grave liability, for the agent may not know when to stop, letting the fun of the game carry him away. However, too little humor is probably the heaviest liability of all, for dedicated and zealous viciousness, or harassment with malice, generates public reactions of anger, con-

---

[1] Counter-harassment is an important subject to citizens faced with harassment from racists and radical rightists. Post-midnight anonymous telephone calls are a favored device of the extremists. An antidote is attributed to Southern publisher Ralph McGill. One of his columns had offended the racists and he was awakened by a three a.m. phone call that was abusive, threatening, and obscene—and anonymous. McGill, the story goes, heard the caller out. When he hung up, the publisher phoned a high potentate among local Negro-haters, whom we shall call George. The call went something like this: "Hey, there, George. This is Ralph McGill. Say, I thought you'd like to know that your folks are right on the job. One of your friends just called up to say he didn't much like my column yesterday. I figured you'd be glad to know how efficient you-all are, and I'm glad to let you know. I'm going to give you a ring and tell you about it every time they phone me up. Maybe we can help each other out. Well, nice to talk with you. Good night, George."

The calls ended two nights later.

155

tempt, and resentment when exposed.

This chapter is dedicated to Messrs. Tuck, Osgoodby, and Peer, and the unnamed Republican stoker from Louisville; for their depredations are effective, yet leavened with wit; they are drollery without an aura of desperation or depravity. These men know and knew how to raise hell without maiming.

CHAPTER 7

Thieves' Market:
The Theft and Purchase
of Votes

THE AMERICAN tradition rules out military force in domestic political conflicts. There have been exceptions. One was the second battle of New Orleans.

In his heyday, Huey Long owned Louisiana as completely as though he had bought it. He ran the state by remote control from the U. S. Senate, through the agency of Governor O. K. Allen,[1] probably the most manipulable public servant since, and perhaps including, the horse that Caligula made a consul of Rome.

There was occasional dissent to Huey's rule, notably from the "Old Regulars" political organization that dominated New Orleans. The Kingfish decided to cripple the New Orleans organization, and he demanded an immediate crackdown on gambling and prostitution, practices which kept city taxes low by keeping public officials' take-home pay high. Mayor T. Semmes Walmsley defied Long's edict. Huey, via Governor Allen, dispatched the

---

[1] Even the Longs laughed about Allen's pliability. As Huey's brother Earl put it, "A leaf blew in the window of Allen's office one day and fell on his desk. He signed it." The state legislature, incidentally, was known as Huey Long's "trained seals."

militia to take over. Infantry, artillery, and cavalry units of the Louisiana National Guard surged into the old city and took over all municipal functions. The date of the primary election was at hand. By coincidence one of the seized offices was that of the registrar of voters, and Long was thus able to prevent election "frauds" which might have returned the popular Mayor Walmsley to power. Long's man won. Louisiana's "dictator" had saved the old city's ballots from any thieves but his own.

In politics, as in other ways of life, it is possible to admire imagination gone wrong while deploring the cause in which it is employed. Thus Robin Hood was a colorful fellow and a selective humanitarian—and a thief. We relish the action and avert our eyes from the fact.

In surburban New York there is an outer suburban community which has not gone Democratic since the decay of the Whigs. Some 35 years ago a local lady became Republican town chairman. Her sensibilities were offended by the blatant cash-and-carry manner in which her predecessors had contracted for Republican votes at $5 a head in a Democratic area in this Republican community. Her political acuity caused her to note that, purchase or not, the Democratic tally was creeping upward year by year in that election district. So, utilizing the imagination that later was to bring her fame in education and public affairs, she contracted with the known Democrats in the area *not* to vote: $5 a head, payable after the polls closed, so long as a check of the names of those who had voted did not include the vote-vendor.

How to prevent enemy votes is half of the process of cheating at the polls. If one has any partisans at all in a district, and enough of the opposition can be kept home, one can't lose.

Less delicacy typifies another method of cheating at the polls. A story resurrected in 1964 on President Johnson illustrates the essence of the tactic. The story was related with particular relish by right-wingers, as though it were somehow unique to LBJ. In fact it had been told a few years earlier in Texas on the conservative governor who magically converted a Johnson win into a thumping defeat—after a few days alone with the ballot boxes. The story probably saw service after the election of Rutherford B. Hayes, and may indeed be as old as universal manhood suffrage.

Little Pedro is crying. "Why are you crying, Pedro?" asks a passer-by. "I am crying for my poor dead father," says Pedro. "But Pedro," responds the man, "your father has been dead for ten years." "That's just it," Pedro rejoins, sobbing now. "Last night he came back to vote for Lyndon Johnson (Coke Stevenson, Rutherford Hayes, or, for that matter, Barry Goldwater) and he no come to see me."

The story was part of right wing exploitation of cloudy passages in Johnson's electoral history. In various versions, including books and campaign tabloids, the tale must have reached a circulation of 20 million or more. Basically, the Johnson miracle at the polls revolved around poll box number 13 at Alice, Texas, and enabled the young Congressman to win his Senate seat by an 87-vote margin.

Robert Sherrill, writing in *Fair Comment*, presented the story in perspective:

"Johnson defeated former Governor Coke Stevenson with the help of George Parr, South Texas' political czar, who 'discovered' 203 more votes—all but one for Johnson—several days after the balloting was over. These 202 Johnson voters had, amazingly enough, voted in alphabetical order. For good reason Stevenson challenged the vote, and he might have won in a court showdown if Justice Hugo Black . . . had not ruled that federal courts have no jurisdiction in a strictly party primary.

"Unquestionably the election was cloudy, but if it cannot be forgiven at least it can be better understood if restored to its historical context.

"First of all, when Johnson lost to Pappy O'Daniel in the Senate race of 1941, the tables were reversed. The morning after the election, Johnson was ahead by 5,000 votes. Four days later he had lost by 1,311 votes. Satisfied with this lesson in practical Texas politics, Johnson did not ask for a recount. But next time he was ready. When he went out for the Senate again, it was against Stevenson, an old hand at dealing with the peculiarities of South Texas voting, who had, when being re-elected governor in 1940, carried Parr's home county, Duval, by the friendly ratio of 3,643 to 53 over his primary opponent." [2]

Dead men have voted. Dogs have voted. Criminals have voted under their rightful names and under aliases. Fictional characters have voted. New York City, long a bastion of electoral respectability, was not always so. The phenomenally successful get-out-the-vote drive of 1844 will illustrate. There were nearly 41,000 qualified voters. Allowing for the suddenly ill, the lazy and the disaffected, the turnout was amazing: 55,000. The dead filled in for the sick.

In recent years, Republican indignation at vote-stealing in Chicago has focused unwelcome attention on that city's voting peculiarities. In many wards virtually every voter is a Democrat. It has been literally impossible for many years to find Republican poll-workers and watchers for these precincts, and in this situation the only limits to skulduggery are the imaginations of the skulduggers. After each election the GOP launches a cry that it was stolen in Chicago, a charge that may well be true.

In 1960 Chicago delivered a Democratic plurality of 319,000 for Kennedy—enough to offset the Nixon vote in the rest of the state and put Illinois' 27 electors in the JFK column with 9,000 votes to spare. Had Chicago fallen short of this sterling clutch performance—say someone had miscalculated and underestimated the vote needed to counter downstate—and come through with a Kennedy plurality of only 309,000, Nixon would have carried the state and the electoral close shave of 1960 would have been even closer: 276 to 246 in Kennedy's favor.

A Canadian salesman got into a cab in front of his Chicago hotel on Election Day in 1960 and gave the driver an address on the near south side, a factory on which he intended to call. The salesman settled back, immersed in his own thoughts, and finally

[2] Review of J. Evetts Haley's *A Texan Looks at Lyndon* in *Fair Comment*, Quarterly of the Fair Campaign Practices Committee, October, 1964.

noted that the fare on the meter was rising astronomically. He looked out and saw he was in a totally unfamiliar section. "Where are we going?" he asked the driver.

"We're going to vote," said the taximan, "then I'll take you where you want to go."

The salesman protested. "I'm not even a citizen," he cried. "I can't vote here. I don't live here. I'm a Canadian."

The driver listened, driving on. He pulled up in front of a precinct polling place and motioned to the door of the cab. The Canadian shrugged and stepped out. "How do I vote?" he asked.

Inside, the salesman was shown politely to a voting booth and given the assistance required—required, that is, by the chief inspector at the polling place. He marked his ballot to the inspector's satisfaction and returned to his cab, and thence to his customer. He was several dollars poorer, but wiser in the ways of stolen votes.

The tradition in Chicago is as old as the celebrated Loop. In the days when Big Bill Thompson, a Republican, was alternately baiting nationality groups and catering to them, he was manipulating voting returns like a circus juggler. Hanky-panky with the Illinois vote goes back to Senate contests before Senators were popularly elected. In 1909 the Illinois legislature belatedly picked William Lorimer for the United States Senate. The solons had been unable to agree on a choice, and, thus deadlocked, who came to their aid but William Lorimer, solving the problem by buying at least one legislator's vote, breaking the deadlock and paving the way for his seating by the U. S. Senate. That body demurred, however, when word reached it of the purchase; Lorimer was not seated.

The big cities enjoy no monopoly on vote stealing; they are more widely known in these terms because the word leaks out faster from a city than from the wide open spaces where men are men and not given to loose talk. There are six states each of which turns out a smaller Presidential vote than, say, Denver County, Colorado; and these states elect twelve United States Senators, thirteen Members of Congress and 25 Presidential electors. In these states, elections are decided by two and three thousand votes, and at this level counting is simple. Of course, two of those six states are scrupulous Delaware and Vermont, but . . .

The election of 1876 was the all-time high-water mark in terms of plain and fancy thievery of votes, popular and electoral, in American Presidential elections. There were four candidates, of whom only two, fielded by the Prohibition Party and the Greenbackers, knew they had lost honestly. The major party candidates were Samuel J. Tilden, Democrat, of New York, and Rutherford B. Hayes, an Ohio Republican.

Northern support for the Reconstruction was dwindling, and liberal Republicans were reacting against tales of excesses by carpetbaggers. In the South, the Amnesty Act of 1872 had enfranchised white Confederate veterans. The end of the Reconstruction was clearly at hand, but white Southern manhood would not wait. Stetson Kennedy, in his book, *Southern Exposure*,[3] illumines some of the ways in which the Democrat, Tilden, polled many more votes than expected.

"Democrats openly threatened that they would 'carry the election or kill the last damned Republican in the South.' The Klan brought its intensive campaign of terrorism to a whirlwind climax. Shipments of arms hurriedly dispatched to military units were confiscated by Klansmen who had been tipped off by railroad officials. On Election Day the locations of many polling places were suddenly changed without notice in an effort to lose the Negroes. The whites appeared with rifles in hand and turned away prospective Negro voters. Many Negroes who sought to vote under escort of United States Marshals were shot, and the Marshals with them."

Tilden won the election, but was about to lose the count. In an electorate of a little over eight million, he polled a popular plurality of a quarter-million over the Republican Hayes.

Each major candidate carried seventeen of the 38 states. The remaining four were contested. Tilden had 184 sure electoral

[3] Doubleday, 1946.

votes—one less than a majority. Hayes got 163 firm electoral votes. The dispute arose over four states. Florida, Louisiana, and South Carolina had nineteen electoral votes among them. Tilden carried the states, but the counts were contested by the dominant, Reconstruction, Republican administrations. Thus the Republican national party organization could contend that the states were in doubt. Democratic election boards certified that Tilden's electors had been chosen. Republican election boards managed to disqualify enough Tilden votes to certify Hayes' electors. So Florida, Louisiana, and South Carolina sent two electoral delegations apiece, one Republican, one Democratic.

The fourth state was Oregon. There was no question that the Republicans had carried the state. The Democratic governor, acting wholly illegally, arbitrarily disqualified one of the three Republican electors—possibly feeling that if Southern Republicans were going to play the numbers game, a Western Democrat could do likewise. He certified a Democrat in place of the ousted Republican. Had the gambit been sustained by the Congress, Tilden would have been the 16th President of the United States. His 184 undisputed votes, plus that of the one unlawful elector from Oregon, would have given him the majority required by the Constitution: 185.

The election was thrown into the Congress. The Constitution set forth the procedure: "The President of the Senate shall, in the presence of the Senate and the House of Representatives, open all certificates and the votes shall be counted."

The Constitution, however, did not specify who should do the counting. The Senate was heavily Republican, and would be sure to count Hayes in. The House, as heavily Democratic since the election of 1874, would certainly elect Tilden.

The unprecedented deadlock frightened the Congress, both as partisans and as national legislators, so it set up an Electoral Commission, designed to be as scrupulously bipartisan as possible. Five of fifteen members came from each body of the Congress, and five from the Supreme Court. The Democratic House chose three Democrats and two Republicans. Reciprocating, in the interest of fair play, public necessity, and political realities, the Republican Senate picked three Republicans and two Democrats. The Supreme Court members were specified to be two Democrats and two Republicans, with these four to pick the fifth, tacitly but firmly understood to be Justice David Davis, an Independent from Illinois.

However, the Illinois legislature, with an eye on the state's 21 Republican electoral votes, opportunely elected Justice Davis to the United States Senate, class of 1876. The four remaining justices then picked a Republican colleague, Justice Joseph P. Bradley of New Jersey.

Early in the actual life of the Commission, Justice Bradley wrote an opinion supporting Tilden's election. Shocked at this blindness to all but the facts and figures, Republican political leaders remonstrated with Justice Bradley, who ultimately found for Hayes, thus tidying up the Commission tally to a party-line 8-7, eight Republicans versus seven Democrats.

So it was demonstrated that who votes is not so important as who counts, a lesson learned with diligence and application by many a political trickster since 1876. However, the increasing vigilance and sophistication of the press, and the ubiquity and speed of news media, have made the Hayes-Tilden manipulation a thing of the past. Never since has a President been elected with fewer popular votes than his rival, even though the Electoral College system leaves room for that eventuality.

Legislators have fought tooth and toenail against automation in the field of votes: namely, the voting machine. Today, with two major manufacturers turning out the device and others producing automatic electronic counters of paper ballots, at least some sections of 48 states use machines. Seven states use voting machines exclusively, and their employment increases steadily. In 1960 half of the total Presidential vote was cast on machines, and by 1964 the proportion increased to 65 per cent.

The voting machine was the first substantial improvement in voting procedures since the introduction of the "Australian ballot" a few decades earlier. The Australian system, the scorn of politicians and the darling only of reformers in the last quarter of the nineteenth century, provided simply that one ballot be printed at public expense, with the names of all candidates on it, instead of individual party tickets which electors might mark and deposit after receiving the ticket from a party worker at the polls.

Adoption of the Australian system gradually in the United States did not end election chicanery, any more than has the voting machine of later date. But the unified public ballot did bring some aspects of the party system under law, in that the publicly printed ballot had to be controlled in its use, and by a public agency. Any paper ballot can be tampered with, and some of the old standard tricks have passed into legend. Early attempts at fraud included marking in another candidate in heavier lead or ink than the voter has used to designate his own candidate. The remedy came quickly: any mark outside the space provided, or any improper mark, voided the ballot.

The response of the manipulators came just as quickly. In the counting process, one could deface ballots voting "wrong" and thus invalidate them. Crooked election inspectors and poll workers took to concealing a bit of pencil lead beneath the thumbnail. A quick counting motion and the ballot was defaced as it was counted. Put back into the box, it later could be examined in the course of a recount and would then be invalidated.

In the early days of the voting machine, a hairpin could jam a machine beyond immediate repair. Paper matches also were used to decommission machines. And a favorite trick, still in use now that the machines are harder than ever to beat, is to cause delay in the line, by running in a batch of organization voters to ask for instructions, help, and general information. The pace of the line becomes so slow that people who must get to work or back to work—voters presumed to be against the organization candidate—will give up in disgust as minutes stretch out toward hours.

Registration abuses are on the wane in the country generally. An exception is the South. As Negro registration increases, so does the temptation for segregationists to intimidate Negroes

subtly, or, occasionally, overtly. Registration irregularities sometimes occur in rural sections of the North, where fast shuffles of
registered voters have been accomplished with some ease. New
York, for example, in many rural towns, has a permanent, *imper-
sonal* registration system, in which almost anyone may register
anyone else. The dominant political organization will enter each
new resident on the rolls, and then advise him of the organization's courtesy and deep personal interest. Some states do not
have registration at all; one may vote on presentation of a tax
receipt, or any identification attesting to residence.

Permanent personal registration, long a goal of the League
of Women Voters, is spreading slowly, and once a county or other
political entity gets the bugs out of the system it works well. One
pitfall new PPR systems have encountered in some places is the
organization of the registration book. In poorly conceived systems, the voter may sign his name, when he appears to vote, just
below his signature for his last previous vote. This enables any
clever penman to vote as often as he encounters names he can
forge with any degree of authority. The foolproof systems of permanent personal registration work from the bottom of the page
up, so the signer's hand covers the last signature he has entered.
If, thus blinded to what his name is supposed to look like, he can
produce a fair facsimile of the last signature, he is not challenged.

The most stringent law is no better than its enforcement, and
there are few areas of human concern that demonstrate the fact
more persuasively than elections. All in all, the fifty states have a
good and sound collection of election laws. Some, indeed, have
attributes so fine that they are virtually exotic in comparison with
national norms. But contested elections are rare, and successful
contests rarer. Candidates often hesitate to challenge their de-
feats. They view the prospect somewhat like Pandora's box, and
fear that next time around *they* might be bitten by one of the evils
loosed from the legendary chest.

When elections are disputed, money is usually the central
factor. For example, in Illinois in 1926, Frank Smith won a Senate
seat in the Republican primary and the general election. How-

ever, the Senate, which, under the Constitution, is the sole judge of the qualification of its members, refused to seat Mr. Smith because of the gross and improper use of funds in his campaigns.

Money was the issue in a contested House race in 1964 when Richard Ottinger of New York spent $185,000—mostly contributed by himself, his mother, and his sister—to win a Congressional election on which, by law, he could spend no more than $5,000. Of course, if Ottinger had been denied his seat for overspending, the Halls of Congress would quickly drain of their population. It is difficult to conceive of more than four or five House Members, if that many, who could have spent less than around $20,000.

Is politics becoming a rich man's game? The entry of more and more rich men into the field tends to make it so. The staggering costs of mounting a Presidential campaign make it so. While primary elections are exempted from Federal statutory limits, they are far from exempt from high cost. Visualize the ease with which John Kennedy in 1960 could shuttle between Washington and the primary contests in West Virginia and Wisconsin, in the family airplane. Hubert Humphrey was reduced by sheer economic necessity to buses and only an occasional chartered plane.

The plight of a man of only modest means was dramatized in the 1952 campaign. California admirers of Republican Vice Presidential nominee Richard M. Nixon had put together a fund of some $18,000 to cover political expenses he could not charge to his Senate budget and could not himself afford. The fund was created to cover postage, extra travel to and within the state, and similar mundane and essential expenditures that were appreciable in total amount.

The Democrats [4] discovered the "Nixon fund" in mid-September. Already smarting badly from the Republicans' holier-than-thou strictures about morality in government and mink coats, the Democrats laid on heavily about immorality, slush funds, bought officials, and the like. Nixon defended his own

---

[4] The actual discovery was made by reporters for some Democratically-oriented newspapers.

probity and the propriety of his fund on nationwide television.[5]

The furor subsided quickly when it became known that friends of Adlai Stevenson when he was Governor of Illinois had put up a similar fund. Actually, there are more than 70 members of the U.S. Senate—and conceivably almost all—who have some such source of money for essential political expenditures between campaigns. In a large state, a Senator will need between *$200 and $300 a week*, year in and year out, just to cover the cost of taping a weekly television commentary for key stations back home. This figure includes postage, the cost of maintaining three sets of tape for each station (one in Washington, one at the station, and one in the mail; they can be re-used) and miscellaneous items, even while the Senator takes advantage of the studio facilities available to him in the Capitol. Also draining such funds are postage for political mail and trips home in addition to those authorized at public expense, precisely à la Nixon.

The money problem bedevils candidate and party organizations impartially. The law, which Congressman Ottinger ran afoul of, is in practical terms a nuisance but not a deterrent. A Senate candidate may spend $25,000, a House candidate $5,000. So committees are organized ad nauseam to receive and spend money for the campaign. No person may contribute more than $5,000 to any political candidate or party. In the Ottinger case, all that was needed was enough committees and enough patience to write out all those checks.

In this instance the real issue was the ease with which the man of means may finance a costly campaign (Ottinger's opponent, rarely visible in the district or the Capitol, was also a man of means). The argument that a rich man doesn't have to steal extends to the logical proposition that he doesn't have to take big sums from potential favor-seekers, which is the real target of all campaign finance legislation. Evasions of the law are general. In

---

[5] The emotional content of the Nixon defense distracted attention from the real merits of his case, the plight of a poor man in politics. The speech, which is remembered best for its ringing endorsement of motherhood, his daughters, and his cocker spaniel, Checkers, passed into political history as The Soap Opera.

1950 Ohio financier Cyrus Eaton gave $5,000 to the labor campaign to beat Robert A. Taft. He also gave a total of $30,000 to his son and seven employees who then generously gave their own checks to the get-Taft movement, totalling, of course, $30,000. Some families regularly contribute from $50,000 to $500,000 or more to the party of their choice.

The difficulty facing the impoverished candidate is where and how to get money without incurring a major obligation to the source. Ideologically, campaign money in dollar bills and fives and tens is just right, but it takes a large pile of them to pay for postage alone. In denominations of 500 and 1,000, those dollars take fewer calls and less shoe leather to amass. Major political efforts would expire if they had to depend for income on many small contributors. As things stand, there just aren't that many.

The suspicion that the poor man may be purchasable hangs over the impoverished candidate. In 1960 Democrats fostered a gag-line to cast this perennial shadow on Nixon *vis-à-vis* millionaire John Kennedy: "I'd rather elect a poor man's rich man than a rich man's poor man."

The law, incidentally, makes any device to entice, coerce, or reward the voter unlawful, regardless of the probity of its motive. Some Rhode Island Goldwater people learned this in 1964 when an enterprising local group set up a raffle to encourage registration *and* voting. New registrants would get a ticket; after voting they would surrender a stub to a party worker and retain the rest of the ticket. The stub would go into a lottery, and there would be fun and prizes for many lucky winners. Launched with fanfare, the scheme was abandoned with haste when it was found that any such device could, under Rhode Island law, cost any participant a jail sentence, fine, and permanent loss of the right to vote or hold office.

Since primary elections are exempt from Federal regulation, they have occasionally proved to be bonanzas for party and candidate. Large contributions can be made to a primary candidate who is considered a shoo-in for the nomination, and the unspent balance can be transferred to the general election fund without accounting. Glen Taylor of Idaho used to raise campaign funds in primary (and general) elections substantially beyond his requirements, and was able to live on the surplus until the next election.

All these are more or less respectable dodges and devices, their acceptability assured by nearly universal complicity in them. Really shady money creates a different problem. A gas lobbyist slipped an envelope into the hand of the late South Dakota Senator Francis Case. It proved to contain twenty-five $100 bills, nicely timed for Case's 1956 campaign. At the time the Senate was considering a bill regulating natural gas producers. During debate on the bill, Case revealed the offer and the fact that he had rejected it. The law was passed, in terms favorable to the industry, but it was vetoed by President Eisenhower, partly because of the Case episode.

One of the juicier elements in the 1964 Bobby Baker scandal was the allegation that a Philadelphia contractor had been paid an extra $35,000 for a job on the Washington municipal stadium. The money, so the story went, wound up in the coffers of the Democratic National Committee, less $10,000 for the "bag man," allegedly Baker. The contractor denied the story and it slid out of the limelight each of the several times the Senate re-buried the Baker case. The contractor was no common man, but Matthew J. McCloskey of Philadelphia, Washington and (later, as U. S. Ambassador) Ireland. McCloskey, described by an associate as "a little old white haired man with a pink cherubic face that conceals a whim of steel," was then treasurer of the Democratic National Committee, a post he had held for many years. It was Matt McCloskey who invented the most popular, and notorious, and simple way to raise political money: the $100-a-plate dinner, which he pioneered for Franklin Roosevelt in 1936.

Periodically reformers draw a bead on party fund raisers with the cry, probably justified to some degree every time, that office holders are being bludgeoned into contributing to party coffers. Actually, financial bludgeoning is a way of life in America. There is not a charitable organization in the land that raises money by the $100 or $500 or $1,000—or even $25—a plate dinner that does not bludgeon diners by finding some excuse to bestow an award on some prominent citizen with hordes of suppliers, or people of means otherwise dependent on his good will. It should come as no surprise that political money raisers will continue to employ the technique found so successful in the sweet name of charity. To be sure, it is rare that a politician in government will put a demand for contributions in writing to the staff of his department, but it happens now and then. Usually, however, the velvet glove suffices. Trouble comes when a Republican feels the pressure from a Democratic superior, or vice versa.

Voluntary contributions are quite all right. The question becomes, how voluntary are they? Semi-voluntary? Indeed, this is the question that is raised time and again about labor union money in politics. It is sometimes suggested that COPE, which raises its budget from voluntary one-dollar contributions by union members, uses pressure to collect. The allegation has never been proved, and probably never will be. Considerably more likely to be true are suggestions of pressure in occasional drives for voluntary political funds by individual unions. Unions may not use any part of dues money for campaign purposes, any more than corporations may spend in political campaigns.

Corporations may, and many do, encourage (so long as they do not *force*) executives to contribute generously to their party. Indirect reimbursement is no problem, for ingenuity is abundant at that level of industry.

On occasion in the past, foundations controlled by politically active individuals have made indirect contributions. The Internal Revenue Service has been examining with a highly jaundiced eye the proceedings of such groups, and has disallowed the tax exemptions of some of them.

Loss of tax exemption for political activity became possible in 1954 when the tax law was amended. Section 501 (c) (3) of the Internal Revenue Code exempts churches and charitable organizations from taxation. The 1954 amendment specified that exempt organizations may not "participate in, or intervene in (including the publishing or distributing of statements), any politi-

cal campaign on behalf of any candidate for public office."
Scholars and lawyers seeking to establish the intent of the
Congress in this particular language are out of luck, for the wording has no legislative history, no record of committee or floor
debate; simply its appearance and passage. The reason: Lyndon
Johnson, then the Senate Democratic Leader, had found right-
wing-oriented foundations circulating, under the guise of "educational material," literature attacking Johnson. He discussed the
problem informally with a number of colleagues and there was
general agreement that the amendment was needed. It was
adopted without fuss, and has generally served well to prevent
organizations indirectly subsidized by their freedom from taxation from influencing the composition of the government.

Literature of the sort some foundation proprietors used to
get away with is no longer a substantial factor in political campaign cost. The bottomless pit is television. If a candidate has
$25,000 he may spend up to $300 or thereabouts on a leaflet and
stationery, and the balance on "the tube." Sometimes it is utterly
essential to get on the air.

Congressman Carl Elliott of Alabama had the fight of his
political life—which he lost—in the 1964 Democratic primary. An
opponent came up with last-minute charges that had to be answered. Elliott bought the necessary TV time, $20,000 worth, and
had to mortgage his car to borrow part of the money. The next
day he lost.

Elliott's problem was unusual for a Congressional District
primary, for Alabama's House delegation ran at large that year,
but it was only a reflection of the kind of financial woes that beset
a Senatorial or gubernatorial candidate, and not even a drop in
the bucket in terms of Presidential campaign finance.

The cost of politics is rising steadily; all of us are in the business of buying votes, like it or not.

In 1964 each of the 70.6 million votes for President cost
about 41 cents.[6] All major committees participating in the 1964

[6] According to Dr. Herbert E. Alexander, Director of the Citizens' Research Foundation, of Princeton, N.J. The foundation is the nation's only
thorough and scrupulous privately-supported observer of political finance.

election for President spent a combined total of nearly $35 million, all but about $6 million of which was spent by the Democratic and Republican National Committees. The total cost of all the elections of 1964 is estimated at around $200 million, up 14 per cent from the $175 million estimate for 1960; and that was 12 per cent higher than the $155 million of 1956; which in turn exceeded by 10 per cent the $140 million estimated for 1952. The change in the status of television from a new medium to an indispensable one is measured in those increases, with inflation only a modest contributing factor.

There are three principal goals that attract efforts to reform campaign finance. First and vital: keeping the political system alive and operating. Second: insulating the politician from favor-seekers bearing gifts (and equalizing the chances of rich and poor candidates to reach the voter). Third: maintaining the confidence of the electorate in the political system, and distributing its costs fairly.

Reform efforts move generally in the direction of direct or indirect government subsidy, with the interim objective of full disclosure of sources of funds. Disclosure of the source of Francis Case's $2,500 from the gas lobbyist, even if Case had *used* the money, would have tended to reduce the pressure for favors that the gift exerted on Case, by setting up a counter-pressure of public concern about the source.

The Commonwealth of Puerto Rico is cited as a precedent by advocates of direct subsidy. The American Territory rigidly limits individual contributions to parties and candidates. The Commonwealth provides funds of $75,000 annually, available to each major political party. The party authorizes expenditures and the government pays the bill, against the party's balance in the government's account. Parties can spend less in non-election years and use the savings for campaigns, but any balance at the end of a four-year cycle goes back into the Commonwealth treasury for good.

Other subsidy proposals include campaign literature printed at government expense—as most states already do with pro and con material about such initiative measures as appear on their ballots. Federal subsidies to television networks have been proposed. Indirect subsidy is involved in suggestions of tax deductible contributions or tax credits up to a specified limit.

Whether the slowly gathering Congressional support for some improvement along these lines will ever reach majority status remains to be seen. Every national effort has collapsed. Even modernization of the ludicrous $3 million limit on national committee spending imposed by Federal law has proven uncommonly hard to attain.

The problem will not go away. The political system belongs to every citizen. If he leaves its support to his rich neighbor down the street he will find it is in effect owned by that neighbor. Eventually the citizen probably will be goaded by concerned groups of his peers into supporting some reform. De Tocqueville noted with surprise that in the America of the early 19th century citizens facing problems formed committees and handled them without recourse to "the authorities."

The spread of information about political finance through the work of the Citizens' Research Foundation and individual scholars and lawmakers can generate the necessary pressures, and ultimately, no doubt, it will. The question is, when?

CHAPTER 8

Index
and Record

"NO GENERAL statement is always true," some sage has observed, "including this one." The adage is particularly apt for the
current vogue of rating members of Congress on a variety of indexes that reflect the biases of the political interest groups doing
the rating.

These indexes do give a general picture of the voting performance of members of Congress. But the point of view of the
rating organization is generally narrow and usually over-simplified. Almost always, the voting index works to the disadvantage
of the Congressman who is a little less doctrinaire—a little more
moderate—than the creed of the rating group.

A number of national groups regularly publish indexes of
voting performance in both the Senate and the House of Representatives. The three most widely known and cited are Americans
for Democratic Action (ADA), the AFL-CIO Committee on Political Education (COPE), and Americans for Constitutional Action (ACA). ADA is ardently liberal and ACA generally reactionary; their indexes reflect their attitudes. COPE is generally liberal, but because of its obvious and legitimate concern for labor
interests, the COPE index occasionally parts company with

ADA's on the selection of key votes.

The American Farm Bureau Federation also rates Congressmen, and from an indomitably conservative point of view, but usually in terms of issues of prime importance to its membership. Its opposite number is the National Farmers' Union, as militant as the Farm Bureau, but liberally-oriented. Both farm groups measure Senators as well as Representatives. The National Associated Businessmen, Inc., only rates House members, and its bias is, naturally enough, conservative.

The 1964 performance of all these groups reflects their political dispositions. ADA gave 100 per cent ratings to three Democrats in the Senate and six in the House, and to no Republican. Its zero scores went to seven Republicans, all but one in the House; no Democrats

ACA found only one Senator, a Republican, and six House members to be 100 per cent conservative. It gave zeroes to six Senators and 35 Congressmen, all Democrats.

COPE bestowed zeroes impartially: four Democrats and five Republicans in the Senate were "wrong" every time; in the House, 21 Republicans and eleven Democrats. Twelve Democrats in the Senate and 94 in the House were 100 per cent "right."

The National Farmers' Union was stingy with its A-pluses, giving none in the Senate and only 28 to Democratic Representatives. Always wrong were five GOP Senators and 38 Republicans in the House.

Finally, the National Associated Businessmen rated only House members, finding 82 Republicans perfect and 98 Democrats hopeless.

ADA, ACA, and the Associated Businessmen compile their own indexes on issues that seem crucial to the groups. Some of the issues chosen by the conservative and liberal groups offer a head-on collision of views, as in eight House votes which ACA and ADA numbered among their key 1964 issues. More often the clashes are oblique. ADA, for instance, listed Senate votes on five amendments to the 1964 tax cut bill as vital, while ACA counted only one vote on final passage. The raters are highly sophisticated watchers of Congress, and they know the variety of ways in which a piece of legislation may be killed without leaving marks.

For example, while an important bill is being considered, a number of amendments to it will be attempted. Some would reduce or increase its benefits, or narrow or widen its scope. Some may try to add special benefits to the main item; others may try to cut away such extras.

When Congressional debate on the final shape of the bill is completed, the remaining question is final passage. There still remain several ways to kill it besides voting a flat *no* on the last roll call. A motion to table the bill may be made, or to recommit it to the committee that studied it before it reached the floor. In the case of a "recommittal motion," there are still several possibilities. If the committee is hostile, sending the bill back for more consideration amounts to tabling it.

A recommittal effort is not necessarily an attempt to bury the bill. The bill may be sent back to committee with specific instructions—for example, to increase or reduce some aspect of it by a specified amount. Often such resolutions also direct the committee to report back to the floor with the revised legislation immediately, or within two or three days.

At last, when the bill comes back from committee, for final consideration on the floor, a bitter-end opponent may move to "strike the enacting clause," killing the language which would establish the bill as the law of the land. When this move fails, the bill is adopted or rejected by whichever house of the Congress is considering it.

There may even be another chance to prevent enactment into law after the House or the Senate has adopted the bill. If there are substantial differences in the final House and Senate versions, the two variations of the bill will go to a conference committee with representatives from both chambers whose duty is to resolve and compromise the differences. Then each house must vote for or against the report of the conference committee.

After any vote, a motion to reconsider may be made. This is done in the hope that enough of the other side will have voted and left the floor so that the members remaining in the chamber can reverse the just-completed vote.

So there are at least seven different opportunities to kill or maim a piece of legislation. In most cases, few of those chances will be record votes that show the public whether a given member voted yes or no.

A legislator who opposes a popular or important measure will try to impair or ditch it before its final passage. If all is lost, and Congressional sentiment indicates that the bill will carry, an opponent may well vote for it on the final roll-call.

Thus, it requires a shrewd observer to tell from the record who is for and who is against a bill, and why—whether on principle or because of some detail it incorporates. The political analysts of the voting index groups are shrewd and sophisticated, and their assessments generally have a high degree of accuracy.

However, the rating organizations represent only their own conception of what is best for the country. Each takes its own rather hard line. There is no compiler of indexes whose viewpoint is sufficiently broad and moderate to find a perfect rating for a Congressman who on one bill or another may anger every one of the rating organizations. Indexes enable the public to find out which Senators and Representatives the ADA thinks are perfect, and the ACA, and COPE, and the farm and business groups. These views of perfection are narrow and imperfect and may be wholly useless to the voting citizen.

What the rating organization sees as heresy, a moderate citizen may count a benison. Suppose a citizen wants fairly liberal, or fairly conservative, representation in the Senate. What help is an ADA or ACA rating of, say, 70 per cent? The downgrading from 100 to 70 may result from the Senator's support of precisely the kinds of legislation that the citizen most favors. Or, it may represent opposition to what the citizen wants. Few moderate liberal voters see eye-to-eye with ADA on every major point, and few moderate conservatives agree item-by-item with ACA.

Worse, there is some inherent distortion in the tests applied by the interest groups to screen out Congressmen who fight a bill out of the public eye, in committee and cloakroom, only to surrender bravely to it on a final roll call. For screened out along with tooth-and-nail foes are also those, ranging all the way from liberal to conservative, who seek to temper or expand a bill in some particulars, or who feel that the present version is unfair to their state or district. Visualize a motion to recommit, say, an imaginary $100 million aid bill, with instructions to the committee to lop off $5 million and report back immediately. The author of such a motion, let us presume, wants the bill passed but wants to cut it by (only) five per cent. Opposition to the bill realizes its enactment cannot be stopped and in an effort to cripple it, however slightly, votes for the motion.

If the (also imaginary) U.S. Committee for Aid finds a handsome collection of Aid opponents in the vote on recommittal, it may select this vote as a barometer of Congressional fidelity to the high principles of Aid, and count a "yes" vote to recommit as a real, obvious-to-the-in-group vote against the substance of the bill. And what shows up in this mixed bag? Some members all for the bill but wanting it modestly reduced, a corps of die-hard Aid-haters, and probably a Congressman or two who quibble with some of the language or don't like the sponsor or committee chairman. In this light, indexing paints "obstructionist" with a brush broad enough to tar some thoughtful moderates along with the hard-nosed real opposition.

The political parties offer to help the uncommitted voter perplexed by the vagaries of ADA-ACA or Farmers Union-Farm Bureau polarized indexing. They come up with their own indexes, laboriously digging out those votes which make the largest possible number of the opposition look as bad as possible by the party's standard of perfection in any given year.

The 1964 performance by the Democratic National Committee is instructive. The Democrats picked 30 issues from the 87th and 88th Congresses for their meter of obstructionism. Twelve of these were votes on bills handled by the 88th (1963–64) Congress, and four of these votes were taken in 1964.

The ADA listed thirteen House issues for 1964, and ACA

nineteen.

ADA and ACA, the rating doyens, respectively, of liberals and conservatives, listed eight identical votes as bellwethers. Not one of the Democrats' key issue choices appeared among the eight on which the left and right flanks agreed.

The Democratic National Committee list covered five farm issues. The liberal National Farmers Union rated only seven Republicans in the entire House of Representatives as having voting records of 50 per cent or better. Yet observe how poorly the Democrats managed to rate them:

RATINGS

Congressman	Democrats		Liberal Groups			Conservative Groups		
	Farm Votes	*All Votes Listed*	NFU	ADA	COPE	NBA	AFBF	ACA
HALPERN (N.Y.)	33	88	71	76	82	47	25	31
LINDSAY (N.Y.)	17	72	58	84	73	72	25	40
MATHIAS (Md.)	0	59	58	72	82	69	50	45
TUPPER (Me.)	50	78	58	56	82	61	25	39
CAHILL (N.J.)	0	59	54	64	64	68	50	50
CONTE (Mass.)	0	55	54	64	55	72	25	50
FINO (N.Y.)	0	55	50	60	64	69	50	40

(Democratic ratings are computed on the basis of votes selected by the Democratic National Committee; other ratings are from six national indexes for comparison.)

The Democrats admitted that Republican Halpern was "right" on all but 12 per cent of their over-all key votes, but they found him two-thirds "wrong" on farm votes. The Farmers Union loved him—71 per cent—and rated him better than all other Republicans and 70 Democrats.

Mathias and Cahill both got zeroes from the Democratic farm indexes. Yet the Farmers Union rated them 58 and 54, and even the conservative Farm Bureau classed them at 50.

Consider the pecking order in the case of Halpern; to the

Farm Bureau, a dreg; to ACA a radical; to the Democrats on farm issues, a measly one-third; to the businessman, below 50 per cent; to the Farmers Union, clearly a good guy; to ADA a whiz—76 per cent; and to COPE?—a hero of the labor unions, 82 per cent!

The Democrats needed Halpern's "wrong" farm vote to pull his record on their overall scale down to 88 per cent—still a higher figure than some members of the Democratic *leadership!*

Actually in the 1964 House campaigns a number of Republicans were able to prove the distortion in some of the Democrats' selected votes. Many Democratic candidates simply listed votes cited in the National Committee's "record of Republican obstruction," never bothering to find out that the target had been on record as solidly favoring the bill in question before and after the parliamentary maneuver on which the Democratic rating was based. The GOP incumbents were then able to riddle the opposition claims. Those who had the attention of their audience won, and those who did not, in general, lost.

Some of the Republicans knocked out of the House in the anti-Goldwater wave were so beset by substantive distortions that they could not choose which one or few to dramatize, and tried to answer all of them, confusing the public hopelessly about the tangle of Congressional procedure.

Newspapers too seldom play a digging and delving role in campaigns where distortion is charged and counter-charged. In some cases the press will print the facts of Congressional voting on disputed issues, but interpretive reporting in a Congressman's own district is virtually unheard of. A few days' study of the facts and an interview with each candidate would enable a competent reporter to record the real impact and direction of the disputed votes. Such a reporter, without calling anybody a liar, without raising the specter of a libel suit or appearing to be partial, would lay the essential facts out for the voters, who then could quickly tell who *was* the liar. Too often, "research" is done by reading press-agents' handouts, and digging is confined to wresting the most striking lead paragraph out of a dull story.

When the press acts as a neutral transmission belt for charges and counter-charges it serves no one, but simply amplifies confusion and conflict to wholly unnecessary, and often dangerous, levels. This is carrying the quest for objectivity to absurd lengths. In these circumstances, parrot-like repetition of the details beneath a dispute amounts to the most flagrant bias.

So, by themselves, without the grain of salt that informed and honest analysis supplies, voting indexes often distort the picture of conduct in office that they purport to clarify. They interpret Congressional careers in the peculiar light of ideological or economic or party bias. By selecting a pattern of votes and measuring all legislators against it, they compose a picture with many sound generalities, and with many weird and distorted shadows among them.

Lacking the expertise to read between the lines, to tone down and modify the image supplied by the indexes, the voter must rely on balanced judgment and the debate of the campaign. It is not enough to believe that the indexes present an ever-fair and always honest measurement of the incumbent. The incumbent's arguments as he attempts to set straight the distorted index-picture must be listened to seriously and evaluated on the basis of comparative believability of the conflicting claims.

The general indexes usually do only general damage. Individual campaigns, however, afford an opportunity for detailed, point-by-point distortion which can be specifically destructive. Through specialized distortion, individual facts about a candidate's voting record can be isolated from their contexts, and regrouped so as to misrepresent an entire career.

The 1964 campaign for Kenneth Keating's seat in the U. S. Senate is an illustration. Robert Francis Kennedy resigned as Attorney General of the United States and came to New York to oppose Keating. Kennedy was disliked by some liberals who had opposed his brother, the President, and he faced predictable anti-Catholicism. He was vulnerable to the "carpetbagger" label, having lived in New York only as a schoolboy, spending his later life in Massachusetts and Virginia. He was thought by many to be ruthless.

His campaign began on a conciliatory note, carefully avoiding any missteps that would magnify existing antipathy.[1] His drivers were armed with road maps and painstakingly briefed on local geography, to spare the new resident the embarrassment of getting lost. He entered on a gentle and serious campaign of showing himself and making known his views. He treated the Republican incumbent, Senator Kenneth B. Keating, with propriety and respect. Kennedy said later he had to do so, because the New Yorker had treated him "very fatherly" in Washington.

Keating's campaign was, with a few departures, good-humored and relevant. He simply tried to project his record, which in general was moderate to liberal, and consistent. Generally it paralleled that of his senior Republican colleague, Jacob K. Javits, with departures from a few of the more ardently liberal Javits positions.

The rating groups found the two New York Senators fairly close together, with all except COPE depicting Javits as the more liberal. ADA found that Keating rated 67 per cent, higher than 56 of his colleagues, half of them Democrats. COPE ranked Keating with Javits at 80, and only found 29 Senators, all Democrats, better. ACA found five Republicans, including Javits, and 40 Democrats more liberal than Keating.

The Keating campaign included appeals to the long list of ethnic groups that comprise so much of New York's electorate. The tactic has been standard in Empire State politics and Keating employed it largely in standard fashion. There were, however, some marginal applications. The Republican chose Italian audiences to make the legitimate point that Kennedy's Cosa Nostra hearings served no useful purpose. They led to no arrests and there were many complaints that they amounted to a publicity stunt staged at Attorney General Kennedy's behest by an obliging Senate Permanent Investigating Committee, which did not even

[1] Opposition pollsters discovered quickly that Kennedy had, in New York, what they called a high "antipathy quotient," or A.Q. This they sought to exploit.

have jurisdiction over Kennedy's proposed wire-tapping bill. Keating said that Kennedy, in exploiting Joe Valachi's testimony, was callously letting the Italian-American community be smeared by the endless repetition of Italian underworld names. Among the snares and deadfalls of ethnic politics, the inference that Kennedy was somehow anti-Italian was read into the barbs. This false inference angered the young Democrat.

Keating, whose efforts to advance Negro rights had been unceasing, told civil rights workers that the Attorney General had walked out on their fight, so he could seek the New York Senate seat. This stung

However, what angered Robert Kennedy most was Keating's commentary on his negotiations for the sale of I. G. Farben assets in the United States. General Aniline and Film was owned by the German combine through a Swiss front, Interhandel, when the Alien Property Custodian seized it in World War II.

After years of litigation, Keating joined in a successful effort to legislate permission for the Attorney General to sell the chemical company without waiting for an end to the protracted legal actions by Interhandel against the U. S. Government. Keating criticized Kennedy for unseemly haste in arranging the sale. He said in effect that the Attorney General had moved in a sloppy fashion in order to get the property disposed of quickly, and that as a result the sale proceeding lacked proper precautions to prevent the money due Interhandel—some 60 million dollars—from falling into Nazi hands.

The Keating charge was scrupulously worded so it did not question Kennedy's motives. But presenting it fairly was so tedious and verbose a project that any prophet might have foreseen what the press would do with it. The payoff words were *Kennedy, 60 million dollars,* and *Nazi.* Kennedy was furious. The implication of some affinity for the Nazis had dogged politicians in the Kennedy family since John Kennedy ran for a Massachusetts House seat in 1946, because of remarks attributed to Joseph Kennedy when he was Ambassador to Great Britain in the early war years. The allegations are false and unfair, and usually appear in whispering campaigns and smear sheets, often anonymous. Here, to Kennedy's eye, was more of the same but with a respectable front.

Keating's advisers were divided on this roster of ploys, but the hard-line faction had won. The Kennedy crew was ready and it swung into action. In the press they cried foul over the Nazi, Italian, and civil rights allegations and innuendoes.[2]

Later, in reflecting on his victory over Keating, Kennedy observed to reporters that when Keating began to attack him personally, he was freed to enter into an aggressive campaign. This he now did.

A newspaper ad and a flyer depicted Keating as a rightist: "By Right-Wing Standards Keating is an Ultra-Conservative." This ad chided him for not rejecting a 1961 "award" from ACA. "Mr. Keating Chooses to Forget His Right-Wing Award," a headline read. A reproduced newspaper clipping cited 136 members of Congress who had won "awards" from ACA in 1961—when ACA ranked Keating *thirty-third* among Senate conservatives. The ad and flyer referred to "this high rating."

Keating had come up with a fairly high conservative rating that year, as he had done occasionally since his career in Congress began. It has been suggested that indexes often are misleading: Keating's ACA conservatism rating has been exceeded on occasion by the Administration's leader in the Senate, Mike Mansfield, among others. To paint a man as an ultra-conservative by rummaging in his past until one finds so flimsy a support for the charge is dishonest enough, but this episode was simply one hit-and-run assault in a long series.

Here were the ingredients of what *Reporter* Magazine called "the sudden deliberalization of Senator Keating." He was said to be *against* aid to education, *lukewarm* toward the nuclear test ban treaty, *against* area redevelopment legislation, minimum wage law extension, Kefauver's drug legislation, school lunches,

[2] They did not file a complaint with the Fair Campaign Practices Committee, because, as one Kennedy staff man put it, "We didn't want to look like cry-babies."

and federally-aided public housing, and he never "added a comma" to the Civil Rights Act of 1964.

The distortions of the Keating record were accomplished with such facility, and such economy of documentation, that they bear close inspection, for they amount to a classic example of how to use isolated excerpts of an incumbent opponent's record against him.

Kennedy literature ("The Myth of Keating's Liberalism") said, "Keating has opposed federal aid to education since 1947. In 1961 he voted to deny $2.55 billion for teachers' salaries and school construction." Actually, Keating had voted against the 1961 bill cited by Kennedy for two reasons: he felt it cheated New York of a fair share of Federal funds; and it did nothing to prevent Southern states from using its grants to maintain segregated schools. The reasons for his opposition to the bill as it finally passed were part of the public record; he had supported one amendment and offered another himself to correct what he conceived as fatal flaws.

The "Myth" leaflet went on: "In 1963 he voted to cut $600 million from the Aid to Higher Education bill." The Kennedy statement implies an amendment to lop $600 million off the bill. There was no such amendment. The fact is that the vote cited was to substitute a three-year House bill for a five-year Senate version because the House bill provided *more* aid money each year and, being for a three-year term instead of five, would be easier to enact. Voting with Keating on this maneuver was Senator Edward M. Kennedy of Massachusetts.

Once on television Robert Kennedy said Keating had voted against a 1959 area redevelopment bill supported by Senator Javits. Later an ad appeared saying Keating opposed and Javits supported a similar bill in 1961. The facts were that both Senators had voted against it in 1959 because they felt it was unfair to New York, and when the offending provision had been corrected in the 1961 bill, both voted for it. Each assertion was half true. But two half truths do not add up to a whole one.

The Democratic State Committee published a flyer citing a

Keating vote on August 18, 1960, to "deny" minimum wage coverage to three million workers in wholesale, retail, and service industries. The bill was actually an extension of minimum wage requirements and, over a three-day period, Keating voted against five amendments vitiating it. Finally Keating voted for a compromise amendment offered by New Mexico Democrat Clinton Anderson, excluding 913,000 workers from the extension of coverage. The "three million" figure never came up. When Keating voted aye on the amendment, he had interesting company: Jacob Javits; the majority leadership, Senators Mansfield and Humphrey; and 83 other Senators. Both New Yorkers and the Democratic leaders, and Senator Kennedy of Massachusetts, then voted together to adopt the amended bill, 62-34.

In a widely used Kennedy TV commercial, New York's Mayor Robert F. Wagner accused Keating of voting "against the late Senator Kefauver's effort to protect the public from dangerous and overpriced drugs." A subsequent newspaper ad said only that Keating had voted against an amendment dealing with drug patents.

The Wagner statement's implication that the Keating vote (for the amendment) opposed Kefauver on "*dangerous* and overpriced drugs" was simply false. The over-simplified approach of the ad omitted a significant fact: the Kefauver amendment, which would have subjected any company realizing a 500 per cent profit on a drug to compulsory licensing, was tabled, not voted down. The motion to table was offered by the Majority Leader, Senator Mansfield. It carried, 53 to 28, and the amendment was shelved. Among those voting to table were Mansfield, Javits, Keating, and Senator Smith of Massachusetts, John Kennedy's designee to fill his old Senate seat until the special election in which Teddy Kennedy assumed it.

A newspaper ad said Keating voted on September 10, 1959, against cleaner-packaged and more nourishing food for the school lunches of needy children. The fact, once again, was only partially represented in the allegation. The vote cited *was* against an amendment to S.1748, and it *did* take place on the date cited.

School lunches *were* included as a mere rider to a long and complex amendment on an entirely different subject. At no time was there any opposition to the clean, wholesome food item, even by the most intransigent Senate conservative. The complex amendment was voted down with Keating's help. Three days later the Senate unanimously adopted the lunch program in a separate amendment.

The Kennedy leaflet "The Myth of Keating's Liberalism" said "Keating has consistently refused to support Federal Aid to public housing." It cited three bills, one in the House in 1950 and two in the Senate in 1959 and 1961.

"Consistent refusal" here was based on three votes in fourteen years. Totally ignored was Keating's truly consistent support for and efforts to expand the Housing Acts of 1949, 1954, 1959, 1960, 1961, 1962, and 1964.

Robert Kennedy told newsmen that neither Keating nor his colleague, Javits, had "added a comma" to the Civil Rights Act of 1964. While it may be true that neither added a *comma*, the fact is that much of the ultimate language of the Act was introduced by the two New York Senators in *seventeen* civil rights bills they introduced jointly in the 87th and 88th Congresses. Both solons were among the bipartisan corps of floor captains for the bill for which Kennedy implied neither did anything, and both were hailed by the Administration's majority leader for their tireless support of the bill.

The Kennedy distortion that got the greatest mileage related to the Nuclear Test Ban Treaty, thanks to a series of unplanned and accidental developments.

Robert Kennedy's passionate commitment to his murdered brother needs neither reiteration nor defense. Robert's antipathy for anyone who impeded John Kennedy at any point can be understood in that setting, and, indeed, applauded. Thus any opposition, or even any reluctance to support President Kennedy's negotiation of the Nuclear Test Ban Treaty naturally generated antagonism, resentment, and, considering the intensity of the man, some contempt.

In 1959, 1961, and 1962 Kenneth Keating was at least cool, and at most caustically critical, of test-ban talk. In 1963, belatedly in Robert Kennedy's terms, Keating came around. First cautiously, then with increasing firmness, he began to support the test-ban treaty. By Robert Kennedy's standards he was a Johnny-come-lately to the cause.

Kennedy scheduled a campaign speech at Syracuse University on October 20. His prepared text, released to the press, included this passage shortly past the middle:

"It is the same with the Nuclear Test Ban Treaty—which my opponent ridiculed throughout the years in which Averell Harriman and Hubert Humphrey and Adlai Stevenson labored to make it a reality.

"On all of these issues, my opponent was behind the challenges of the times. Not once did he anticipate a challenge. To some of them, like the Nuclear Test Ban Treaty, his final response was adequate. To far too many—like aid to education, or college scholarships, or housing—his final response was totally inadequate.

If Kennedy had left it at that—or if indeed he *did* so—there would have been no Test Ban problem. It would not have entered the campaign, and the focus would have been on the reiterated distortion of Keating's record on other issues. But two additional Kennedy appearances were scheduled in Syracuse that day, one at the University's Morley Field House, and another at a $50-a-plate Democratic dinner.

The Associated Press, in Dispatch number 380 of October 20, reported the dinner speech at Syracuse:

"Kennedy also charged the [sic] Keating 'ridiculed' the Nuclear Test Ban Treaty and did not speak out for it until after passage was assured."

The Syracuse *Herald Journal* covered Kennedy's visit. Reporter Joseph V. Ganley wrote that in speeches at the University and the dinner, "Kennedy accused Keating of voting against Federal Aid to Education, housing, urban renewal, the Nuclear Test Ban Treaty . . ."

189

Every public figure knows that reporters sometimes mis-hear, mis-remember, or misquote. Every reporter knows that public figures, faced with one text and several audiences, often interpolate and parapharase.

Keating complained to the Fair Campaign Practices Committee of distortions by the Attorney General on the subjects of education and the Nuclear Test Ban Treaty.

It is ironic to note that the fair campaign group had imposed itself on Keating's attention in a way unrelated to either issue. A scurrilous pamphlet had been authored by a right-wing professional anti-Communist named Frank Capell.[3] Titled "The Strange Death of Marilyn Monroe," it implied that the actress' death was not a suicide, but the result of a murder arranged by Mr. Kennedy after an unsatisfactory liaison with Miss Monroe.

Fair Campaign Committee agents in New York and Los Angeles believed that the pamphlet, in a lurid red cover, was about to be circulated *en masse* in New York during the Senate campaign. The Committee routinely contacted the Keating forces to arrange for an immediate and pungent repudiation of the Capell tract if indeed it did appear in bulk. The Keating group agreed immediately and cooperated fully.

A few days later, Keating released to the morning press the text of a letter of complaint against Kennedy that he had prepared for the Fair Campaign Committee. Kennedy, whose vilest traducers have never accused him of slow reflexes, had an answer in the same editions of Friday morning, October 23.

The staff of the Fair Campaign Committee first learned of the exchange in the papers. At 10:05 a.m. two messengers elbowed each other through the narrow doorway of the Committee's offices on New York's upper Madison Avenue. One bore the text of the Keating charge; the other the Kennedy response. The Committee staff works through week-ends in the last month or so of campaigns, often around the clock. The Keating charges were complex and based on numerous citations of the *Congressional*

[3] Capell was later convicted for his part in libeling California Senator Thomas Kuchel.

Record. Both the Committee's researcher, Frederick F. Andrews, and I worked over the week-end studying the complaint, seeking documentation from Keating, and studying that.

The Kennedy answer to the complaint was briefer, simpler, and easier to comprehend. It was a four-sentence letter dated October 22, and the crux of it was: "Enclosed is a statement I have issued in reply to Senator Keating [sic] charges. This statement is, in my opinion, a complete refutation of the charges he has made to you."

The accompanying statement [4] jibed at Keating for "running to the Fair Campaign Practices Committee to complain about documented recitation of the facts about his record" while Keating was making "false charges" about a Kennedy " 'deal' with the Nazis, being anti-Italian, running out on the civil rights program," and telling Jews that Kennedy was supported by Egypt's Prime Minister Nasser. [5]

Then the Kennedy statement said that Keating was only "an interested observer" of the test ban debate "until the day before the voting began.

Kennedy went on to quote three isolated passages from a Keating speech in the *Congressional Record* to "document" the assertion that Keating had "ridiculed" the treaty just before its endorsement by the Senate in 1963.

In his prepared Syracuse text, Kennedy had confined the "ridicule" assertion to 1959. Reporters quoted him as laying ridicule of the treaty to Keating right up to the moment of passage.

But here, *in response to a charge of distortion made to the Fair Campaign Practices Committee,* Kennedy specified the Keating "ridicule" on the very last day before the Senate vote.

Actually, the speech Kennedy now cited began with Keating endorsing the treaty, went on to acknowledge and answer "the to my mind hypothetical and never successfully proved disadvantages," and ended with a plea for support of the treaty without

[4] Full text of the Kennedy statement appears in Appendix III.

[5] The story of Arab support for Kennedy, and what amounted to a jurisdictional dispute between Nasser and American Arabs over who disliked Keating more, appears in Appendix IV.

any hampering restrictions.⁶ Into this kind of support the new
Kennedy statement read ridicule.

Robert Kennedy carries with him, for good or ill, the image
of a realist who measures the facts and finds solutions for the
problems they delineate. It is difficult to believe that he could
have read the Keating speech, even scanned it more than fleet-
ingly, and read ridicule into realism

However, he is a man whose loyalty is nationally known, certainly so far as the late President is concerned. It is easier to assume that his loyalty downward to his staff is unquestioning than
it is to ascribe to him the monumental falsity required to analyze
one of his own superior traits—realism—as ridicule in another.

On this perhaps charitable assumption, I concluded a week-
end-long review of the Keating-Kennedy dispute on Monday
morning, and dispatched to Kennedy a letter.

After a routine request for documentation on the anti-
Keating allegations about education, the letter ⁷ read:

"As to the Nuclear Test Ban Treaty, I say with deep regret
that I read your statement with dismay. Mr. Keating has provided
documentation for his complaint, enumerated in the enclosed
copy of his letter to us, which demonstrates conclusively that your
description of his position on the Test Ban Treaty is not only false
and distorted, but also appears to be either a deliberate and cynical misrepresentation or the result of incredible carelessness,
touched with luck."

A paragraph of documentation followed, and my letter went
on to point out that whoever put together the quotations attributing ridicule to Keating "had to pore through 240 lines of the Senator's *Congressional Record* speech of September 20, 1964, beginning at page 16713, before finding the first of three isolated passages which you lump together to describe his attitude."

After a summary of the Keating speech, my letter concluded:
"I trust you will be able to correct this grievous flaw in your research operation that this dishonest and unfair distortion re-

⁶ Full text in Appendix V.
⁷ Full text in Appendix VI.

veals."

The letter was personal and confidential, intended for the eyes of no one but whoever opened Kennedy's mail and whoever else relayed it to him. It was harshly worded so it would blast through the protective layer around any public figure and come to the attention of Kennedy himself. Within a couple of hours Kennedy researcher Adam Walinsky, a brilliant young lawyer who had left the Department of Justice with Kennedy, was on the phone to justify the contention that the excerpts from the Keating speech reflected Keating's own views and that they indeed amounted to ridicule.

By this time the Committee had acquired full documentation from Keating and partial documentation—from the Committee's own resources, based on Kennedy staff citations of dates and votes—from Kennedy. A Keating campaign figure phoned to inquire if the Committee would brief the editorial writers of the *New York Times* and the *Herald Tribune* on the situation. For years the Committee had given occasional background briefings to the press on campaign controversies, but never oustide its own offices. I was asked to go to the papers for the briefing. I refused, and was reminded that the Committee had the only complete set of the Keating documentation in New York. (It had been assembled between Friday and Monday.) Unwilling to let the material out of the Committee's possession until the tangled education matter could be reviewed further, I relented and agreed to send the staff researcher, Fred Andrews, to the papers with the files and to answer questions purely for background.

In the confusion and haste of the moment, I inadvertently slipped the carbon copy of the confidential letter to Kennedy into one of the file folders. Andrews left for the papers, with the folder containing my letter to Kennedy, and was met in the lobby of the *Times* by a Keating staffer.

This precise situation had never come up before. Never had anyone from the staff gone to a newspaper office for briefing. At the *Times* the basic questions were answered, and when he left, Andrews inadvertently left part of the Keating documentation behind.

Two blocks south, at the *Herald Tribune*, Andrews was embarrassed to realize he had left key material at the *Times*. The Keating man asked about the Committee's communication to Kennedy and Andrews confirmed that such a letter had been sent. The editorial writer asked to see it and Andrews showed it to him, off the record. Not only was the Committee treading on unfamiliar terrain, but this was the researcher's first campaign on its staff, and he had not as yet taken on the almost paranoid concern for security that grips the agency's four-man crew at this period.

A reporter, Martin Berck, was in the room, and asked if he might see the letter. As Andrews put it later in a memo to me, "in the confusion surrounding what part of the conversation was on the record and what part off," he handed the letter over. Berck asked if he might copy it. Andrews, assuming that it was clear that the letter and any Committee response to questions was off the record, permitted him to do so. Berck, assuming that the surrender of the letter to him put it on the record, announced that he intended to print it; he had seen it, had gotten it honorably, and could not erase it from his memory. Andrews demurred, Berck insisted, and the interview ended.

It was an hour or two later when I learned the first bits of fact in the situation. I phoned the *Tribune* to seek withdrawal of the letter. The paper was sympathetic but adamant. I pleaded, threatened, blustered, and cajoled, to no avail. The letter appeared in Tuesday morning's *Tribune* and the fat was in the fire.

Activity at the Committee's cramped offices alternated between thinking aloud, meditation, anger, and despair. I phoned the Committee Chairman, Charles P. Taft, in Cincinnati. He was at home, ill. We agreed on the text of a telegram of apology to Kennedy, making clear that the publication of the letter was unauthorized.[8]

I relayed the text by phone to Kennedy's press man, Debs Myers, who demanded more concessions and a more apologetic

[8] Text of the telegram as finally sent appears as Appendix VII.

tone. I said that I wanted to release the statement, but that if Myers wanted to argue for more concessions with Taft he might do so, and gave Myers the Cincinnati phone number. Myers agreed to call back promptly so a final version could be agreed on.

At this stage, late evening of Tuesday, October 24, the deadlines of the morning papers were approaching fast. I had not yet seen Andrews in person to get a blow-by-blow account of how the letter actually got into the hands of the *Herald Tribune*. I assumed the letter had been acquired by some bit of stealth and the draft of the Committee telegram to Kennedy said as much.

. . A *Times* man, R. W. ("John") Apple, phoned from Albany to inquire about the telegram. I read him the draft text, cautioning that the wording might be changed, pending a call-back from Myers at the Kennedy headquarters, and agreeing to call the news desk at the *Times* if the text were changed. Then Andrews came in and acquainted me with the facts, including the fact that the letter had not been dishonestly acquired by the *Tribune*. A call to Myers to ask what resulted from his conversation with Taft revealed that Myers had not placed the call. I told the Kennedy press man of the change in wording about the newspaper. Myers said he would release the text of the apology telegram at once. The *Times* desk was called and the telegram's language corrected. A call from the *Tribune* revealed that Myers had already released the telegram in its early version without checking back with the Committee. Now in addition to the angry Kennedy forces, the Committee confronted a newspaper which found itself accused of dishonesty instead of, perhaps, an excess of diligence.

Next morning word reached the Committee that one board member, Ralph McGill, had resigned after reading the letter, on the grounds that the letter purported to represent the judgment of the entire Committee [9] and he had not been consulted.

---

[9] A re-reading of the letter would have revealed that, with two exceptions ("We are interested in further documentation . . . and [Keating's] letter to us . . ."), the only first person pronoun used in the letter was "I." There were several personal references that should have made it apparent that the letter was not a full Committee letter, much less a Committee

Soon two Kennedy team-members arrived at the Fair Campaign Committee office. They were supplanted by another pair, and then, one at a time, two Kennedy partisans on the Committee's board arrived. A hectic conference ensued, interrupted by phone calls and messengers. The whole thing was clearly a misunderstanding. All that was needed was a withdrawal of the letter. And perhaps another apology. Perhaps Felknor should be fired or resign. Andrews could be sacked, with an abundance of blame, and all could be forgotten if not forgiven. The Kennedy aides had brought with them new evidence which proved that Kennedy had not made the offending statement at Syracuse. Perhaps this new evidence could be the basis for a letter of withdrawal.

A long distance call came in from another Democratic board member: what the hell was going on? He had been alerted by Kennedy press man Debs Myers.

Version after version of a letter of withdrawal was drawn up, amended, and discarded. At several points the three private rooms in the office were commandeered by visitors, and staff people were forced to borrow the phone in a nearby office for private telephone conversations. At length, by about five p.m., a statement was agreed upon and the Kennedy people departed.[10]

It was not until the following Friday that I discovered the final distortion of the Kennedy campaign. The vaunted "new evidence" simply repeated what Kennedy claimed he had said at Syracuse about Keating ridiculing the test ban treaty in the past. Thus, by "proving" that he had never accused Keating of latter-day ridicule of the treaty (despite the testimony of two newspapermen at Syracuse who recorded him to that effect) the Attorney General diverted everybody's attention from the fact that while denying that he said Keating ridiculed the treaty *in 1963*, he went on to "prove" Keating's "ridicule" *in 1963* by quoting him out of context. A new ploy entered politics: distortion (and

judgment, but a communication from the Committee director to the former Attorney General.

[10] The complete statement appears in Appendix VIII.

sleight-of-hand) to defend against charges of distortion.

The tactical results of the Kennedy counter-foray were impressive. Shaken by the unfair position in which the publication of my letter had put Kennedy, the Committee was for all practical purposes taken out of play so far as the remainder of the Keating complaints were concerned.

Actually, the Committee found itself in a cross-fire between the Kennedy camp and the *Herald Tribune,* and both were playing for keeps. Both were dealing with particles of absolute fact sufficiently isolated from their context to present wholly false impressions. So what started out as a luckless misadventure that was unfair to the Attorney General [11] wound up as a net plus for him and unfair to Senator Keating, since Kennedy claimed that the Committee's withdrawal of the letter was complete vindication for him. After the election, the *Times* and *Herald Tribune* published interviews which the new Senator-elect had granted before the votes were in. He said he would have lost if the Committee had not withdrawn that letter. The estimate is probably not accurate, for Kennedy won by some 600,000 votes—while Johnson was beating Goldwater in the state by two and a half million. Had the Kennedy margin been on the order of 100,000, it might have been a different story.

The Kennedy-Keating saga should not be construed as a suggestion that the new Senator from New York is personally or deliberately dishonest, any more than any candidate who lets excesses and distortions by his staff represent him in public. But it does suggest that every candidate should be alert to the possibility, the danger, that eager aides, more concerned with scoring points than with presenting facts fully clothed, can make him seem a sophistic, deliberate, and cynical twister of his opponent's record.

Neither should that sorry episode imply that the Democrats

[11] Because the Fair Campaign Committee does not issue public findings. The Committee also was hurt by the affair, both financially because of cancelled pledges from Kennedy supporters and by a general (and natural) negative reaction to the mishandling of the episode. By the fall of 1965, visible negative effects on the Committee had been overcome.

have a corner on the market when it comes to distortion. To the shame of the business of politics, both parties play it in varying degrees at different levels. Every man of principle and sense when he is holding Congressional office confronts the responsibility of leading and following his constituents, of representing the nation and the district. He must finally filter his responses to the challenges of legislation through his own judgment and biases, which, after all, hopefully formed part of the basis on which he was elected. In these moments the legislator is alone with his conscience and judgment. It is only the rare one who never wavers. The majority compile records that make them vulnerable to attack by any candidate who is willing to justify an isolated fact by its own accuracy and without regard for the context. By such standards, anyone can lose, for by them the Red Chinese *were* agrarian reformers and Hitler *was* a road builder and Mussolini *did* make the trains run on time.

Thus one may be forgiven for wondering what moves honest men to stay in politics, when so much conspires to drive them out.

CHAPTER 9

The Whipping Boys: Cruel and Unusual Punishment

THROUGHOUT American history various organizations have become political whipping boys, punished not only for actual misdeeds, but also for imagined ones. Freemasons, labor unions, and large corporations are examples. These days, however, an uncommon lot of whipping boys suffer cruel and unusual punishment. And linking the name of any of them with a political candidate is enough, in the mind of the misinformed, to disqualify that candidate for office.

Near the end of the 1964 campaign, a Young Republican Campaign Committee of Westchester County, New York, published a pink sheet for distribution throughout that influential suburban county. "H.H.H. and the A.D.A.," it was headed. Ten questions on a checklist were accompanied by Yes and No boxes. At the bottom of the list, citing H.H.H.'s role as a founder of the ADA, the Westchester Young Republicans explained that "Mr. Hubert Humphrey, Democratic V.P. candidate says 'yes' to all ten questions—this is the man who *could* be one heart beat away from the Presidency."

Most of the questions were trickily worded extractions from the context of genuine ADA positions, one was wholly false, and two so distorted as to be unrecognizable as ADA positions. There was no attempt to document the false statement that Humphrey supported them. "We should resume normal relations with Castro?" read one. Others: "We should recognize the East German government?" and "We should continue massive aid to foreign governments regardless of how they use it?"

Another flyer, peddled in southeastern Pennsylvania, painted a similar picture: "Hubert Humphrey Could Become the First ADA President if the American People are Fooled into Electing Johnson in November.—Remember Hubert Would Then Only be a *Heart Beat Away* From the Top Job." Neither of these tracts gave the names of the persons responsible, as Federal and state law require.

The Pennsylvania piece attributed to ADA support of "Govt. control, Govt. planning, Govt. financing or Govt. takeover in every field." It implied that ADA opposed loyalty oaths because loyalty oaths attempted "to keep Communists out of our Government." This checklist concluded with the observation that "The Senates [sic] Internal Security Subcommittee and the FBI are also cherished ADA targets—but *not* the Communists and Soviet Spies whom the two agencies have unearthed!!!!"

Another GOP leaflet and a full page newspaper ad appearing in a number of cities asked, "What is ADA?" It posed a frightening answer, including the comment: "The political organization, Americans for Democratic Action, (ADA) has become a synonym for fellow-traveler, for Communist sympathiser, for advocate of 'soft' policies toward Russia."

The quotation was attributed to Robert L. Riggs, chief of the Washington Bureau of the Louisville *Courier-Journal*. It came to Riggs' attention at the end of the campaign, and he viewed it with profound distaste, for reasons he set forth in a steaming letter to Dean Burch, chairman of the Republican National Committee, the day after the election.

Wrote Riggs, "This distortion is as dishonest a bit of political chicanery as I have encountered in nearly forty years of covering campaigns. It is a cheap trick to make me appear to say the exact opposite of what I actually did say."

Riggs went on: "Inasmuch as your party scored such a huge success in Tuesday's elections by the use of this distortion, I assume you will file it away for further use in the next campaign. I earnestly request that you file this protest along with the folder containing the ADA ad so that when your people drag it out for the campaigns of 1966 and 1968, they will not be able to pretend they didn't know what a piece of deception it is . . .

"Having covered in 1948 the first convention of Americans for Democratic Action, I was moved on February 2, 1962, to comment upon the hatchet job which had been done on that organization. In my piece, I wrote—

" 'One of the greatest image-making jobs of *the* current *political* era is the one that has been done on the *organization* named *Americans for Democratic Action*. This job has been done in reverse, performed by its enemies rather than by its friends. So successful has it been that the *ADA*, which was organized for the specific purpose of forcing Communists to keep their hands off worthy causes, *has become a synonym for fellow-traveler, for Communist sympathizer, for advocate of "soft" policies toward Russia.*' [1]

"A few months later, when Thruston B. Morton was in a Senate race with Wilson W. Wyatt, Morton's people published a pamphlet entitled 'The Danger of ADA and Wilson W. Wyatt. Wyatt had been the first president of ADA. To support their contention that ADA was a dangerous outfit, Morton's people quoted me as saying [precisely what the 1964 pamphlet attributed to Riggs]."

Noting that he had complained on the earlier occasion by letter, and in the *Courier-Journal* by editorial, but had gotten no response, Riggs said he was "strangely unmoved" by use of the distortion in 1964, "sustained by a calm conviction that the people

[1] Italics supplied to indicate which words the Republicans selected for the deception.

using it were headed for an historic drubbing at the polls."

Riggs concluded by promising "to be equally calm the next time the geniuses that operate the Republican Party feel there is some mileage to be gained by running against so ferocious an outfit as the ADA. I just want your records to contain this guidance for someone who might have a relatively weak stomach for distortions."

Perhaps Riggs was too hard on the Republican chairman, for the transient hatchet man who was thought to have prepared the surgery on the actual quote for the 1962 Kentucky campaign was not in evidence at the National Committee in 1964. In any case, two weeks later Burch did reply, apologizing for the distortion and reporting "what I trust will be effective action to prevent further use of the advertisement." He deeply regretted "any embarrassment this spurious quote has caused you [Riggs]."

However, the Republican chairman was a logical recipient for the complaint and Riggs obviously addressed it to the office, not the man. This was appropriate enough, for the Republicans at various organization levels have been capitalizing on their carefully constructed image of ADA for years. In fact, the party's investment in the straw man of ADA was substantial enough so it might explain why Burch regretted embarrassing Robert Riggs but not ADA.

What is Americans for Democratic Action, and how Red *is* its program, classed by a House Republican Policy Committee staff report back in the 1950's as "laundered communism"?

Americans for Democratic Action was established in 1947 to prevent further Communist successes with the American liberal community. In that era the Communists were making the greatest possible mileage out of the respectability of wartime support for the gallant Soviet. But they were pushing farther and faster than thoughtful and perceptive American liberals were prepared to yield. Having taken advantage of the wartime situation, in many cases to enshrine gains they had made altogether clandestinely in the prewar years, the Communists now were moving to dominate labor, and to infiltrate the Democratic Party and influence its platform and nominations in 1948. ADA grew out of a handful of liberals who saw the threat and concluded that it could only be turned back by responsible liberals with more sophistication and political savvy than was usual.

Sometimes defenders of ADA so concentrate on the organization's freedom from Communist taint that they almost paint a picture of a quasi-conservative group. Nothing could be farther from the truth. ADA was conceived as, and remains, a band of dedicated, militant liberals led by brilliant, skilled and realistic politicians. They are specifically and frankly anti-conservative. But they are anti-conservative entirely within the democratic tradition. Far from conspiratorial in approach, they proclaim their goals widely, loudly, and frankly, and pursue them through study, publication, and persuasion. Their policies are set at national conventions which are so un-secret that leaders lament that they do not draw *more* attention from press and public. ADA is a left wing group, but efforts to equate its left wing status with Communism or disloyalty are either demonstrations of ignorance or dishonest efforts to spread such ignorance.

In domestic matters, ADA believes in economic planning. It is vaguely Keynesian and specifically Galbraithian in outlook (John Kenneth Galbraith was a founder). It believes in diligent government pursuit of full employment; in government intervention to limit recessions; in concentrating tax reductions heavily in the lower brackets; in increased Federal spending in education,[2] public housing, transportation, health, and welfare. It supports metropolitan planning (long a favorite target of the remote right; another advocate of metropolitan planning is Barry Goldwater). It urges anti-poverty action by the Federal government and wants to strengthen social security, minimum wage laws, public assistance payments. ADA was an early supporter of Medicare and believes government responsibility should go even further. It urges greater efforts to protect the consumer. It was an early advocate of repeal of the McCarran-Walter Immigration Act.

[2] Some rabid anti-Communists see danger here; free public education for all the children was advocated in the *Communist Manifesto*.

ADA is a militant advocate of strong civil rights legislation. It played a major role in persuading the 1948 Democratic Convention to adopt a strong civil rights plank and has been in the forefront of every subsequent responsible effort to advance Negro equality of opportunity. It is anti-filibuster and anti-poll tax, pro-sit-in and pro-legislation to prevent the abuse of voters' literacy tests.

In international matters it is equally liberal. ADA advocated the Truman Doctrine and economic and military aid to European countries threatened with Communist subversion. It supported the Marshall Plan, freedom for West Berlin, defense of the Republic of Korea, NATO, the Mutual Security Program, and favors a strong national defense as a cornerstone of a positive foreign policy. It supports the United Nations and a permanent UN armed force. It believes in substantial and long-term foreign economic development. It advocated the Nuclear Test Ban Treaty and urges negotiations toward general and complete disarmament based on effective inspection and control, and it wants consideration given to unilateral initiatives to improve the atmosphere of such negotiations.[3]

ADA wants mutual withdrawal of Soviet and western armies from East and West Germany. It supports *de facto* recognition of East Germany: recognition of the fact of Communist control of East Germany. This does not mean approval or full and normal diplomatic recognition, as ADA's detractors always imply and sometimes state, but it does mean the possibility of direct discussions on current issues with a government we now legally pretend does not exist.

ADA also supports negotiations toward recognition of Red China and her admission to the UN, predicated on a Formosa settlement. Neither the German nor the Chinese position implies moral support or moral approval, but simply a recognition of the real fact that, however wrongly, China is controlled by the Reds, as is East Germany.

[3] Critics often scramble this sequence, sometimes ignorantly, sometimes dishonestly, to portray ADA as urging unilateral disarmament.

There are a couple of political issues that continually arise in campaigns to paint ADA red. The organization does not believe in loyalty oaths beyond the fundamental one prescribed in the Constitution. And it advocates the abolition of the House Committee on Un-American Activities.

The interpretation is always that the ADA takes these stands because the oaths and the Committee are effective weapons against the Communists. The fact is that the organization believes precisely the opposite, that they are not successful in deterring Communists.

The group's charter specifically debars Communists from membership. When it was founded, Communist infiltration of initially respectable liberal causes, and Communist creation of ostensibly respectable causes designed to appeal to liberals, were commonplace. Within a year of its founding ADA spotted the Red domination of the Progressive Party effort for Henry Wallace and Glen Taylor, and harried the Communists involved into full public view. It is a basic tenet of ADA that the real Communist danger to the United States lies precisely in this area of infiltration and espionage, and the organization has demonstrated its ability at locating, combatting and outsmarting the comrades in the political arena.

It was in the McCarthy era, when the organization was in its infancy, that the pro-Communist tag first appeared. The rightists of that day assumed that everyone who was not with them was against them; and that anyone who did not pursue their own tack in fighting Communism was an anti-anti-Communist. There certainly is such a thing as anti-anti-Communism, and many American liberals have been and are guilty of it. The leadership of ADA, however, has not included them; nevertheless, the tag has stuck so far as latter-day extreme reactionaries are concerned. Conservatives, real conservatives, may and ought to be just as hostile to ADA as the liberal body is to the conservatives. But real conservatives will fight in the open and by the rules, which do not include smearing the opposition. ADA is lonely on the left end of the spectrum of political respectability and the reason is that

ADA itself pushed the Communists off the edge.

Americans for Democratic Action recognizes that liberals can turn back the radical left more effectively than conservatives can do it. It has a little trouble recognizing the opposite side of that coin. ADA-ers tend to gather in alarmed knots and fulminate about the radical right, often with as distorted a view and as little opportunity for stimulating useful action as characterizes arch-conservative perceptions and attitudes about the liberal-Communist borderline. Neither end can see clearly past the middle.

A constant source of right wing propaganda laced with racism is the New Orleans headquarters of Kent and Phoebe Courtney, patrons of the Conservative Society of America and publishers of a newspaper, *The Independent American,* and a series of pamphlets ranging from intense to rabid. Among the latter is a variety of leaflets known as the "Tax Fax" series. One of these in 1964, "HUBERT HUMPHREY The Flaming Liberal," took out after HHH and ADA, and then linked the Democratic Vice Presidential candidate with another group.

"In addition to being a leading member of the ultra-Socialist organization known as Americans for Democratic Action, Hubert Humphrey is also a member of a semi-secret, New York-based, Communist-appeasing group called the Council on Foreign Relations."

Near its end the leaflet quotes approvingly "Admiral Chester Ward, USN (Ret.)" in attacking a "pet scheme" of Humphrey and the Council on Foreign Relations.

It is true that the "semi-secret, New York-based, Communist-appeasing group" did list Hubert Humphrey as a member in 1964. Another name on its roster was that of Rear Admiral Chester Ward.

Admiral Ward is the co-author with Mrs. Phyllis Schlafly of one of the 1964 political paperbacks, *The Gravediggers,* whose thesis is that the grave in which Khrushchev promised to bury the United States was being dug by arch-liberal intellectuals influential in the Kennedy Administration, and that these liberals were, as one chapter heading put it, "Far to the Left of Even Humphrey."

What kind of "Communist-appeasing group" could house Even Humphrey and Even Ward? Even more names in favor with the right appear on the roster of the Council on Foreign Relations, among them a trio whom Goldwater named to advise him on foreign policy in the 1964 campaign: Lucius Clay, Richard M. Nixon, and Adolph W. Schmidt. The roster also included nuclear physicist and hard-liner Edward Teller, former Ambassador Spruille Braden, Admiral Lewis Strauss, and Robert Strausz-Hupé. On this list also were former President Eisenhower and Secretary of State Dean Rusk, and the grandson of President Grant and the grand-nephew of Grant's Secretary of State Hamilton Fish, and 1,436 other distinguished and influential Americans of the widest possible diversity of responsible political and economic views.

The Council on Foreign Relations was conceived by a corps of Woodrow Wilson's advisers on the peace treaty that concluded World War I. It came into being as a meeting and discussion group for distinguished citizens who were personally interested in the study of foreign affairs. As an angler's club of wealthy men will buy and stock a stretch of trout stream, so the council acquired and equipped a place to pursue its interest, and hired sufficient staff, now numbering some 75 scholars and clerks.

It was incorporated under its present name in 1922, and began publishing *Foreign Affairs*, possibly the most influential quarterly in the world. In 1927 CFR published the first edition of *The Political Handbook*, an annual listing of foreign countries and their governments, political parties, and press. The next year it added an annual survey, now titled *The United States in World Affairs*.

From its incorporation the Council has held frequent meetings addressed by distinguished foreign guests. In 1923 a system of study groups was initiated for concentrated study by small groups of members on international problems of common interest and substantial importance, "to study the problems before they become issues."

The question of why the CFR should *want* to study the problems is one that has obsessed many residents of the remote right. Kent and Phoebe Courtney offer a lurid answer in their paperback book, *America's Unelected Rulers:* "And there it is—spelled out! the grandiose, megalomaniacal plans of the One Worlders to govern the United States via the system of 'High Councils' and 'private citizens'—all under the control of members of the Council on Foreign Relations."

The Courtney book opens chapter one with a quotation from a 1961 right-wing newsletter, "The Dan Smoot Report." Mr. Smoot, a professional former FBI man from Dallas whose alarums and excursions against the dangerous radicals everywhere to the left of Barry Goldwater stimulate the glands of radicals everywhere to the right of the former Senator, takes a deadly serious, wide-eyed view of the Council on Foreign Relations as "The Invisible Government," a theme he used to title a subsequent book on the CFR.

Following the Smoot quote in the Courtneys' book is one from Richard Rovere's *Esquire* Magazine spoof on "The Establishment," which the Courtneys and virtually the entire right wing took with utmost earnestness as a bonafide map of the world of *Realpolitik*. Rovere said in his sardonic "exposé" that "The directors of the Council on Foreign Relations make up a sort of Presidium for that part of the Establishment that guides our destiny as a nation." Thus Rovere, in the Courtney application, "corroborates Mr. Smoot's statement." Mr. Rovere's view is that Mr. Smoot's view would make pretty funny reading, too, if it weren't so widely believed.

The Council on Foreign Relations is not exactly amused by the Smoot estimate that the CFR is trying to destroy the national sovereignty of the United States, but it is not rushing into print to denounce Smoot. "The Council takes the position that such assertions are so lacking in reason as to defy serious consideration," says a sedate memo taking cognizance of the shrill indictment by the Dallas newsletter operator.

From the beginning the Council decided its discussion sessions would be private and off the record, to encourage complete candor and free exchange of ideas. Thus the group is seen as semi-secret, or, as some of its worried foes put it, super-secret.

It would be difficult for any group with the resources, intellect, concern, and political potency that CFR members possess to be anything but hugely influential. Most brilliant and prominent Americans who are deeply interested in foreign policy belong to it; others seek inclusion in its roster, limited in the by-laws to 1,450, half within 50 miles of New York. When a government, corporation, foundation, or university post dealing with foreign relations at an exalted level needs filling, what is more natural than casting an eye over the CFR membership rolls? One goes where the ducks are. The membership roster of this private organization, unlike those of most others, is published in an annual report and is available to the public on request, thus providing a handy guide for locating its "super-secret" conspirators.

The conspiracy-oriented right wing naturally assumes that major accomplishments which it either does not understand or does not approve or both are the fruits of a conspiracy. So, of course, does the conspiracy-oriented left wing. And indeed the occasional incorporation into the government of men—and at least once a whole organization—from the CFR provides fuel for the extremists' fires. As World War II began in Europe—two years before American involvement—the Council began studying postwar planning. In 1942 the entire study group became the nucleus of the State Department's Advisory Committee on Postwar Planning.

This sort of thing, viewed by the far right, becomes domination of the government by the cryptic CFR, invisible government, unelected rulers.

When Robert A. Lovett prepared, in 1947, to assume the duties of Under Secretary of State to George Marshall, he asked the Council to brief him on U. S. foreign policy problems. Joseph Kraft, in an article in *Harper's Magazine*, in July, 1958 ("School for Statesmen"), quotes Lovett on the impact of the briefing: "I came away from the session with the firm conviction that it would be our principal task at State to awaken the nation to the dangers of Communist aggression."

There is one agency in the United States that would gladly defend CFR's right to study and associate freely, and simultaneously support Kent Courtney's right to impute treason to it. The agency, of course, is that perennial whipping boy, the American Civil Liberties Union. In every election year, ACLU is called a Communist front or a transmission belt to the Soviets.

ACLU labors under the handicap of believing in equal justice under law, plus the further crippling burden of taking seriously the Constitution of the United States, including all of its Amendments, even the Bill of Rights. Time and again it has demonstrated its concern for the civil liberties of the most inflammatory left wingers and right wingers with an impartiality that defies matching.

The ACLU opposes prior censorship, the practice of ruling a kind of expression out of bounds before it is uttered. It opposes punishment of citizens for simply advocating or teaching even the most revolutionary philosophy; overt revolutionary acts, it feels, may properly be punished or forbidden, but not the expression of revolutionary ideas. ACLU opposes government financial aid for religious schools no less ardently than it opposes religious exercises in public schools. And it opposes any invasion of the freedom of students and teachers to learn and teach.[4]

ACLU is for the right to associate and assemble freely. It is for full public access to government information. It is for freedom of religious—or irreligious—belief and expression.

When the American Civil Liberties Union was organized in 1920, it was with full awareness that the people whose civil liberties were most likely to be violated often were the most unlovable of individuals. To protect the rights of the most exalted citizen,

---

[4] Its detractors list its sins, but carefully neglect to mention moderate or conservative figures who have espoused similar ideas. One such forgotten man in this context is the late Senator Robert A. Taft, now idealized, in selective memory, by the radical right. Taft believed that a Communist, for example, should be free to teach in American colleges, so long as he didn't try to convert students to Communism.

ACLU folk argue, the rights of the lowest and meanest must be protected. The anti-German hysteria of World War I fanned the spark that flamed into ACLU. The abuse of Japanese-Americans in the Second World War aroused as much concern for the loyal Nisei. This consistent concern for the hapless victims of war-induced hysteria led the late General Douglas MacArthur to say of ACLU founder Roger Baldwin when he retired in 1950 that his "crusade for civil liberties has had a profound and beneficial influence upon the course of American progress. With countless individuals finding protection in the nobility of the cause he has long espoused, he stands out as one of the architects of our cherished American way of life."

ACLU supported the defense of Sacco and Vanzetti whom the Commonwealth of Massachusetts electrocuted as Wop Anarchists because they could not prove their innocence of the Braintree Payroll Robbery. It defended the Tennessee teacher, Scopes, who faced jail for teaching evolution. ACLU defended American Nazis in the early days of World War II when their rights of assembly were violated. ACLU fought the ban on James Joyce's *Ulysses* as obscenity. It has fought government security efforts that encroached on the Bill of Rights, and private anti-Communist programs when they resorted to blacklisting of performers. It has stood up for the rights of the German American Bund and the Scottsboro boys, the Ford Motor Company and the United Auto Workers. It has attacked unions and employers for violating the civil rights of members and employees. It has fought school prayers and defended a Catholic parish against discriminatory ordinances, fought the government to defend the civil liberties of Hearst and Jones & Laughlin Steel; and it has fought Southern lawyers for their reluctance to represent Negroes.

The ACLU also opposes the Communist Registration Act, and supports civil liberties for Communists as well as left and right wing anarchists, Nazis, and fascists.

Some Americans see resort to the Fifth Amendment as tantamount to conviction. These think it pro-Communist to advocate the same liberties for Communists as for non- and anti-

Communists. So ACLU, since its earliest days, has found itself accused of pro-Bolshevism and all its latter-day equivalents.

Even biased men who examine the facts are forced to recognize that ACLU is not disloyal. As early as 1939 then-Congressman Martin Dies of Texas noted in proceedings of the House Committee on Un-American Activities, then a special committee known generally as the Dies Committee, that "This committee found last year, in its reports, there was not any evidence that the American Civil Liberties Union was a Communist organization." [5]

More recently, Committee Counsel Richard Arens was interviewed in 1960 (April 25) over television station WILL-TV in Urbana, Illinois. The interviewer, a journalism instructor at the University of Illinois, referred to a local controversy in which ACLU was embroiled. "Have you found it to be subversive?" he asked Arens. "Has it been investigated?"

The Committee lawyer responded. "The American Civil Liberties Union, ACLU, has never been investigated by the Committee on Un-American Activities nor has it been found to be a communist front by the Committee on Un-American Activities or so far as I know by any governmental agency."

The San Francisco Examiner put the whole matter of ACLU and its role in society into useful perspective in an editorial supporting a recruiting and fund drive, on April 21, 1956: "Wherever it believes [constitutional rights] are being violated or whittled away, it seeks to intervene and test the matter in court. At all times it is concerned with the rights of the individual, not the individual himself.

"You may sometimes disagree, as we do, with the ACLU's choice of cases or its interpretations of the Bill of Rights and other constitutional guarantees. But this is an area where disagreement and dissent have gone on throughout the life of our Nation; if agreement were universal, no ACLU would be needed."

And the Houston Chronicle focused sharply on the impartiality of the organization when it pointed out editorially that an

[5] Transcript, October 23, 1939.

American's rights "are not chance tidbits, to be given or seized. These rights are fundamental. Deny them to one citizen and they are denied to all citizens. The ACLU upholds that proposition when it defends a communist or a General Walker."

The pairing was not metaphorical. ACLU did indeed stand up for the former general, when he and the law ran afoul of each other in the University of Mississippi integration crisis of 1962.

General Walker, from his home in Dallas, cheered embattled segregationists at the University of Mississippi with the message, "Send word that Ted Walker is coming." At Oxford, Walker strove to rally the white supremacists. He was arrested and taken into custody, to the outraged cries of the radical right and very nearly no one else—except ACLU.

Walker was arraigned at once and transported to the Federal Center for Medical Prisoners at Springfield, Missouri. The next day, unrepresented by counsel, not even present himself, Walker was ordered by a United States District Court to be subjected to psychiatric examination, to determine whether or not he was mentally competent to stand trial.

There were only a few things wrong with the procedure, and they probably would not occur to a non-lawyer, unless he, by some wild mischance, had been subjected to the same improper indignities.

The government was within its legal rights. But its freedom to follow this high-speed procedure, however urgent the need, is what disturbs many American conservatives. Roughly comparable proceedings have disturbed liberals, particularly when the victims have been liberals. "They ought to hang the bastard" is a phrase that the right reserves for bastards of the left, and, symmetrically enough, vice versa.

However, in this instance, concern was not manifested only on the right. The same "fellow traveling, pro-Communist, pseudo-liberal, dangerous left wing radical" agency that pried into the Jim Crow legal treatment accorded the Scottsboro boys rallied to General Walker: ACLU. It was not surprising; it was consistent.

Abashed at the indignity of possible ACLU defense of General Walker, the right supplied its own civil liberties advocate, in the person of Robert Morris of Texas and New Jersey, president of the recently formed Defenders of American Liberty.

When Walker was arrested, on charges of insurrection, the ACLU wrote Attorney General Robert F. Kennedy and released the text to the press. Temperately but cogently, ACLU Chairman Ernest Angell criticized the Justice Department for "the procedure under which General Walker was taken into custody and transported . . ." The letter recited the indignities to which Walker was submitted, and conceded the government's power to act as it had. "We think, however, that its application in this case was improper . . . a far better procedure to insure a defendant the due process of law would be to give Walker notice of the proceeding and allow him to be represented by counsel, and present himself."

Angell noted that this fairer procedure was "followed, at least in the [courts of the] Southern District of New York, and is beyond doubt the preferred procedure.

"This failure to honor a due process standard, admittedly under difficult circumstances, is heightened by the press reports that Walker will be detained for psychiatric examination for a sixty to ninety day period . . . we urge that the examination of Walker be completed as expeditiously as possible so as to avoid even the impression that he is being detained to deny him bail, or a speedy trial guaranteed by the Sixth Amendment on the charges against him."

At about the time the ninety-day period foreseen by the ACLU expired, the U.S. Attorney dropped the charges against Walker and he was released, when a grand jury considering the circumstances shut up shop without indicting Walker or his six fellow-subjects of inquiry.

Although ACLU had proven again that its concern extended all the way to the right fringe, the organization got scant thanks from the denizens of that sector. By the time of the 1964 elections, about twenty-one months after Walker's release, ACLU was again being smeared as pro-Communist by some of Walker's warmest admirers.

Walker's warmest admirers probably include nearly the whole membership of the John Birch Society, which while hardly a whipping boy of the ADA-CFR-ACLU sort, is coming to be treated in similar fashion.

The Birch Society can be located in the political spectrum in several ways. Among radical rightists, the society today probably belongs near the left middle. In the band of responsible participants in the American political system, the Birchers belong outside and to the right.

Like the Communist Party, and other extremist groups, the Birchers have much that is good in their body of doctrine and their code of practice. But there are also potent evils, which, along with the good aspects, spin a web of confusion.

The Birch Society figures mainly in political campaigns through guilt by association. Only a few candidates who have publicly acknowledged their membership in the Society have run for major office.[6] In such cases Society membership has been and ought to be an important issue: the voters must determine whether the approach of the Society to government and politics reassures or frightens them.

However, the whipping boy problem appears in earnest at the secondary level of involvement: when a candidate is endorsed by leading Birchers or supported by them or has worked closely with them.

Thus in 1962 a new smear phrase, "soft on Birchism," appeared for the first time in national politics.

Steven B. Derounian was an ardently conservative Republican Congressman representing a wealthy and fast-growing Long Island surburban district in New York's Nassau County. He consistently got a high but not a perfect score from Americans for Constitutional Action and a low but not zero score from ADA.

Derounian, as a member of the Republican Congressional campaign committee, stumped for several other candidates, in-

[6] To be sure, in some cases JBS candidates have been attacked shrilly and unfairly as fascists, an appellation the Society does not deserve.

cluding Edgar Hiestand and John Rousselot of California, then the only two members of the Congress who acknowledged membership in the John Birch Society.[7]

The Democratic Party had been edging up on the Nassau County GOP, and in 1962 Derounian's opponent was a lawyer (and ACLU board member) named George Soll. Derounian sneered about soft-headed liberals, and recorded messages (which could be heard upon dialing a publicized telephone number) hinted that the Soll-ACLU position on censorship virtually made the Democrat a peddler of pornography. Soll's organization bridled at this innuendo, and assailed Derounian for his campaign efforts on behalf of the two California Birchers. Derounian won that year, but in 1964 the attack was mounted again, this time by a television producer named Lester Wolff.

The liberals had everything going for them. The Goldwater candidacy was attracting masses of Republicans to the Democratic column. The anti-Derounian forces in 1962 had begun to draw blood with the Bircher angle, and the candidate this year, Wolff, was an articulate, attractive and persuasive campaigner.

Derounian was the "darling of the Birchers." The 1962 activities for Hiestand and Rousselot were paraded and brandished. Derounian blasted back that the tactic was a standard of dirty campaigning, that he had campaigned for the two as Republicans and not as Birchers, and that this was a smear from 1962 that was being warmed over and dished up again. But the Wolff people made the "darling of the Birchers" tag stick and down went Derounian.

In the closing week of the campaign, two of Wolff's campaign workers called the Fair Campaign Practices Committee to complain that Derounian was unfairly invoking the name of the Committee in attacking the Democrats' linkage of Derounian and the Birchers. To each caller I put this question: "You don't like it when the Republicans use guilt by association to tie up Demo-

[7] The California legislature, managed by the Democrats, had redistricted after the 1960 census, and had drawn the lines of the Hiestand and Rousselot districts so it would have required an Act of God to elect them. Derounian was unable to deliver that, and the voters retired Hiestand and Rousselot.

crats with Communists; what's the difference when you use guilt by association to make a Bircher out of a right wing Republican?" One of them muttered that it was true Derounian had campaigned for the Birchers, and that was the only way to win. The second, a youth, deferred to a senior member of the Wolff staff, a woman, who tearfully conceded, "I'm not very proud of our campaign, but he [Derounian] is so firmly entrenched that that's the only way we'll ever get him out."

Liberals have long been offended at guilt by association. In the McCarthy era they had enough of it to make them thirst for revenge. When they do seize the chance to take revenge on a vulnerable conservative or reactionary the action can be understood, but it does not have to be admired.

"Soft on Birchism" as a smear phrase has nearly the same kind of potency as "soft on Communism." The impact of claimed association with a "Birch front" is nearly as great on the left as that of the analogous "Red front" on the right. Not all reputed fronts, Red or Bircher, actually are that.

One reactionary organization that pre-dates the John Birch Society is Americans for Constitutional Action. Unlike Robert Welch's creation, however, ACA is just inside the right-hand edge of political responsibility. It was conceived as a frank antagonist of ADA on the left, while the Birch Society was set up to expose and root out the treason its leaders see as dominating the government and the American society.

ACA, in this early period of the new American right, has some Birchers in its leadership just as bona fide liberal organizations had some Communist leaders in what a generation ago was the new American left. And a number of ordinary arch-conservatives have joined the Birchers today, just as many ordinary arch-liberals swallowed the Communists' bait yesterday.

Today many liberals see in "interlocking directorates" on the right the mirror-image of what the right wing remembers and occasionally still sees as a kind of sinister interlocking on the left.

A high ACA rating is seen by some liberals as one hallmark of a radical right Congressman. Barry Goldwater's approval of

ACA is read by these types as approval of the John Birch Society.

At the height of the 1964 campaign, a book appeared which abounded in over-simplified equations of this sort. It was *Danger on the Right,* by Arnold Forster and Benjamin Epstein,[8] general counsel and national director, respectively, of the Anti-Defamation League. The authors insist that the timing of the volume was accidental.

The Forster-Epstein book appeared under the auspices of ADL, and the research that went into it was done by the ADL staff. That staff is seasoned, scrupulous, and consistently accurate. Their research for the book is characteristically scrupulous.

Unfortunately, alarm at the very real danger on the right seems to have tricked the authors into precisely the same guilt-by-association that they fear and deplore on the right. They somehow lost a perspective that their agency's biographer, John Roche,[9] retained. A year earlier Roche acknowledged that he was afraid of the John Birch Society, but that his fear was somewhere near the middle of a long list, "between my fear of college presidents and my fear of being eaten alive by piranhas."

Danger on the Right distinguishes between the Radical Right and Extreme Conservatives, noting as it does so that "if the Extreme Conservatives are not card-carrying [10] Birchers, they often make common cause with them, and the similarities between their views are often more compelling than the differences*."

Thus it is possible for *Danger on the Right* to go directly to Americans for Constitutional Action. Its founder, retired Admiral Ben Moreell "himself has no affiliation with * the John Birch Society . . . But if Moreell is scrupulous in avoiding any personal connection with Welch and the Birch Society, he is not quite so scrupulous about those who serve with him as leaders of ACA.

[8] Random House, 1964.
[9] Chairman of the Department of Political Science at Brandeis University, President of ADA, and author of the history of ADL's first half-century, *The Quest for the Dream* (Macmillan, 1963).
[10] Note here, and in subsequent starred passages, the recurring rhetoric of guilt by association.

"He believes that the political and organizational affiliations of his closest associates in the leadership of ACA are none of his business*."

Then are listed five organizations to which Moreell has belonged along with Birchers; one Moreell friend and ACA treasurer who is on the editorial advisory board of *American Opinion* (Charles Edison); one vice chairman who "has been listed as an Endorser * of the Birch group (Bonner Fellers); and thirteen other supporters with "clear ties * " to the Birch Society.

With the Radical Right (JBS) and the Extreme Conservatives (ACA) thus "inextricably intertwined*," Forster and Epstein—and their eager readers who are opposing a clutch of Extreme Conservative candidates—have their whipping boy, and they proceed to lash him.

ACA in 1962 had endorsed four "card-carrying Birchers," Forster and Epstein continue. "It would be difficult, indeed, to make any valid ideological distinctions between Birchers such as Rousselot and Hiestand (who were defeated) and such successful candidates as Representatives James Utt of California, John R. Pillion of New York, Bruce Alger of Texas, Donald Bruce of Indiana, August Johansen of Michigan, and a number of others plainly far, far Right in their political thinking."

The book does not suggest who the others might be, but the Democratic opponents of the 41 Republican Congressmen defeated in 1964 may have sketched out a list, since the 41 losers had an average ACA rating of better than 75 per cent.

Actually, Messrs. Forster and Epstein use to describe ACA one really all-purpose passage which can be modified, by substituting only four words, to fit any organization to be condemned, left or right. (The replaceable words are italicized.)

In short, these leaders of *ACA* support, with disturbing impartiality, organizations that are radical and organizations that claim to be *conservative,* underscoring clearly the ideological blur that exists between the Radical *Right* and the Extreme *Conservative* and the difficulty of making distinctions between the two.[11]

[11] The exercise is from pages 181–182 of the Random House hard cover

The ADL is itself the subject of smears and innuendo. Bigots make much of its Jewishness; it was founded in 1914 to defend Jews against the traducement of their anti-Semitic neighbors and its concern has always included other minorities and the proper functioning of the American society and its political system. The League has been falsely accused of pro-Communism and loosely accused of an Extreme Liberal bias, rooted in the real and entirely legitimate liberal orientation of a great many of its leading figures.

Victims of any manner of aggression are tempted to reply in kind. But at the foundation of our society is the assumption that injured members will exercise restraint in redressing wrongs done to them, and will leave punishment to just laws justly administered. Excesses by any individual, whether through physical mayhem or violence by distortion of the record, or guilt by association, are as gross an offense to our system as excesses in the name of the law.

ACLU is fond of quoting an English printer who was first pilloried for producing unlicensed books, and then banished by a Parliamentary committee in 1652. His name was John Lilbourne, and he said, "What is done unto any one, may be done unto every one."

edition. Copyright 1964 by Anti-Defamation League of B'nai B'rith. A possible set of replacement words is offered for convenience: *ADA, liberal, Left, Liberals*. Or, for that matter: *ADL, non-partisan, Jew Marxists, Liberals*.

CHAPTER 10

Technique and Ethics: the Hare and the Tortoise

THE HISTORY of political pamphlets in America is as old and as honorable as that of the republic. The pamphlet was devised to place before the eyes of readers facts and arguments that could not be presented as effectively in any other way. Shorter, cheaper, and more ephemeral than books, the pamphlet may be discarded as soon as it is well-thumbed. It exists to address The Crisis of the moment.

Political pamphlets fell on evil days when modern mass media made it cheaper and more effective to reach voters their way. Although they never disappeared entirely, pamphlets gave way to newspapers, radio, and television, and left the political literature field largely to flyers and handbills, which were even older in usage, and shorter, and cheaper.

Then the paperback revolution hit the book publishing business. In five years, to 1960, production of paperback titles multiplied five times and one book in three was published in soft cover. High-speed printing presses, which had paved the way for truly mass media, were part of the reason, but the biggest factor was distribution.

Publishers' Weekly has estimated that in 1964 there were fifty paperbacks referring substantially to the Presidential election. Of these, fewer than half had considerable sales. Nine titles were by Goldwater or about him in terms favorable or neutral; two favored Johnson similarly. Two opposed Johnson. One of these was merely a coloring book, the other a bitterly critical but essentially honest hatchet job by former newsman Frank Kluckhohn. There were five anti-Goldwater paperbacks, and the biggest seller, by Fred J. Cook, was nearly as honest as the Kluckhohn book against Johnson.

Each of the foregoing books was published by a firm in business before and after the 1964 campaign. The success of all of them, however, was dwarfed by the sales of three quite different paperbacks that descended in a paper landslide on voters in 1964.

One of these was *A Choice Not An Echo,* by Phyllis Schlafly. Mrs. Schlafly saw "secret kingmakers" in New York choosing every Republican nominee since Landon on the basis that their choices were suitably "America last" in outlook. The book urged Barry Goldwater's nomination because he, unlike the choices of the "secret kingmakers," would not be "easy to beat."

The "easy-to-beat" candidates of the kingmakers, and Mrs. Schlafly's preference, Goldwater, appear below with their percentage of the two-party vote in the eight elections involved:

Landon 1936	Willkie 1940	Dewey 1944	Dewey 1948	Eisen-hower 1952	Eisen-hower 1956	Nixon 1960	Goldwater 1964
37.5	45.1	48.3	47.7	55.5	57.9	49.9	38.9

William Randolph Hearst, Jr., who reviewed the Schlafly book for *Fair Comment,*[1] said of it, "I have just put down, with a bewildered sigh, a book of fantastic political indictments. It is called *A Choice Not An Echo.* Confusing as the title is at first

[1] October, 1964.

glance, it becomes the more so as one plods through . . .

"In her venturesome compilation of supposed incidents, largely conjectures based on clippings scissored from newspapers and periodicals, Phyllis Schlafly has composed a structure of warmongering, 'America last' plots that left your reviewer totally unconvinced."

The second of what came to be known as 1964's "dirty books," or, less accurately, "hate books," was *None Dare Call It Treason*, by John Stormer, who helped the right wing take command of the Missouri Young Republicans. Stormer's thesis was that left wingers of both parties, "the secret revolutionaries and those they have brainwashed," are in command of "America's retreat from victory," in pursuit of a "new world order," the whole scheme financed by tax-exempt foundations. Stormer tells his readers what to do: learn the enemy, enlist others, and take action. The enemy may be learned by study, he says, and the book closes with a reading list which, it notes, may be obtained from any of the John Birch Society's American Opinion Libraries. Citizen enlistment may be in established organizations "like the John Birch Society." The action suggested is to get into politics and "elect a President and a Congress with the will to win *and* the courage to 'cleanse' " the government of those who "have aided the communists down through the years."

"*Treason*" is heavily footnoted, with references to speeches and material inserted into the endless Appendix of the *Congressional Record* by McCarthy, Jenner, Velde, and other rightists, testimony before various Congressional committees, and right wing publications. The unsophisticated reader tends to accept this abundant "documentation" as proof (after all, the *Congressional Record*), rather than as unsupported assertion, which it very often is.

One highly sophisticated reader, the conservative scholar Russell Kirk (in the *New York Herald Tribune's* "Book Week" for October 11, 1964) noted that "sometimes Mr. Stormer cites as authorities certain newsletters of dubious veracity; and he recommends some serious books cheek by jowl with productions of ignorance and prejudice . . . Averell Harriman, according to Stormer, is a 'longtime Soviet apologist'! By implication, he tars John Foster Dulles with the same brush."

Last of the big three paperbacks was the hate-Johnson book by sometime Texas historian J. Evetts Haley, *A Texan Looks at Lyndon*. Haley saw Johnson as wholly immoral and wholly cynical. He even saw sinister implications in the fact that Lee Oswald had made an overnight stay in Jim Wells County, Texas, where, Haley says, Johnson stole his first election to the Senate in 1948. As Miami newsman Robert Sherrill, a Texan, wrote in his *Fair Comment* review, "an impressive amount of research has been ruined by Haley's hatred for his subject. The result is a book of grotesque perspective . . . a book in which normal actions, seen through a steaming mirage of hate, take on strange and dreadful shapes."

Another critic, editorial page editor A. C. Greene of the *Dallas Times Herald*, called the book "so outrageously, surreptitiously wrong that it is almost impossible to isolate the heavy, thick aura of wrongness and define it."

"The result," Greene concluded, "is a book which will appall decent men and women and the President. The only fit word I can find for it is evil."

These remarkable publications, oil of fact watered with opinion, hearsay, and occasional falsehood, and shaken vigorously by their authors, were ladled out to an incredible number of American citizens. Mrs. Schlafly's work, explicitly designed to foster the Goldwater nomination, continued to sell throughout the campaign. Two million copies of it were printed, and estimated sales have ranged upward from one and a half million. Stormer's and Haley's books sold more than *six million* copies each (more than seven million were printed).

All three of the runaway best sellers were published by the authors. Mrs. Schlafly set up her Pere Marquette Press as an order-taking office in Alton, Illinois, near her home. Mr. Stormer's Liberty Bell Press in suburban St. Louis outgrew his home and wound up sharing quarters with a beauty parlor in Florissant,

Missouri. The Palo Duro Press, Haley's publisher, remained in his home at Canyon, Texas.

The high-speed presses necessary for the economical production of paperbacks were open to the three author-publishers on a routine commercial basis. The nation's two largest printers of soft cover books produced the Haley and Stormer works. Distribution, however, was another matter. The publishers found substantial difficulty in getting their wares into the market through regular channels. In at least one case, that of the Stormer book in Cleveland, the wholesale distributor that did handle it, Klein News, got its copies from the area coordinator of the John Birch Society at a rate of 20 cents per copy with the right to return all unsold copies. The printer of *None Dare Call It Treason* said some one million copies had been shipped to the Birch Society and various American Opinion Libraries, and at least 100,000 copies of the Haley book were handled similarly.

Distribution difficulties, of course, began with the reluctance of established publishers to handle such manuscripts. Libel suits, though unlikely because of the tendency of public figures to ignore rather than fight this kind of attack, still were a possibility, and one that could wipe out even a substantial publisher. Moreover, as one spokesman for a big house put it to *New York Times* writer Geoffrey Vincent, "Nobody I know wants to get into the hate dodge."

The future impact of such home-published latter-day pamphlets is difficult to assess. For one thing, the Goldwater candidacy was a phenomenon that is unlikely to be repeated at any early date: it took 28 years of Presidential victories and relatively narrow losses for "me-tooism" after Landon before the "real conservatives" got another day in court, and the Republican Party is not likely to repeat in 1968 what laid it so low in 1964.

In pre-convention politics, a new rationale for Goldwater, or for a new Goldwater, along the lines of the Schlafly book of 1964, is likely. In the more general realm of the Stormer book, the thirst of the radical right for new explanations of how it all happened is unslaked, and will continue. The President-hating audience also is substantial, and the line of hated Presidents is broken only here and there from Washington to Johnson, as witness the continued success after Kennedy's death of Victor Lasky's *JFK, The Man and the Myth*.[2] The Lasky effort, however, should not be classed with the irresponsible *A Texan Looks at Lyndon*.

The established publishers and distributors hesitated or refused to handle the three tracts, and except by ardent partisans of the author-publishers, the fact can be understood in terms of aversion to "the hate dodge" and fear of libel.

The almost universal refusal of newspapers—broken only rarely and then just two or three weeks before Election Day—to review the books is much more difficult to understand. To be sure, the books were not, for the most part, on display in regular bookstores. They were difficult to take seriously, and could be classed as political pornography. The Republican National Committee had disavowed them, but they were found in most states in local GOP headquarters, and in almost all of the Citizens for Goldwater-Miller headquarters.

Newsmen, like other citizens, were deluged with unsolicited copies in the mail. Individuals bought copies in lots up to 500 and more to give and mail to friends, acquaintances, and benighted liberals who revealed themselves by signing liberal letters-to-the-editor. But they were a major political manifestation of 1964 and it was dishonest of the newspapers to ignore the fact of the books or the arguments they contained. A few—notably the *Chicago Tribune*, the *New York Herald-Tribune*, the *Washington Star*, the *Denver Post* and the Knight Newspapers—did outstanding jobs of covering and reviewing the books, but this is a responsibility that could and should have been met earlier and more widely.

Unfortunately the "dirty books" were not the only application of high-speed printing presses to the craft of deception in 1964.

In October, a periodical named *Fact* stirred national controversy when it published the results of a pseudo-scientific "psychi-

---

[2] New York: Macmillan, 1962.

atrists' poll" about Barry Goldwater's mental fitness to be President of the United States. The *Fact* affair became one of the low-comedy lights of 1964. The publisher of the young and struggling magazine, Ralph Ginzburg, had once published a sophisticated sex magazine called *Eros*. He had been convicted of sending pornographic material through the mails, specifically *Eros* and a couple of companion pieces.

All this led liberal columnist James Wechsler to note in the New York *Post* that Ginzburg was "heretofore chiefly renowned for his concern with matters erotic rather than neurotic." Wechsler thereupon had himself some thousand words of fun with the patent absurdity of long-range psychoanalysis of a Presidential candidate whom virtually none of the analysts had ever seen in the flesh.

A memorable paragraph put the article (and Wechsler's innocence of pro-Goldwaterism) into perspective:

"For anyone encountering this column for the first time, it should be recorded that I have never been accused of any pro-Goldwater bias. There are approximately 973 reasons why I believe his election would be a national disaster. But the notion that his candidacy should be subjected to public psychiatric evaluation by men who know nothing more about him than what they have read in the newspapers seems to me a disservice to the profession. The enterprise is reduced to vulgar absurdity by a lengthy introduction in which publisher-editor Ginzburg offers his own latrine analysis of Mr. Goldwater's psychological deficiencies."

Ginzburg had rented, from a broker of mailing lists, the American Medical Association's roster of more than 12,000 psychiatrists. He sent these doctors a simple questionnaire: is Barry Goldwater psychologically fit to be President of the United States? One in every seven of the AMA's psychiatrists responded! Nearly two-thirds of the respondents—1189, ten per cent of the whole—said Goldwater was unfit. *Fact* published a wide selection of the responses. Many of the "unfit" verdicts simply bristled with psychiatry's formidable jargon, with pompous expertise and with quackery. ". . . Never forgiven his father for being a Jew" . . . "behavior which has a schizophrenic quality" . . . "adolescent desire to attract attention by provocative or belligerent statements" . . . "paranoid traits" . . . "sensitivity to questions about his honesty and integrity—obvious unconscious substitutes for masculinity" . . . and finally, "any psychiatrist who does not agree with the above is himself psychologically unfit to be a psychiatrist."

Slightly more than half as many long-range observers (675 of them) found Goldwater fit, but their responses were more restrained than those of the enthusiastic anti-Goldwater psychiatrists. ". . . Opportunity for the public to choose between conservatism and modern socialism . . . he is a sane man" . . . "statements, when not distorted or misinterpreted, indicate him to be a thoughtful, capable person . . ."

The anti- comments from the psychiatrists, of course, were nothing more than standard cocktail-circuit hyperbole for nonprofessional people who hated or feared Goldwater, but coming from doctors of medicine who practice their healing arts upon the human psyche they raised embarrassing and disturbing questions about the ethical level of the craft and the psychiatrists' own professional competence. To be sure, note of this may have been taken by the 10,000 psychiatrists who ignored the *Fact* query, and was taken by the 571 who did reply that they could not judge Goldwater's fitness at long range. This 4.6 per cent of the AMA's psychiatrists who were charitable enough to answer Ginzburg and responsible enough not to abuse their profession and the public's avid gullibility found their finest expression in a letter from one Dr. Hubert Miller of Detroit: "If you will send me written authorization from Sen. Goldwater and arrange for an appointment, I shall be happy to send you a report concerning his mental status. The same goes for you."

Republicans believed the undertaking was supported by Democrats, and pointed to a $100,000 advertising campaign for the magazine featuring the Goldwater issue, to suggest that a floundering publication could not spend money like that without a big infusion of money from someone with an axe to grind. If this suspicion is correct, as it probably is not, the sponsor certainly was not any official Democratic agency. When the Goldwater edition was mailed early in October of 1964, the Fair Campaign Practices Committee released, in its quarterly bulletin, *Fair Comment*, a series of statements by concerned political and medical groups. John Bailey, the Democratic National Chairman, noted in his denial of knowledge, or approval or intent to use any part of the survey, what other critics overlooked in their denunciation of the medical and scientific breach of ethics and sense. He pointed out that "the long-distance analysis of any candidate by questionnaire is not responsible journalism."

Other denouncers were the AMA, the American Psychiatric Association, the American Psychological Association, the Republican National Committee and the Fair Campaign Practices Committee, which had alerted the Republicans and Democrats to the content of the poll and coordinated the simultaneous rebuttal of the Goldwater "exposé." The American Psychological Association, like its sibling psychiatric body, had been upset by the poll since the questionnaires were mailed out in the summer of 1964. The psychological group spoke up early and firmly to Mr. Ginzburg, stating that it was advising its total membership that any member even *responding* to the questionnaire would be brought up on ethical charges. The psychologists also insisted, successfully, that publicity and advertising placed after the date of their confrontation with Ginzburg contain no suggestion that the poll included psychologists, as the original notices had done.

The mass media lend themselves well to the exploitation of emotion. Motion pictures, and now television, because of their evocative ability, are especially well-suited to distortion. Since the early days of the movies it has been attempted. In 1934, when Upton Sinclair was running for governor of California on his utopian program of EPIC, or End Poverty In California, alarmed movie moguls made their studios available for the creation of utterly phony newsreels attacking Sinclair and his panaceas. Actors and actresses played the parts of citizens selected at random and interviewed "for our cameras." They acted out with shock, grief, and outrage their fears of what lay in store should the mad genius be elected. Reason (and dishonest arguments) prevailed, and the state was saved for the radical right of a generation later.

Reminiscent of the anti-Sinclair newsreels was a 1964 effort to rally moral America to Barry Goldwater. The story broke two weeks before the election when the Democrats, for whom Dick Tuck had obtained a copy of a film called "Choice," showed it to the press, and precipitated a chain of events that led several days later to the abandonment of the movie. The sponsoring organization, "Mothers for a Moral America," had been invented by Citizens for Goldwater-Miller to present the $65,000 film. It was scheduled to be shown to the nation's housewives on $35,000 worth of NBC network Friday afternoon television time. A real, live Mother had been found and imported from California for the occasion. The Fair Campaign Committee challenged the Republicans to avow the film or scrap it. Goldwater saw it and at the last minute repudiated it as "racist." „

The story had begun less than a month earlier, on September 22, 1964. On that Tuesday afternoon, Citizens-for-Goldwater aide Russell Walton sat in a second floor suite of the Beverly Carlton Hotel in Beverly Hills, California, with three movie makers and a shorthand reporter.[3] The trio was to produce and direct the film. Walton described the "documentary" he wanted, as part of what was to be a larger special films project. It must stress the "national prevalence of juvenile delinquency, crime, moral degeneration, narcotics; and the facts that women are afraid to walk on the street at night, the parks are empty after dark—parents are fearful for their children, husbands for their wives . . . we want to show that the country's moral standards are in a serious decline." He summarized: "Remind the people of the moral crisis in America, the rising crime rate, rising juvenile delinquency, narcotics, pornography, filthy magazines. We want to just make them mad; make their stomachs turn."

[3] Whose report was also obtained by Dick Tuck for the Democrats.

230

The director, Henry Ludwin, got the idea. "Appeal to their basic emotions," he said.

"Yes, raw, naked emotions," Walton said. "Arouse them." Walton suggested that the film makers "take this latent anger and concern which now exists, build it up, and subtly turn and focus it on the man who drives 90 miles an hour with a beer can in his hands and pulls the ears of beagles, and leave them charged up to the point where they will want to go out and do something about it." [4]

Walton misremembered the "Harlem race riots" and said the "head of CORE" had "wanted to get 1,000 Negroes, and he said, 'There are only a thousand policemen, and I want a thousand Negroes who are willing to die,' and he wanted them to go out and kill the policemen. This is pretty violent."

And *almost* half true.

Walton warned the movie men against showing any action that could "be determined a police brutality. You have to have calm, dedicated police, law-enforcement officers who are really trying to protect the public as opposed to a Bill [sic] Connor who doesn't give a damn, he just wanted to beat some heads."

A film maker addressed the question of a narrator, "one of these Ronald Reagan types." Walton demurred. "I don't know. He has quite a reputation of political association."

Walton spoke of rural audiences for the film. "They think that the big city is something evil," he said, "that it is a sinkhole, it produces narcotics and crime. This film will obviously and frankly just play on their prejudice . . . We are catering to the Midwest. We should carry the Midwest like nothing. They have a very high level of morality in the Midwest supposedly, so we are just going after that too."

The Goldwater advocate repeatedly came to the point: "The basic emotion is the fear and the anxiety of parents for their children's safety, for the safety of their wives, the safety of their

---

[4] The spectacle *is* diverting— the man driving 90 miles per hour, holding onto a beer can with both hands, pulling the ears of at least a pair of beagles, with who knows what.

homes. 'Tonight maybe the glass will shatter and someone will come into our bedroom.' Then we provide them with the solution for it: Morality must start at the top, it must start with the White House, with the Administration."

Walton had an example or two: "Wife-trading, the jet set, and that whole damned rat-pack situation." He summarized: "The public by and large feels that Johnson cannot cope with the moral problems because he is immoral himself, so there it is, there is the issue."

The movie technician asked, "How do we come to the conclusion that he is immoral himself?"

Walton ticked off the evidence: a stolen election, Bobby Baker, Billie Sol Estes, the Johnson television monopoly in Austin, the Johnson wealth, the McCloskey-Washington Stadium kickback allegations, the big city political machines, the race riots.

"We want to find film on all of this?"

Walton confirmed: "Yes, powerful film, real gut film."

Finally, after off-the-record discussions, Walton concluded: John Kennedy, like him or not, "was moving America to a period of greatness . . . Then this guy, Johnson, by an act of God, moves in and has not only allowed all this immoral stuff to start, he has literally destroyed all the work that Kennedy had started to accomplish, and the Kennedy people feel this . . . This guy Johnson is nothing but a political animal. Kennedy was a principled man and I think you can hit a lot of Democrats right in the guts with this."

Producer Raymond R. Morgan spoke: "He said, 'Ask not what your country can do for you, but what you can do for your country.'"

"I think you can twist that," Walton said. "You can twist it subtly because Kennedy is respected by both parties, and this respect is growing."

Twist it subtly they did. And the script could have been written by the prophet Jeremiah. It was narrated by actor Raymond Massey, whose conservative leanings were not so visible as "one of these Ronald Reagan types," and it was narrated with somber power and righteousness.

To prescription, the Kennedy image was invoked, and twisted. The noble young leader had been moving the country toward greatness, then was slain. Now, in eleven months, immoral leadership had visited the land with desolation and evil, and all was undone. More sorrow than anger. Oh, that our tragic loss should plunge us into immorality, filth, vice, drugs, sex, crime. The wise, noble voice of wise, noble Dr. Gillespie, Dr. Kildare's mentor and leader, was tinged with sadness—until the dawning prospect of yet another noble leader: who but Barry Goldwater?

Under, around, and often over that splendid narration was a score of strident and frenetic jazz.

The film showed a black sedan careening through the night. Out of its window hurtles a beer can. If you miss it the first time, you will have another chance, and another. There is a riot scene. Negroes looting, Negroes rioting, Negroes picking merchandise out of a shattered display window. Strippers disrobe. Teenagers perform bizarre dances. Rioting whites, for impartiality. More looting Negroes; once more the black sedan ejecting beer cans. A topless bathing suit, filled to overflowing by some blonde. Riots, raids, drug-smuggling paraphernalia, a Mardi Gras shot of a man wearing only a fig leaf. A long, lingering shot of a rack of pornographic books, centered on the title *Jazz Me Baby*.

The Republican National Committee wanted to promote bland efforts like the homey Barry-Visits-Ike-Down-on-the-Farm film. They felt it essential to counter the mad-man label. Citizens for Goldwater wanted "raw, naked emotions," to "make their stomachs turn," and "leave them charged up," to sing a profane little mass for the slain leader and "twist it."

Yet those who defend the morality and the propriety of "Choice" find another dexterous manipulation of "raw emotion" to be utterly indefensible. The ethics of political appeals to emotion appears to be measured in the familiar terms of whose ox is being gored.

At the very start of the campaign Republican Chairman

Dean Burch cried foul at a Democratic television spot announcement. A winsome little girl appears in a meadow, wholly ab-
sorbed in picking the petals off a daisy as her voice counts: "One,
two, three, four, five. . . ." At "ten," a male voice is heard, over-
riding the girlish tones, louder and louder: "Ten, nine, eight . . ."
The familiar ominous tone of the countdown. ". . . four, three,
two, one, *zero*." The screen goes black, the child is obliterated,
and the screen fills with the stunning, fiery umbrella of a nuclear
explosion. The shape distends into the dread mushroom cloud,
and shock waves ray out and off the screen. Now the somber
voice of Lyndon Johnson: "These are the stakes. To make a
world in which all of God's children can live, or go into the dark.
We must either love each other, or we must die." The screen goes
into the dark. One line of type appears, white on the black void:
"VOTE FOR PRESIDENT JOHNSON ON NOVEMBER 3." The voice of doom
urges the point: "The stakes are too high for you to stay home."

A *Wall Street Journal* story at the end of summer had detailed Democratic TV plans, and accurately predicted the spot.
The Republican chairman had read the story and a few days later
met with John Bailey and Fair Campaign Practices Committee
Chairman Charles P. Taft. The occasion was the Washington
press conference at which the party leaders endorse the Code of
Fair Campaign Practices as the traditional start of the fall campaign.

When the first of these biennial rituals took place in 1954, the
party leaders, then Republican Leonard W. Hall and Democrat
Stephen A. Mitchell, had at one another while the ink was still
wet on their newly-signed Code. Nearly every time since then one
party head, and sometimes both, has launched a cry of foul and
taken out after his opponent. Dean Burch won the toss in 1964
and harpooned John Bailey on the spot—about the offending spot
described in the *Wall Street Journal*.

Burch bitterly criticized the Democrats' portrayal of Goldwater as a trigger-happy militarist who would set off bombs heedlessly. John Bailey rejoined that the image of Goldwater had been
created by the Senator himself, and that the Democrats could

hardly be blamed for exploiting it.

When the bomb spot appeared, it bore out Burch's fears. The advertising agency which created it, Doyle Dane Bernbach, Inc., defends the spot as an entirely proper presentation of the central theme of the 1964 campaign, nuclear responsibility.

Hosts of Democrats disagreed, reportedly including Hubert Humphrey, who was quoted as describing the spot as "unfortunate." Hundreds of Democrats phoned local television stations to complain, and wrote bitter letters to the Democratic National Committee and the Fair Campaign Practices Committee.

The advertising agency pursued the theme, and soon another little girl appeared on the nation's screens, this one with her mommy and an ice cream cone. Mommy quickly pointed out that ice cream cones used to be poisoned with strontium-90 but weren't any more. Unless all the other mommies wanted to see fall-out from bomb tests come back to poison their little girls with dirty old strontium-90, they had just better elect President Johnson, because "there's a man who wants to be President and if he's elected they might start testing [bombs] all over again."

More protests followed the ice cream spot, and the Fair Campaign Committee relayed these citizen complaints, along with the formal Republican protests, to the Democratic National Committee. The Democrats did stop scheduling the spots, although they never publicly acknowledged doing so.

As a matter of fact, Goldwater had created the image the Democrats were exploiting, just as John Bailey had said.[5] But exploitation need not engender distortion. The bomb spots oversimplified grossly. Furthermore, they employed a tactic the Democrats found shocking when it was used against them later in the

[5] One of the most damaging "Goldwaterisms" was a suggestion that the United States could expose north Viet Nam supply lines by defoliating the jungle with low-yield atomic weapons. The few Goldwater partisans among syndicated columnists were outraged that the Democrats would use the quotation against the Senator. They pointed out that although Goldwater had suggested atomic defoliation as a possibility, he had also added that it was a course he did not think we would follow. This was true enough of the Senator's most recent television comments, but the fact was that he had raised the defoliation possibility several times previously, without the observation that we probably would not do it.

campaign: quoting a candidate's past utterances against the candidate today.

Another of the 1964 TV spots showed a Social Security card being torn in half, while the announcer said, "Goldwater has said he would change the system. Even his running mate admits that the voluntary plan would wreck your Social Security." Goldwater had discussed making participation in Social Security voluntary for certain groups and under certain conditions, but he had spent a large share of his stump time in the 1964 primaries and in the general election campaign denying that he would change the system and pointing out that he had voted for extending it. In desperation as his varied antagonists continued to flail him with the outdated "voluntary" remarks, he finally said he could think of no other word but "lie" for allegations that he would impair the system. Yet the spot appeared. Goldwater *has said*. Well, when? Never mind, he said it. The episode was remindful of bitter racists quoting an earlier Johnson against civil rights, to beat the 1964 Johnson, a champion of civil rights.

Much closer to the mark, and more effective, was a classic interpretation of an earlier Goldwater observation that it would be just as well if the eastern seaboard were sawed off and allowed to float out to sea. With script-writing of this caliber, Doyle Dane Bernbach hardly needed editors. They filmed a plywood map with the eastern seaboard being sawed off and floating out to sea. Their spot, lacking the desperate overtones of the bomb commercials, brought the Democrats huge merriment, no complaints, and certainly some votes.

The head of the Democratic National Committee's account group at Doyle Dane Bernbach, generally regarded within the advertising business as high on anybody's list of the few best agencies, explained to writer Pete Hamill for the *New York Times Magazine* why the Democrats' ad campaign did not mention Humphrey. "We just don't feel that people vote for Vice-Presidential candidates," agency executive James Graham said. "We're selling the President of the United States."

One client among many. Airlines, El Al; Automobiles, Volkswagen; Confections, Cracker Jacks; Culture, Lincoln Center; Presidents (1964 model), Lyndon B. Johnson. Doyle Dane, as the agency is known in the trade, is proud that its television commercials have never shown a cross-section of the human stomach; this is a barometer of taste.

The election campaign has one valid purpose: to reveal the policies and beliefs and strengths of the contenders. Barry Goldwater would have been more fairly represented if a cross-section of *his* stomach (perhaps to show that he had some strontium, too) had been flashed on the nation's screens. Campaign ethics cannot tolerate hyperbolic magnifications of what one side *thinks* the weaknesses of the other side to be, and especially when the stakes are as high as the very survival of humankind.

The Democrats insisted in 1960 that the opposition and the voters were obliged to accept John Kennedy's word as to whether he would be the Pope's servant first and America's second. The Republicans took him at his word, and the issue was raised only by bigots. The GOP *could* have conjured up some great spots with burning martyrs. But it didn't.

Goldwater in 1964 simply could not get any Democrats to listen when he outlined his views on nuclear responsibility, so completely disguised in the Democratic little-girl-and-daisy spot. If the Republicans had responded in kind they would have run the "morality film" over and over until the (strontium-laden) cows came home.

So the issue of nuclear responsibility was handled, in 1964, on a basis of what would work, not what would come to grips with real facts. Cracker Jacks, anyone?

Television is not unique in its capacity to rally emotion and to distort. Its elder sister radio still can do a workmanlike job of deceiving, in some cases more aptly and smoothly than television.[6] The 1963 campaign for governor of Kentucky is a case in point.

[6] Of course the techniques of editing video-tape are not yet as widely known as in the case of audio-tape recordings.

The issue was integration; Breathitt, the Democrat, was depicted as a "stooge" of President John and Attorney General Robert Kennedy, eager to force integration at every level. The campaign was already dishonest; a fraudulent flyer distorted Breathitt's positions on integration and implied that he advocated racial intermarriage. Now a 30-second radio spot went out over the state supporting Republican candidate Louie B. Nunn. The President of the United States, John F. Kennedy, spoke first:

"Good afternoon, ladies and gentlemen. I would say that over the long run, we are going to have a mix. This will be true racially, socially, ethnically, geographically, and that is really, finally, the best way."

Then came the announcer: "Breathitt supports this Kennedy policy. Vote against it. Vote Nunn."

Unlike an audio forgery that had come to light a few years earlier, in which opponents of "socialized medicine" had forged an entire radio speech on tape in the name of a United Steelworkers official, the Republican spot in Kentucky used the President's actual voice, from a Presidential press conference on September 12, 1963. The official transcript begins thus:

"THE PRESIDENT: *Good Afternoon. Ladies and gentlemen,* I want to stress again . . . [the nuclear test ban treaty. Twenty-two pages later a reporter engaged the President in this colloquy (the passages used in the radio spots appear in italics):]

QUESTION: Mr. President, a Negro leader who helped organize the March on Washington says that he feels you are greater than Abe Lincoln in the area of civil rights. Apparently a lot of other Negroes support you. The latest poll showed that 95 per cent probably would vote for you next year. Now, in your opinion, Mr. President, does this political self-segregation on the part of the Negroes, combined with continued demonstrations in the North, pose any problems for you as far as the electoral vote in the North is concerned next year?

THE PRESIDENT: I understand what you mean, that there is a danger of a division in the party, in the country, upon racial grounds. I would doubt that. I think the American people have been through too much to make that fatal mistake. It is true that a majority of the Negroes have been Democrats, but that has been true since Franklin Roosevelt. Before that a majority of them were Republicans. The Republican Party, I am confident, could get the support of the Negroes, but I think they have to recognize the very difficult problems the Negroes face.

So in answer to your question I don't know what 1964 is going to bring. I think a division upon racial lines would be unfortunate, class lines, sectional lines. In fact, Theodore Roosevelt said all this once very well way back. So *I would say that over the long run, we are going to have a mix. This will be true racially, socially, ethnically, geographically, and that is really, finally, the best way."*

Lawmakers are only beginning to eye the possibility of regulating such abuses. They are becoming more frequent as bright young political robots see foolproof opportunities to use not only a man's words but his very voice against him. A generation earlier Walter Quigley noted that he could find the dynamite to destroy a career from its possessor's utterances over the years. What he would have given for audio tape! A cheap tape recorder, a razor blade, and six inches of Scotch tape; libel-proof use of the candidate's own voice to make a "scallawag" of him.

Tacticians at the National Republican Congressional Committee pioneered another kind of radio distortion in 1954, a little drama that may have held the seeds of the Goldwater "morality film" then a decade in the future. Printing presses roar in the background, and over them is heard the voice of the ubiquitous professional neutral, the announcer: "Those are the printing presses of the Communist Party. Listen to them!" The presses roar louder, then fade under the announcer: "The date is April, 1954. Those printing presses are turning out the official Communist Party line."

A Russian-accented voice is heard over the sound of the presses. "Defeat the Republican Congressional candidates in 1954! That is our order from Moscow. Return America to a New Deal type administration! Moscow orders that!"

Now the announcer concludes with some business about the Red blueprint. "Don't take orders from Moscow! Vote for a Republican Congress . . ."

Even the telephone is a vehicle for electronic smear in this electronic era. The method is akin to certain public services offered by the telephone companies. You dial a prescribed number and get the correct time, a current weather report and forecast, or a few words of oleaginous uplift from a clergyman. The practice of dial-a-smear emerged along about 1962. Scattered individual candidates used it in Congressional and local races. The phenomenon went national when a young right-wing physician named William Douglass, of Sarasota, Florida, conceived it as a weapon in the battle to "save our sick country" from the Communists who have seized control of the government and the communications media.

The Liberty Bell, or Let Freedom Ring, Network operates across the country and more outlets are added from time to time. Subscribers pay Dr. Douglass $20 a year for his messages, and agree to use a certain quota in addition to those they prepare themselves. The telephone company says it is permitted to exert no control over the content of messages. It simply rents the equipment and the telephone line to the subscriber for a modest monthly charge, which in New York City comes to about $23 a month—a modest enough price for the superpatriot to pay for one last chance at saving liberty.

The messages are a potpourri, sometimes referring to national candidates, like "socialist" Hubert Humphrey in 1964, and often to national figures not currently involved in a campaign. Eisenhower is a Communist agent; read all about it in Robert Welch's book, The Politician. Jacob Javits has a "100 per cent pro-Communist voting record," Martin Luther King is "a fake humanitarian . . . nothing more than an instrument for furthering the cause of Communist world revolution."

As local political candidates apply the technique to their campaigns, as they have begun to do in every region, the tactic is becoming commonplace at election time. The sponsor need not identify himself,[7] or he may contrive a high-sounding paper organization or a patriotic sign-off like "Let Freedom Ring." All he then need do is advertise the telephone number by word of mouth, radio or local newspapers. He can then sit back, confident that voters, ever curious, are fighting each other to get a chance at the constantly busy number, and the message, over which no control but the flexible conscience of the candidate can be exerted.

So in the decade ended with the Johnson-Goldwater election, technical developments in communication have offered to revolutionize dirty politics. If a publisher will not accept your screed, good candidate, publish it yourself. The printing houses who produce the paperbacks for the nation's biggest publishers will be happy to work for you, and if you get the volume high enough you can get your cost per copy down below a dime.

Has your opponent said something inflammatory at some point—any point—in his career? Dramatize it, by all means. Retain an advertising agency, but be sure to get the best. If they can sell soap, why can't they sell you?

Look over your rival's past speeches; you may find a place where he says, for instance, "The dirtiest word in the English language is Nigger! Nigger! Nigger!" In the South you can use the whole statement; in Negro areas you can clip it a bit so he is just saying "Nigger! Nigger! Nigger!" Remember the signs on the paper towel dispensers in economy-conscious public schools. Why use two when one will do? Politic like that. Why use the whole truth when half will do? "Half a truth is like half a brick; you can throw it twice as far."

Technical experts operating in an ethical vacuum introduce the sewage that pollutes the stream of American politics. They are far more numerous than the authentic dirty politicians. Dirty politicians get found out, and voted out. The slick pros operate

[7] The Bell System finally arranged in 1966 to make the true name and address of each operator known on inquiry, and to insist that the message itself include such identification.

behind the shield of their anonymity, once, or twice, or a few times removed from the candidate himself, remote enough so the anger their tactics generate may be vitiated by the time it finds its way to the candidate, and certainly before it reaches them.

The invention of movable type made it possible for articulate advocates of political causes to extend their persuasiveness beyond a single audience. Tom Paine's arguments for throwing off the British yoke utilized the technique of printing for a straightforward political purpose. The Coffin Handbill against Andrew Jackson used the same technique for a dishonest one.

Motion pictures, radio, television, the high-speed printing press, all have augmented the means of communicating political ideas. Today's argument, true or false, can span the nation in less time than it took Paine's printer to set the type for the title of his Crisis Papers.

The possibilities for abuse of the electorate by dishonest political advocates are not quite unlimited. But they are limited *only* by laws of minimal effectiveness and, more hopefully, by the politician's willingness to observe the ethical restraints that he expects the opposition to honor.

Technical developments are the hare of the fable. Political ethics is the tortoise. Can the tortoise win?

CHAPTER 11

The Survival of Politics

SOCIETY has remedies for the political ills which this book has described. At bottom these ills are human failings rather than political *per se*. Granting that man cannot be perfected, at least he can be exalted on occasion, persuaded frequently, and restrained almost always. Exaltation and persuasion cannot be reduced to formulae; restraint can, and so the role of the law in curbing dishonest and scurrilous election campaigns is the easiest place to start. Like laws against murder, theft, or any other antisocial action, election laws will continue to be broken. Therefore it is important to remember that legislative reforms are only a partial and imperfect step in the right direction.

However, the step desperately needs to be taken. Our election laws are shockingly out of date. An increasingly urban nation, we vote in November, waiting until the farmers' crops are in. The lag between election and inauguration of a President was originally four months, in order to give the electors time to get the word, assemble, vote, and notify the President-elect. Messages and people could then travel as fast as a river boat or horse.

In 1933, when people could travel by Ford Trimotor, the election-inaugural interval was cut to two months. And there it stands to-day, although people can travel as fast as sound and messages are transmitted at the speed of light.

Laws governing voter registration and the actual conduct of elections have been trimmed and patched, and in some states wholly revised, so that at least they employ today's terminology and at best they do a fair job of prescribing honest elections and honest counts. The room for improvement is vast; for example, Arkansas only recently removed a *constitutional* prohibition of voting machines.

Permanent personal registration and voting machines or electronic counters for paper ballots should be the rule of practice in every state. It is ironic that voting machine manufacturers are more concerned about proper registration systems than many legislatures; the manufacturers realize that sloppy registration can permit flagrant fraud even with machines, and they cannot afford to have their machines mute parties to unfair practices for fear of ruining the good name of the voting machine.

State regulation of voting in Federal elections should not impose a residence requirement on citizens moving from other states in the case of Presidential elections. Residents moving about within any jurisdiction ought to be able to vote for any office serving that jurisdiction. That is, a Chicagoan who moves to Springfield, Illinois, the day before Election Day should be permitted to vote for Governor and U.S. Senator.

Although many eminently qualified experts, notably including most of President Kennedy's Commission on Voting Participation, oppose literacy requirements for voters, I believe strongly in such a requirement, so formulated as to eliminate most possibilities of abuse. Proof of completion of sixth grade in a public or private school in the United States should be adequate proof of literacy. In the absence of such proof, a standardized and simple test should be administered by election officials. In the literate and complex age in which we live, ability to read simply is not too great a burden to impose on those whom we ask to choose our government.

If the registration and qualification of voters is handled moderately well by our laws, the purported regulation of campaign finance by the Federal Corrupt Practices Act and 28 states is a scandalous anachronism. Under these absurdly unrealistic laws, every serious candidate for major office is either a lawbreaker or an obscure loser. Budgets that must include the costs of television time and chartered airplanes are "regulated" by laws conceived for an era of handbills, coal-burner railroad trips, and two-cent stamps.

Such fiscal restrictions as most states and the Federal law impose *cannot* be obeyed by a candidate who wants to present his position to a decent fraction of his constituency. Apart from the moral dilemma with which they confront the candidate, and the validation they supply to voter cynicism, these laws engender and make inevitable a voter contempt for law itself. When we scoff at the laws that govern the selection of our lawmakers, we erode the very base of the American political process, the democratic election of a representative government. Thus cloaking our legislators and legislatures with dishonor, we provide for the creation of laws in an atmosphere we disdain.

Spending limits imposed on candidates and parties should be abolished; 21 states impose no limit, and Florida restricts spending only to money in the campaign treasury, thus outlawing deficit spending.[1] Full publicity for all contributions of more than $100 should be rigidly required. An important step in such requirement should be to make it impossible for the Clerk of the House of Representatives to impede access to financial reports by reporters or any interested citizen at any reasonable hour. Violation of the publicity requirement, or hampering public access to the information, ought to be punishable by a stiff penalty.

Since television has emerged as the major cost factor in urban and state and national campaigns, its availability to candidates and parties must insure fair treatment for both sides. The

[1] Section 99.161(6).

problem is extremely difficult, but its solution cannot be put off on that ground. The "equal time" provision of Section 315 of the Communications Act desperately needs revision, but the question is how to revise. The broadcaster cannot be saddled with the obligation to provide equal time to a frivolous or insubstantial candidate for "reply," yet a voice cannot be denied third party or independent candidates who have a real or potential following that is substantial.

The easiest way to address the problem probably would prove to be government subsidy of campaign TV time, but subsidy should exclude spot announcements, on which candidates spend an ever-increasing share of their budget. The rationale for subsidy is simply that television has become as important to the electoral process as the registration of voters and the provision of polling places, cost items which are borne unquestioningly by government at the local level. In any solution, however, subsidy or no, provision must be made not to exclude the maverick who has a serious message and potential. Share of vote at the last election, or petition signatures, offer a realistic approach.

The difficulties faced by candidates—and broadcasters—in areas where several political jurisdictions are served by a single group of TV outlets also must be taken into account. The Congressional candidate in Newark, New Jersey, cannot afford to buy television time to reach listeners in New York, Connecticut, and other New Jersey districts as well as his own, and the broadcaster can ill afford to lose the bulk of his audience while a local candidate talks to a fraction of the total TV audience. Here the best prospects for progress appear to be in voluntary cooperation by local broadcasters, sharing the responsibility equitably, perhaps with all stations in an area agreeing to allocate the same segment of time to political messages. In this fashion in New York City for example, nearby Connecticut candidates might use Channel 2, New York City hopefuls Channels 4 and 5, those in Long Island Channel 7, Westchester County Channel 9, Putnam and Rockland Counties Channel 11, and New Jersey Channel 13. Every local channel would be in use for local political messages simultaneously. Whether or not this particular device would work, it is certain that some approach will succeed in time. A major deterrent to any solutions in the area of political broadcasting has been the traditional attitudes that broadcasters and politicians have had toward each other, each on his guard and demanding total surrender from the other. One breakthrough on this score was a National Conference on Broadcasting and Election Campaigns, which the Fair Campaign Practices Committee held in 1965. Such confrontations, in which each side attributes some good faith to the other and each acknowledges that the other faces thorny problems, will open the way to useful legislation and voluntary action.

One area of election legislation remains, and it is the most difficult to address because it comes closest to legislating morality. One man's meat tends to be another man's poison; an attack may seem perfectly fair to one observer and utterly foul to another. Smear is even difficult to define precisely, and harder still to deal with in legislation. Its most troublesome aspects have been summarized by the Fair Campaign Practices Committee. In its basic criteria for evaluating fair and unfair campaigning, the Committee boils the question down to these elements: is the attack true? is it relevant?

Libel laws are the standard refuge for a person who has been lied about in print. Politicians, for the reasons suggested earlier, rarely take to the courts. Indeed it was all but precedent-shattering when California's Senator Thomas Kuchel acted through the courts against a handful of radical rightists and fellow-travelers who circulated libelous material suggesting that he was a homosexual.

Yet there are remedies for the ineffectuality of libel laws in protecting politicians. Here and there they actually appear on the books, although they are rarely tested in the courts.

Oregon has a political criminal libel law [2] that was enacted half a century before it was first put to use in 1960. It requires the state's attorney to act through the courts when a candidate is

[2] Oregon Revised Statutes, Section 260.370.

libeled, thus freeing the candidate from the image of a "bad sport." When a group of zealots concocted a list of lies, half-truths, and oversimplifications all implying that a Democratic candidate named Monroe Sweetland was a pro-Communist, the state acted. One leader of the fervent band of "anti-Communists" was convicted, and placed under a suspended sentence. Superficially the suspended sentence appears inconsequential, but in this case it was a substantial deterrent. The culprit was in effect placed on probation for two years, with his political activities subject to court scrutiny; any further dabbling with political libel and he would be jailed to serve the sentence.

Like most libel legislation, the Oregon law covers false statements reflecting on a candidate's "character, morality or integrity." The Sweetland case fell afoul of the act because in the course of "proving" him to be a Red the document impugned his morals and character repeatedly and falsely. Simple proof of falsity is never sufficient to convict; libel laws require proof of damage to *reputation*. Here is the biggest defect in the Oregon law and in the general libel laws as they relate to candidates. The distinction between damage to *reputation* and damage to *political prospects* needs to be drawn sharply.

Some states do indeed distinguish, among them Massachusetts, Minnesota, Utah, and West Virginia. Their laws prohibit false statements that are politically injurious, but to be actionable, the falsehood must be uttered knowingly. Michigan prohibits politically injurious false statements without requiring proof of knowledge that they were false.[3]

A further hazard confronts the candidate who has been lied about in Congressional dialogue or in some speech or statement that has been read into the endless Appendix of the *Congres-*

[3] Massachusetts: Chapter 56 section 42. Minnesota: Chapter 861 section 210.11. Utah: section 20–14–29. West Virginia: section 218 (5)(e) and 218 (5)(f). Michigan: section 6.1915 and 6.1931(s). Other states are Alaska, which includes radio broadcasts: sections 15.55.040 and 15.55.090; Florida: section 104.271; Mississippi: section 3174; North Carolina: section 163–196 (10); Ohio: section 3599.09; Washington: section 29.85.070; and Wisconsin: section 12.17.

sional Record. Henry Wallace once noted sourly that if you read far enough back in the *New York Times* you could find everything that anybody ever said. The observation is as valid for the *Congressional Record*, and the almost infinite testimony before Congressional committees contains some of the most baldly false and wholly unsupported assertions ever contrived by the imagination of man. Yet these assertions are privileged matter inasmuch as they were uttered under Congressional immunity, and the immunity is conditionally extended under the law to their repetition outside the Congress.

Thus if a far-sighted and dishonest legislator wishes to lie with impunity about a prospective opponent, he need only plant his falsehoods in advance in the record of his legislature, whence they can be disinterred when needed. The conditional privilege against libel attaching to such testimony needs to be delimited, but the job will not be easy.

Radio and television also have raised a libel problem that did not exist in the "good old days" on which so much of our law is based. A candidate in one state may be libeled by a broadcast originating in an adjacent state. The libel laws and court practice and the mechanics of serving subpoenas are likely to vary so widely between the states that it might be almost impossible to sue. Serious thought should be given to an interstate libel statute to govern such situations. Thought has been given by at least one Congressional leader, Walter Rogers, the Texas Democrat who is chairman of the House Subcommittee on Communications and Power.

Finally, American legislators would do well to explore the English law permitting court injunctions against repetition of a false statement. In California, especially, there has been recent experience with injunctions against particular kinds of compaign literature that violate some aspect of law. The most obvious episode was the Nixon-sponsored postcard "poll" of California Democrats. However, the poll could be enjoined not because it was loaded with false implications but because it sought, even though in an effort to seem genuine, to raise money for what ostensibly was an organization of Democrats.

Perennially, one of the most troublesome aspects of smear in election campaigns is the anonymous leaflet or other publication. The Federal government outlaws unsigned literature in campaigns for Congress and the Presidency, and 38 states forbid it within their own boundaries. But the spread in terms, degree of identification required, penalties, and enforceability is colossal. Some states, following the Federal government, require only the name of the person responsible. Many others, among them New York, California, New Jersey, and Illinois, require name and address. The New Jersey law is one of the better statutes, in that it requires name and address of the person responsible for the publication or, alternatively, the person paying the bill. If either of these is an organization, the name of a responsible officer acting for the group is required. The New Jersey law goes on to require that the printer maintain full particulars, including a sample of the document, quantity, price, names, and dates, and that he make this record available for inspection by any interested person at reasonable times over a two-year period.[4]

Most of the anonymous literature legislation either specifies campaigns for political office or has been interpreted that way by the courts or the attorneys general. Unfortunately, this excludes school board elections, a category in which some of the wildest contumely regularly appears, very often anonymously published. Ideally, anonymous literature should be rigidly banned from any election for any public office in the land, from school board member to President.

There are two reasons for requiring identification. Philosophically most important is the fact that an informed voter needs to know the source of a political argument in order to evaluate it fully. Second, and important after the fact, is the libeled candidate's right to be able to locate his accuser for rebuttal or legal action.

[4] Title 18 U.S. Code section 612. New York: Penal Law, section 781-b; California: section 12047; New Jersey: sections 18:5–82.35; (3); 19:34–25 (j) (3); 19:34–38(i); 19:34–38(i); 19:34–38.1; Illinois: sections 26-1 to 26-4.

A model anonymity law would require name and address of sponsor, and if the sponsor is a committee, the name and address of the officer authorizing the printing. Established state and national party committees ought to be exempted from these requirements so long as each piece of literature carries a registered and recognizable graphic device—for instance the star or the eagle—with accompanying initials. Unauthorized use of these symbols should be punished as severely as forgery, which, after all, is precisely what it would be.

Penalties for circulating unsigned literature should be uniform. A mild penalty, such as a $500 fine in a local campaign, $1,000 in a Congressional or statewide election, and $5,000 in a Presidential campaign, should attach to first offenses. Second and subsequent offenses should result in jail sentences *and* (not *or*) fines of increasing severity.

Civil libertarians sometimes argue that prohibiting anonymous literature is an abridgment of free speech. But Justice Holmes noted that freedom of speech does not convey a right to shout "fire!" in a crowded theater. When we consider unsigned literature in political campaigns, literature whose source and credibility are impossible to determine, we are dealing not with the lives of a few hundred moviegoers, but with the life of the Republic.

The American Civil Liberties Union has reviewed the question of anonymity in campaign material on several occasions. Each time it has concluded that the state may properly require identification of literature whose aim is to elect members of the government, although ACLU is hostile to any blanket banning of anonymity.

There is some Congressional sentiment for outlawing a new brand of anonymous political comment, that offered by the recorded voices of radical rightists over "dial-a-smear" phone numbers around the nation. The telephone companies, goaded by the Anti-Defamation League and the National Council of Churches, have begun to react and the Bell System companies have changed their tariffs to require that any local "station" carrying one of the familiar hate messages carry in the text of the message the name of the subscriber whose telephone is so used. If independent companies follow suit, as is likely, legislation would seem to be superfluous, for the basic problem is identification. However, one persuasive argument for legislation is that a law could penalize violators in terms more substantial than mere loss of telephone service.

Other inventions in this area will certainly require regulation when they come into general use. One such is a device which can automatically dial a number and play a recorded message, not relinquishing the line until the message is completed, even if the person called hangs up. Barring new abuses which demand legal remedy, it would seem prudent to wait until the precise requirements of legislation in this area become apparent, and then to deal with automatic telephoning in one comprehensive package.

The Mississippi election law contains an attractive supplement to the prohibition of anonymous literature. It is a requirement that any political document include the approval of the candidate for whose benefit it is circulated, or a statement saying that such approval was not obtained.

Stanley Kelley, Jr., corresponded with Mississippi political figures about this act, Section 3176, in preparation for his articulate and penetrating book, *Political Campaigning*.[5] Professor Kelley reported that Mississippi candidates did not find the law to be burdensome. Such a provision would benefit the electorate and the political system if it were applied to—and enforced in— every state.

The right of reply to political charges embodied in Section 315 of the Federal Communications Act has substantial merit, provided that it can be enforced without abusing the right itself. For instance, such candidates as New Jersey's pig farmer who has been a perennial pretender to Presidential candidacy should not qualify for time or space equal to a Republican or Democratic nominee.

The laws of Florida, Mississippi, and Nevada contain right-

[5] Washington: The Brookings Institution, 1960.

of-reply provisions with regard to printed election coverage, and of these the Nevada law, which stipulates equivalent space and position in an early edition of the publication concerned, is the best. In this way, insofar as it is possible, a damaging charge can be refuted in the same medium and to the same audience.

Florida law also contains a stipulation against last-minute attacks, a campaign ploy that causes vast confusion in every election year. Any charge that can stand examination, with rare exceptions, can be made early enough to give an opponent time to rebut it if he can. Florida prohibits any new charge in the last eighteen days before Election Day unless notice of the charge has been served on the candidate attacked.

Unfortunately, the Florida courts have interpreted the law to apply only to printed matter. This is half a loaf, to be sure, but it completely ignores the possibility of last-minute defamation over the broadcast media. More comprehensive legislation, properly drawn and enforced, can make roorbacks a thing of the past for all practical purposes.

Election laws should, where possible, make the punishment fit the crime. When a candidate himself violates the law against his opponent, the penalty should be fine or imprisonment for an unsuccessful candidate, with the alternative of voiding the election if the smear-artist wins. Minnesota makes such a provision in its law, and as recently as 1965 a legislative seat was vacated in an action growing out of such a case. The legislation limits the role of the court in such cases to the gathering of evidence, which then is turned over to the legislative house concerned for trial.

Finally, every election law ought to provide for any responsible citizen to initiate legal action against a violator of the election law in the event of non-feasance by the state's prosecutor or an excess of bonhomie on the part of a winner reluctant to press action against the loser. The weakest link in the entire chain of election laws is the impunity, even disdain, with which prosecutors ignore violations, and simply fail to prosecute.

The immediate responsibility for legislative action along these lines rests squarely on the politician in his role as lawmaker.

Congressmen and state legislators know full well the immorality and unrealism of the laws, but they are timid about correcting these glaring weaknesses. There are several reasons for this timidity. One that is important in relation to campaign finance laws is the self-serving howl many of the news media and "opinion leaders" set up at every suspicion of a proposed legislative pay or expense increase or anything, like subsidy, that smacks of giving money to the politician.

This reaction ignores the realities of campaign cost and seeks only to prevent increased expenditures rather than to find out how costs can be met, modified, or avoided. The root of such hostile demagoguery is not public-spirited concern about the rising costs of democracy. If it were, those publishers and broadcasters doing the howling would be applying imagination to public problems as diligently as they seek business economies through computers and automation. The root of the rancorous denunciation of "political spendthrifts" is rather the same contempt for politicians that underlies so much of the trouble in our political system.

Legislative improvements in the realm of campaign costs and practices also depend on the integrity of the politician as candidate, and on the political organization. The lawmaker who will not correct inadequacies in the law for fear he might some day trip over more stringent legislation in a campaign of his own deserves exposure rather than sympathy.

Similarly, the political party organization that postures righteously in the public gaze but keeps a smear artist or two on the payroll deserves exposure, and the only place it can come from is inside the organization. The procurement or diversion of funds for such projects as the 1965 Martin Luther King write-in attempt in all likelihood was accomplished with specific approval of some responsible person within the Republican National Committee. Continuing efforts by prominent Republicans to find whose skeleton is in that closet are evaded to this day. The GOP has no monopoly on this kind of political delinquency, but simply possesses the most offensive recent example of it.

Political parties in the United States are a wonderful improvisation which grew by trial and error, fertilized by the remains of attempted parties too parochial to survive. The westward growth of the United States changed the parties and the system. So did the development of the telegraph; and slavery, immigration, and war; and public education; and the telephone, radio, modern newspapers, motion pictures, and television. This evolution continues, and will correct many of the ills of the party system, in time.

As the parties evolved, so did the convention. Invented by a narrow party that quickly slid into oblivion, the convention was taken up by broader and more viable parties. The convention's length and timing are criticized today, and both will change in time. The 1964 conventions were unnecessarily long and boring; yet who could have spared an hour of maneuvering time at the Democratic convention of 1960?

Television is modifying the convention, but it should not dictate its shape. Who ever said that television should cover every minute of any convention? The medium in its early years was overcome with the idea that the best coverage was the most coverage. So television fastened its unwinking eye on conventions from beginning to end, uncritically capturing exhilarating debate and banal time-filling devices.

Now that television has gained the confidence of youthful maturity, and thanks to the real development of TV journalism as a different and useful variety of reportage, broadcasters are complaining that party conventions are too long and boring and costly to cover. What is called for is some adjustment to the realities of jet planes and television by the parties, and some discrimination in what to cover and what to ignore on the part of the broadcasters. Analogies between broadcasting and the press are tenuous at best, but a newspaper publisher who decided to print no other news and no ads so his paper could reprint every syllable of a national convention would be kidnapped by his staff and rushed off for mental tests.

Let the networks convert the prospect of truncated and selective convention coverage from threat to promise. The parties will benefit, and might even make bold to exclude reporters occasionally without apologizing. The locked door to the smoke-filled room has fallen from grace along with secret diplomacy, but both traditions had many useful attributes.

Campaign techniques change with the information media, and the tendency is to pursue a new development headlong so as to reach more people faster or more cheaply. It is many a year since politicians deliberately reflected on the efficacy and the ethics of political persuasion in an effort to place printing, broadcasting, and filming techniques in a philosophical *and* pragmatic frame.

The ever-present lag between technology and ethical considerations profoundly affects the prospects for election law reform. It is not enough for a problem to be foreseeable or visible: its dangers must be palpable before a remedy will be forthcoming. Thus when newspapers are giving way more and more to television as a political medium, anonymous literature laws are moving from the handbill era into the newspaper era and including advertisements among the messages that must be identified. Now that automatic telephone *calling* systems are perfected, automatic *answering* systems are coming under Congressional scrutiny.

Not yet under any scrutiny save that of an occasional scholar or advertising executive is the political application of the whole spectrum of motivational research, including advertising appeals to emotion, the exploitation of psychological predispositions to buy, and the use of television commercials to vend public officials. In general, political public relations consultants talk baldly of changing the candidate's image to increase his appeal, to win the voters his record frightens; only an occasional hair shirt type protests.

The news media themselves owe more careful treatment to politics and politicians. When mere recital of statistic-like facts will not convey the whole picture, the media should provide interpretive reporting, balancing their coverage, reporting in depth, ferreting out facts and substance. Readers and hearers should be guided to the essence of both sides of controversial issues. The press should declare a voluntary, cooperative moratorium on new charges in the closing three or four days of a campaign, as some papers do now. Exceptions should be limited to those rare, thoroughly documented cases where the public interest demands exposure.

Finally, it is the voter on whom the load of political responsibility falls most heavily. How can he resist being conned; avoid the trap of cynicism; seek, identify and evaluate real facts; stand against the pressure of special interests and spinners of chilling yarns of conspiracy and betrayal?

The American electorate is evolving, along with the parties. Once only male, Protestant Christian freeholders could vote, and only the literate minority among them played any larger part in politics. The restrictions withered away over the years, and the electorate continues to change rapidly with advances in Negro registration and the assault on pockets of illiteracy. Now a larger, more diverse, more literate electorate is confronted with more political information, through better and better reporting and analysis, and through seeing and hearing political events. This electorate needs to ponder the ethics of political persuasion along with the politicians who seek its consent.

The responsible citizen is plagued within his own ranks by those who refuse to participate in the American political system. The citizen who so values his "independence" that he will not enroll in a political party is really forfeiting independence, because he abandons a share in decision-making at the primary level: the choice of the candidate. The adult who knows better but is too lazy or fastidious to *do* better reinforces the cynicism of political hacks for the electorate at large, and seals their control where it exists. The high-minded and foolish citizen who stays home on Primary Day forfeits the field to the hack, and the smear artist, and the grafter, and the crook.

The voter who sees or hears a charge he doesn't know to be true or cannot prove should challenge a party worker on either side to prove or disprove it. The sensible voter will assume that any anonymous charge is false, and will refuse to credit or pass along more than he can see or prove.

Participation in the American political system makes self-government a reality. Abdication of that participation surrenders the government to others. The responsible citizen is jealous of his rights as a voter and as a partisan, and is angered at anybody's attempt to hamper or cripple the system. The voter who deceives himself about political realities by falling back on cynical mottoes like "politics is a dirty business" enables politics to become a dirty business.

Another internal threat to the voter is the polarizer, who sets himself and his party up as the embodiment of good, relegating the opposition—and its dupes—to the role of evil personified. Here is the radical rightist right alongside his counterpart from the left. Our man is the moral one; the other is the devil's agent.

It is natural enough that humans band into groups pursuing common interests. Segregationists naturally will coalesce with other segregationists to advance their conviction that the Negro is inferior and should be isolated from whites. Integrationists as naturally will unite to proclaim the iniquity of segregationist doctrine. The two groups naturally and inescapably are polarized against each other on ideological grounds. This is well enough. The mischief to the political system appears when either of these groups seeks to make over the political parties in its own image. Success in this endeavor would transform the basis of the American parties from consensus to ideology, creating precisely the kind of party structure that Washington and Jefferson feared and that the American political climate cannot support.

Ideological conflict in human affairs is as old as Cain and Abel, but the good-guy-bad-guy polarization is rarely as clear. Ideological attitudes and related facts do not come in neat packages, carefully wrapped, sealed and stamped "this side up." There is not always a *south* pole opposite every citizen's conception of *north*. One party or faction can polarize against another, or even against most of the society, without reciprocation. The anti-Mason Party arose outside of orthodox American politics because of the reaction of its members to the power of Masons in both major parties. No Masonic Party developed. The Know-Nothings polarized against unrestrained immigration, the foreign-born in general, and Catholics in particular; they took on the whole political spectrum. There was no anti-Know-Nothing party. The Dixiecrats polarized against integration, not against the whole fiber of the Democratic Party, whose elements included loyal Southerners just as cool to integration. The separate appearance in the same year, 1948, of the Communist-manipulated Progressive Party did not add up to a genuine polarization, either, although the two third-party efforts were mutually hostile.

The Communist Party is polarized against the whole of American life, singling out real abuses where they exist and imagining ones that do not exist. But the polarization is not reciprocated, for almost all reputable elements of the American society are working one way or another at the real abuses, and the national opposition to the encroachment of the Communists is self-defensive, rather than an across-the-board set of oppositions on each specific point. Communists are for education; so is the American consensus, as it is also for civil liberties for Communists. If the Communists did not threaten to pervert and destroy the American society, Americans generally would not object to them, any more than Americans object to calendar reformers or Biblical literalists or vegetarians.

Today's radical right is polarized against the Communists. But the problem is that the radical right reads everyone outside its own bounds as a Communist or a Communist stooge or dupe. The society at large is not polarizing *itself* against the right extremists; it is merely trying to elbow aside their excesses while remaining alert to such relevant facts as may stand out in the right extremist chorus of weird maladies and weird remedies.

Myriad reasons are advanced to explain why ideologically-based political parties fail in the United States. The simplest explanation is the same reason that coral does not thrive in fresh water: the environment is just not right.

The consensus party endures on American soil because it is the *party* which does the hammering out of issues and positions on issues, in purely party, and Congressional, and convention debate. The party comes to represent a broad section of the nation.

What emerges from the deliberations and in-fighting within a consensus party is some degree of *national* consensus. Lyndon Johnson in 1964 represented such a consensus and the fact that his landslide was so overwhelming simply underlines the fact that Barry Goldwater only represented one faction in what had been a Republican Party consensus. John Kennedy and Richard Nixon both reflected consensus party politics and the result in 1960 was a horse race, the closest since 1888.

Europeans find it difficult to understand the ease of transition from one American party administration to another. Russians find it impossible, for the American conception of consensus party politics cannot be translated into the Russian political experience. So the Russians settle for unbelief instead of understanding, and after the fashion of any conspiracy theorist, turn to their own propaganda for an answer that will fit: there is no real difference between parties—both are the tools of Wall Street imperialists.

Although conspiracy theorists, left or right, do not realize it, there is only one thing more deceptive than insisting on being told only what you want to hear: that is telling *yourself* only what you want to hear. It remained for Robert Welch of the John Birch Society to name the key to the mental gyrations of the left and right extremists: *the theory of reversal.* If what you hear doesn't fit your *weltanschauung*, apply the theory of reversal. Turn what you hear upside down and everything will come out all right. Thus Welch interprets as a lie every Communist statement that would threaten his rationale if it were true, remaining free to accept Communist assertions that appear to support his theory. The Communists use the same technique. Red Propaganda described the Kennedy-Nixon choice as that between the gold dust twins of Wall Street warmongers; both of the American parties are Wall Street fronts. And with Johnson-Goldwater? Ah, the real fascists have taken over the Republican party, while the less dangerous, run-of-the-mill Wall Street imperialists are running Johnson. If it doesn't fit right-side-up, by all means turn it up-side-down. *Then* it will fit.

The topsy-turvy logic of the extremists can and does confuse and mislead concerned citizens. The Communist pretense to be truly liberal is an historic example, and the radical right's masquerade under the banner of conservatism is a new one. One result of these two incursions has been to downgrade the terms *liberal* and *conservative* to the point where they are, to a large degree, semantically worthless. Another has been the creation and the baiting of whipping boys. In time it becomes traditional for liberals to believe that Americans for Constitutional Action is merely a front for the John Birch Society, and it becomes similarly part of the conservative formula that Americans for Democratic Action has a program of "laundered communism." So the extremists, who cannot comprehend what really goes on in American politics, who neither understand the system nor trust it, manage to infect the real liberals and the real conservatives with some of their blindness, mistrust and incomprehension.

The United States of America needs a moral tightening in its political system. These thoughts have been a suggestion for action. Not all of the legal remedies possible will be adopted, and their adoption would only restrain but not eliminate abuses. Careful, thoughtful, critical listening to political argument, and citizen anger directed through the ballot box can ultimately have more effect than legislation.

One basic accomplishment that *is* possible is most badly needed. That is a will to cease imputing evil to one's fellow-men and saintliness to oneself. If the conservative and the liberal will agree with the moderate that today's world is better than the destruction of today's world, they can find the key to political survival. The conservative, liberal, and moderate branches of the political family are brothers. They are free to fight among themselves, and they do and always will, but they must not let interlopers from outside the family tear one of them apart.

Probably the greatest responsibility for improvement is the long-range one of the educator. America's youth need to be taught to read and listen critically, to understand and develop values, and to make competent judgments. The society needs responsible citizens, not moral and political eunuchs.

The American political system is under threat from the Communist world and from the radical right. The system can withstand nuclear threats, and spies, and traitors, and agitators of every persuasion, but there is one threat from within it cannot withstand nearly as long: cynicism and apathy. The gravest enemies of the American people are in their own ranks. These are the citizens who sow suspicion; the citizens who absorb it uncritically; and the citizens—celebrated in the first ten chapters—who offer to both breeds of cynics support for their simple, false solutions.

Appendixes

Code of Fair Campaign Practices

There are basic principles of decency, honesty and fair play which every candidate for public office in the United States has a moral obligation to observe and uphold, in order that, after vigorously contested but fairly conducted campaigns, our citizens may exercise their constitutional right to a free and untrammeled choice and the will of the people may be fully and clearly expressed on the issues before the Country.

THEREFORE:

I SHALL CONDUCT my campaign in the best American tradition, discussing the issues as I see them, presenting my record and policies with sincerity and frankness, and criticizing without fear or favor the record and policies of my opponent and his party which merit such criticism.

I SHALL DEFEND AND UPHOLD the right of every qualified American voter to full and equal participation in the electoral process.

I SHALL CONDEMN the use of personal vilification, character defamation, whispering campaigns, libel, slander, or scurrilous attacks on any candidate or his personal or family life.

I SHALL CONDEMN the use of campaign material of any sort which misrepresents, distorts, or otherwise falsifies the facts regarding any candidate, as well as the use of malicious or unfounded accusations against any candidate which aim at creating or exploiting doubts, without justification, as to his loyalty and patriotism.

I SHALL CONDEMN any appeal to prejudice based on race, creed, or national origin.

I SHALL CONDEMN any dishonest or unethical practice which tends to corrupt or undermine our American system of free elections or which hampers or prevents the full and free expression of the will of the voters.

I SHALL IMMEDIATELY AND PUBLICLY REPUDIATE support deriving from any individual or group which resorts, on behalf of my candidacy or in opposition to that of my opponent, to the methods and tactics which I condemn.

I, the undersigned, candidate for election to public office in the United States of America, hereby endorse, subscribe to, and solemnly pledge myself to conduct my campaigns in accordance with the above principles and practices, so help me God.

Date _____   Signature _____

special report on Religion in the 1960 Campaign

The Fair Campaign Practices Committee has been deeply concerned for more than a year with the dangers involved in the injection of religious issues into the 1960 campaign. With the cooperation and co-sponsorship of the National Conference of Christians and Jews it recently brought together a distinguished group of religious leaders of all faiths for a two day discussion on a full, frank and friendly basis.

On the basis of this discussion the Committee feels that it can lay down some simple principles which we hope will commend themselves to American voters.

1. It is proper and desirable that every public official should attempt to govern his conduct by a personal conscience informed by his religious faith.

2. No candidate for public office should be opposed or supported because of his particular religious affiliation. A campaign for a public office is not an opportunity to vote for one religion against another.

3. A candidate should be judged by his qualifications for the office he seeks, and by his position on issues relevant to that office. He may properly be questioned about such issues and about the bearing of his religious faith and conscience on them. A candidate's religion is relevant to a voter's decision, but only so far as it bears on such relevant political issues.

4. Stirring up, fostering, or tolerating religious animosity, or injecting elements of a candidate's faith not relevant to the duties of the office he seeks are unfair campaign practices.

5. Intelligent, honest, and temperate public discussion of the relation of religious faith to the public issues will, as it has already done, raise the whole level of the campaign.

Participants in the Washington conference were:

Rabbi Bernard Bamberger, Congregation Shaaray Tefila, New York and President, Central Conference of American Rabbis.

Rev. Dr. C. Emanuel Carlson, Executive Director, Baptist Joint Committee on Public Affairs, Washington, and a director of Protestants and Other Americans United for the Separation of Church and State (POAU).

Dr. William Clancy, Catholic layman, Education Director of the Church Peace Union.

Dr. Carl F. H. Henry, Editor, Christianity Today.

Msgr. George Higgins, Director, Department of Social Action, National Catholic Welfare Conference.

Rev. Dr. Winthrop S. Hudson, Professor of Church History, Colgate Rochester Divinity School.

Dr. Lewis Webster Jones, President, National Conference of Christians and Jews.

Msgr. Francis J. Lally, Editor, the Pilot, Boston.

Rabbi Uri Miller, Temple Beth Jacob, Baltimore, and vice president, Synagogue Council of America.

Rev. Dr. A. T. Mollegen, Professor of Christian Ethics at Protestant-Episcopal Theological Seminary in Virginia.

Dr. C. Arild Olsen, Executive Secretary, Department of Christian Life and Work, National Council of Churches.

Rev. George Papadeas, Pastor, St. Paul's Greek Orthodox Church, Hempstead, New York, representing Archbishop Iacovos.

Rev. Gustave Weigel, S.J., Professor of Ecclesiology, Woodstock College, Maryland.

Mr. Taft served as moderator for the discussions.

JOHNSON - HUMPHREY KENNEDY CAMPAIGN COMMITTEE

9 East 42nd Street
New York, New York

FOR RELEASE
P.M.'s Friday
October 23, 1964

Press Contact:
Debs Myers, 421–7720

Robert F. Kennedy said today (Fri.) that his Republican opponent did not state his support of the Nuclear Test Ban Treaty during the debate on the floor of the the U.S. Senate until the day before the Senate vote began and then gave it only "grudging and cautious" endorsement.

Mr. Kennedy, the Democratic candidate for U.S. Senator, said Senator Keating in a speech on the Senate floor on Friday, September 20, remarked that the treaty "has heightened tension" and "may well create unforeseen difficulties" before giving the treaty his grudging support.

Mr. Kennedy's comments were made in response to a complaint made by Senator Keating to the Fair Campaign Practices Committee, Inc.

"It is ironic that Senator Keating should go running to the Fair Campaign Practices Committee to complain about documented recitation of the facts about his record in light of the false charges he has made about me concerning a 'deal' with Nazis, being anti-Italian, running out on the civil rights program, and the advertisement in Jewish newspapers saying President Nasser of Egypt is supporting my candidacy.

"The Congressional Record shows that from the time the Senate debate on the Test Ban Treaty began on September 9, 1963, until the day before the voting began, Senator Keating preferred to be an interested observer. He asked questions and made a few comments but did not rise to address himself directly to the issue and announce his final position until Friday, September 20, 1963. There was no Saturday session and the Senate vote began on Monday.

"In a matter as important to all of us, to our children, and to our children's children, the junior Senator from New York should have been in the forefront of the struggle instead of on the sidelines.

"The Congressional Record shows the ridicule to which Senator Keating held the Treaty, even suggesting it might be a 'trump card' for the Communist world, before he finally gave some grudging and cautious approval.

"The Congressional Record of September 20, 1963, shows on page 17620 * that Senator Keating's position was stated in part as follows:

" '. . . considering all areas of the world, the treaty will probably not, at least in the short run, reduce existing political tensions. Let me be very specific on this point. I believe there is already some evidence that in Europe the treaty has heightened tension . . . In Asia the treaty has undoubtedly heightened Soviet prestige at the expense of Red China . . . In other parts of the world, such as Africa and Latin America, the test ban treaty gives the Soviets the opportunity to pose as worldwide peacemaker. The treaty of Moscow can be a trump card if local Communist groups play it right. In short, all over the world the test ban treaty may well create unforeseen difficulties for the United States and make a lot of trouble for our policymakers . . .'

"The record is equally clear on Senator Keating's record of opposition to aid to education, despite his air of hurt and feigned sense of outrage and wounded pride.

"The phrase 'Federal Aid to Education' has common usage and only one meaning in Washington: it means *general* federal aid to education. Such a bill was before Congress starting in 1946—and the fact is that Senator Keating opposed this bill repeatedly—in 1957, 1960, and again in 1961.

"He refers to several specialized bills which he supported but avoids noting that these smaller bills were introduced specifically because the major bills—which he opposed—did not achieve passage. The overall federal aid bills which Senator Keating opposed provided for at least $1.5 billion on every occasion. The 1961 bill, for example, would have meant $120 million for New York State.

"Senator Keating concedes he voted in 1963 to cut $600 million from the Aid to Higher Education Bill. Senator Keating's attitude was reflected in his characterization of federal aid to education as '. . . simply a handout of federal funds . . .' (July 26, 1957) He also said 'New Yorkers can take care of education in New York.' (May 25, 1961) As might have been anticipated, Senator Javits and Senator Keating were on opposite sides of these votes in the Senate."

* Some confusion arose over page numbers, since the *Record* in permanent binding is numbered differently from the copies distributed daily. Kennedy and I used different bindings although the texts were identical. This page in Kennedy's material was page 16715 in mine.

APPENDIX IV

Kennedy campaign workers were bitter over Keating flyers that quoted Egyptian President Gamel Abdel Nasser as saying, "Ken Keating and his ilk must disappear from the American scene."

The Action Committee on American-Arab Relations picketed Keating and issued three flyers, the first attacking both Senate candidates, the second urging a vote against Keating, and the last finally endorsing Kennedy.

Kennedy staff people maintained that the Action Committee was a Keating front. Meanwhile, the executive secretary of the Action Committee, Dr. Mohammed T. Mehdi, came to my office with a complaint against Senator Keating because of the Nasser quote on his flyers. Keating had said that Nasser was working against him, Dr. Mehdi protested. Mehdi said it was the American Arabs, through the Action Committee, who were assailing Keating's "extremist pro-Israeli position." Nasser had nothing to do with the affair, Mehdi insisted, and Keating should prove his assertions or apologize to the 50,000 to 75,000 members and friends of the Action Committee.

APPENDIX V

From the Congressional Record—Senate

Sept. 20, 1963, pp. 17619–21

(Passages extracted by Senator Kennedy appear in
bold face. Salient passages which Senator Kennedy
failed to quote appear in *italic*.)

Mr. KEATING. Mr. President, preparatory to making a statement of *my reasons for supporting the partial nuclear test ban treaty*, it might be of interest to have a brief rundown of the trend of mail on this subject. It is a matter of some surprise to me that before the treaty was negotiated, my mail ran 10 to 1 in favor of it. Since then, the evidence of support has dropped gradually until opinion became evenly divided about the first of September. And since that time, my mail has reflected a slight edge for the opposition. Cumulatively, it amounts to over 10,000 letters, and is a little over 3 to 1 pro.

I mention this point not because I or any other Senator, I am sure, feels that it is his responsibility to vote on all issues exactly in accordance with percentage breakdowns of mail from his constituents, but rather to point out how difficult, not to say how completely impos-

sible, it would be for any Senator to be guided entirely by the response of his constituents.

Most of the mail I have received in opposition to the treaty makes the point, which, in other circumstances, is a very valid one, that the Russians have broken 50 out of 53 treaties, so why should we trust them now.

Others write—and I quote a typical letter:

Wasn't the stumbling block to a test ban treaty our insistence on onsite inspection? True, each year we were ready to accept fewer inspections, but we did insist on some. Now we are offered a no-inspection treaty and we are supposed to be thrilled with it.

That is a fair question, but the answer to it lies in the treaty itself and in the tremendous advances in the technology of test detection. The treaty only bans atmospheric testing and every single expert that

I am aware of has indicated his belief that no significant nuclear tests can take place in the atmosphere without detection by the United States. If underground testing were included, that would be a valid objection and the whole treaty would be something very different indeed. But as of now, I am convinced by the expert testimony that we can inspect and monitor this ban very effectively with the equipment and techniques that we now operate from the United States and overseas, as opposed to a ban on underground testing which would require onsite inspection.

It is perfectly true that the Soviets cannot be trusted to abide by treaties that we are not able to enforce ourselves. That we have learned to our sorrow, not only from Yalta and agreements on access to West Berlin, but most recently from the agreement last year to neutralize Laos. But we do not have to trust them in this treaty because the Russians simply cannot conduct any kind of testing under the treaty that will make a serious difference in weapons development without our being immediately aware of it.

So I feel that the question of trust is altogether beside the point. If the question of trust were the point involved, I would have quite different views about this treaty.

Another point made in my mail which I believe also deserves to be explicitly dealt with is the possibility of Soviet use of Red Chinese territory in testing. The so-called Kremlinologists tell us this is impossible—and at the moment I entirely agree. They say that one of the reasons the Soviets signed the treaty was to embarrass the Red Chinese, and that reconciliation is impossible.

That point of view looks reasonable today, but then, who would have thought that Tito and Khrushchev would ever be embracing one another the way they did not long ago? The fact is that times change, policies change, and peoples, especially national leaders, change. In Communist countries a change in leadership can mean a totally new orientation. But there can be no question under the express terms of this treaty that if the Soviets should patch up their differences and start testing on Red Chinese soil or if, indeed, the Red Chinese should start testing in the air, then this would be considered as one of the extraordinary developments justifying U.S. abrogation of the treaty.

Some of the other arguments made against the treaty seem to me considerably less weighty. One opponent writes:

Being in favor of that nuclear treaty is another step in the wrong direction. I for one much prefer nuclear war at once.

Another writes:

If you vote for this treaty, we'll never vote for you again, not even if you run for dogcatcher.

Well, let me make it perfectly clear that I have no plans to run for dog-catcher. It is an honorable office, but it is not my present intention to be a candidate for dogcatcher. It is not my intention to run for any office on a "nuclear war now policy." Anyone who wants nuclear war now or any other time, had better vote for someone else for Senator or dogcatcher.

The great bulk of the mail I

have received opposing or favoring the treaty, I am sure represents the reasoned and sincerely held convictions of the writers. Although I certainly do not agree with all of the arguments of treaty supporters, I entirely reject the explanation one correspondent sent me. She wrote:

I'm sure you realize the people who are against it are a little lazy and don't all get to write to you. The people who are for it are encouraged by the Communist fronts and are pushed into writing to you.

This effort to equate support of the treaty with Communist sympathy is the last resort of those who have run out of valid arguments.

Out of all the thousands of letters I received, however, there is one that really puzzles me. It is from a civil defense official who warns:

The microscopic amount of fallout from an airburst bomb would cause several orders of magnitude less possible birth defects than the custom of men wearing underwear and trousers which keep the temperature of the body higher than nature intended.

That makes it sound as if the most constructive thing any of us could do is take off our clothes and stay on the beach.

So much for the mail. *I am supporting the test ban treaty because in my own considered judgment it is a useful measure and in the interest of the United States.* In sum, what the treaty provides is basically that the United States and the Soviet Union do not intend to undertake any further nuclear tests in the atmosphere, in outer space, or under water, unless something should occur to cause either power

to change its mind. It is not a binding, ironclad commitment, since the withdrawal clause in the treaty would make it possible for any signatory to withdraw should extraordinary events jeopardize the supreme interests of the country. In something of an understatement, the Senate Foreign Relations Committee report terms this "a remarkably flexible provision." That, it undoubtedly is.

Moreover, even though this treaty has been widely hailed as a "first step," there is considerable variation of opinion as to what it is a first step toward. The preamble asserts the principal aim of the United States, Great Britain, and the Soviet Union as being "the speediest possible achievement of an agreement on general and complete disarmament under strict international control in accordance with the objectives of the United Nations."

Even though I recognize that this catch phrase has been adapted part and parcel from Soviet propaganda and in effect means virtually nothing, I think it is unfortunate—I concede this—that it should have a place in a serious treaty of this type. The fact of the matter is that if the United States, Britain, and the Soviet Union actually wished to achieve such an agreement, it could have been achieved 10 years ago.

It is, I very much fear, this kind of language which has found its way into this treaty as well as other government publications, that does have the effect of alarming many people and filling the coffers and ranks of some of the organized groups who oppose this treaty. The virtue of the treaty is that it is realistically limited to what can be accomplished today that is within the realm of the shared interests of the United States, the Soviet Union, and Great Britain. It is not only the John Birch Societies that become incensed when the treaty is depicted as the first step in general disarmament, but also a lot of quite serious and responsible and conscientious Americans who would oppose general and complete disarmament. In fact, I have not yet met any responsible person anywhere who believes such a course is possible. This language in the treaty, therefore, only encourages the opponents and confuses the basic issues that are involved.

Besides not being a step toward general and complete disarmament, there are a lot of other things both desirable and not desirable that the treaty does not do. For instance, over the long run, considering all areas of the world, the treaty will probably not, at least in the short run, reduce existing political tensions.

Let me be very specific on this point. I believe there is already some evidence that in Europe the treaty has heightened tension. Combined, as it has been in many people's minds, with the possibility of a nonaggression pact or some agreement on the status of Berlin, it has aroused very deep fears not only in Germany, but also in France and Britain, of some kind of a private United States-Soviet deal. Should we accept in any kind of juridical document the status quo of the satellite countries of Europe, we would be greatly strengthening the hand of the Soviet Union in its international relations, and we

would be weakening NATO. The more these questions are discussed, the more such matters as access to Berlin, inspection of key transportation junctions, are discussed, the more nervously will we be viewed by our European allies, the more will we be strengthening the hand of General De Gaulle in his efforts to dominate the European continent. In short, although this treaty itself has been welcomed everywhere except in France, it clearly puts the United States on its mettle.

In Asia the treaty has undoubtedly heightened Soviet prestige at the expense of Red China. But it would be most unrealistic to expect the Chinese to take this lying down. The Chinese are now engaged in an ideological dispute with the Russians as well as long-term hostilities with the United States. They may well feel that the best way to strengthen their hand is to stop talking and to start acting perhaps by renewing their warfare against India or seeking to move directly into southeast Asia. In any case the treaty is a challenge which I would not expect them to take lightly. Certainly the last 2 months has heightened tension throughout Asia from Pakistan to South Korea, and there is well justified fear that the end of the monsoon season will mark the beginning of the military season for Peiping.

In other parts of the world, such as Africa and Latin America, the test ban treaty gives the Soviets the opportunity to pose as worldwide peacemaker. The treaty of Moscow can be a trump card if local Communist groups play it right.

In short, all over the world the

test ban treaty may well create unforeseen difficulties for the United States and make a lot of trouble for our policymakers.

In discussing this matter and in expressing my support for the treaty, I think we would be unrealistic not to recognize the difficulties that are posed by the signing of the treaty and its ratification.

Let me make it perfectly clear, however, that I do not think rejection of the treaty would eliminate these tensions, but only urge, in referring to these matters, that we see the situation as it is and be prepared for the next set of challenges.

What is more, if the pledges solemnly given by the President and Secretary of Defense to maintain U.S. readiness are to be redeemed, the treaty will require stepped up expenditures on surveillance techniques and devices for measuring nuclear radiation. It will put our military and intelligence people in the position of having to study and evaluate even more carefully the even less readily accessible results of underground Soviet testing. The pressure will not be off, it will merely be turned in a different direction; and I think it is very important that all of us recognize that the pressure will not be off.

In the development of antimissile missiles, the test ban will probably offer some disadvantages, but undoubtedly in the years to come, the problems of missile defense will increase in geometric progression to the advances in the art of missilery itself. There is no ultimate weapon and we may find it is a better defense to make our missiles superior to Soviet defense, than to try to perfect a missile defense. In short, instead of an antimissile missile, what we may really want in the long run is an antiantimissile missile. There is no evidence that the lack of further atmospheric testing will significantly hamper that development at all.

As to large 50- to 100-megaton weapons, our Government has already made the decision not to proceed with further development of these weapons. If that decision was wrong, we may suffer, but the fault will not be the test ban, but rather the conclusion reached before the ban was even considered.

In short, we must see the treaty for what it is, a very limited agreement. It has two important advantages that outweigh the, to my mind, hypothetical and never successfully proved disadvantages. These are, first, the end to radioactive fallout. Although this menace may indeed be exaggerated, there seems little doubt that increased radioactivity in the atmosphere could eventually have a serious effect. No one can be certain that additional cancers or birth deformities have not resulted from higher levels of fallout. The fact of the matter is that as long as we do not know precisely what causes a birth deformity or what makes a cancer grow, it is the better part of wisdom to end the contamination of the air that has, by statistical study, at least, contributed to them.

Recent studies have very clearly pinpointed the increased incidence of childhood cancer in cases of prebirth X-rays. Although we do not know nearly as much as we would like to about birth deformities, and in fact about the many and subtle ways in which radiation can affect living and future generations, the fact remains that no one has been able to show any benefits from a general increase in radiation levels, and medical studies are indicating, with increasing impact, the possible dangers.

So I look upon this as the first basis for support of the treaty.

Secondly, the treaty is important in hampering—though not, of course, fully preventing the proliferation of nuclear weapons—atmospheric testing on the part of other nations. Although this treaty clearly does not prevent other nations from proceeding if they are ready to undertake underground tests, the inconvenience and expense may well apply a brake—a brake which would be in the interest of the Soviet Union as well as the United States. In short, the treaty represents a limited effort to reduce what has been one of the most conspicuous, if perhaps not actually one of the most serious, threats to world peace in the post-war decade. It is a limited vehicle to achieve a limited, but certainly desirable, result.

For that reason, I believe it would be a very serious mistake to attach to the treaty any of the reservations or understandings that have been proposed to date. There is nothing I personally would welcome more, and nothing I feel would be more in the national interest at this time, than the withdrawal by their sponsors of each and every one of these reservations or understandings.

One of the understandings, for instance, provides that U.S. participation in the treaty does not involve any degree of recognition of the East German Government.

What about North Korea and North Vietnam, if they should ever desire to accede? What about Outer Mongolia, which we do not recognize but which has acceded? Should they not also be specifically mentioned? To raise this issue formally as an understanding to the treaty adds nothing substantive to our determinations on East Germany, but it might well confuse the situation with regard to other countries. And a vote of rejection of such an understanding would cloud the East German issue.

Another understanding, with regard to U.S. right of withdrawal immediately in the event of Soviet violation, has been thoroughly clarified by the Secretary of State. We would abrogate the treaty, we have made it clear, if the Soviets cheat.

Another understanding with regard to peaceful nuclear explosions brings a wholly new element into the actual treaty, and in my view could open a loophole for Soviet and other testing that we might later regret. In any case, in my judgment, it deserves a lot more study and attention before being incorporated in this document.

The issue of use of nuclear weapons in the case of armed hostilities has similarly been clarified beyond doubt.

Also, the desire to insure that any and all amendments to this treaty be submitted to the Senate is important and worthwhile. Such a requirement is basic constitutional law. The President and Secretary of State have already assured the Senate they would comply with such a requirement. If the Senate voted to add specific language to this treaty to that end, it might seriously imply that amendments could be made to other treaties, in which such language does not appear, without the advice and consent of the Senate. If the Senate voted not to add specific language, it would leave the issue as regards this particular treaty, up in the air. It is my hope, therefore, that the assurances of the President will be accepted and no effort made to complicate the situation by such an amendment of the resolution of ratification.

Every one of these points has been answered satisfactorily time and again by the President, the Secretary of State, and the Secretary of Defense. To include them in the treaty would add nothing but confusion and ill feeling for other signatories. To vote not to include them might leave these very questions up in the air. It seems to me it would be very unwise for the Senate to be put in the position of having to vote on any of these points, which to my mind are perfectly clear now and would only be confused by a Senate vote.

Another reservation recently introduced would require that the treaty not come into effect until all the delinquent Soviet assessments to the United Nations are paid. Nothing, it seems to me could be more extraneous to the subject matter of the treaty, and in fact, no more germane than would be a reservation postponing the effective date of the treaty until the United States balances its budget. Needless to say, I favor a balanced budget for the United States, and for the United Nations, and I favor all nations paying their debts and obligations, but I do not see what that really has to do with a limited test ban agreement.

Certainly we are right to be concerned about Soviet delinquency in the United Nations and to do everything we appropriately can to encourage them to pay up. Soviet actions in this session of the United Nations, including the question of paying their share, will be a good test of how much the Soviets really mean in their new peace offensive. It will be a good indication of what we can expect in the future, but it is no test at all of the validity of a ban on atmospheric nuclear explosions. It would be extremely unfortunate if the Senate were to meander down this byway and lose sight of what we are really here to ratify and secure.

Finally, with respect to the reservation that Soviet military personnel be required to leave Cuba before the treaty comes into effect, I doubt there is any Member of Congress that has for so long expressed greater concern than I have over the Cuban situation. If I thought such a reservation would encourage the Soviets to withdraw from Cuba, I would back it, but I am not such an optimist as to believe that this is a constructive move toward getting the Russians out of the Caribbean.

They are going to leave Cuba, and other points only when we make things so tough for them, by economic and political and other pressures that it does not pay them to remain there any longer. We are not going to talk them out of Cuba —any more than we talked them out by passing a tough resolution last September, a resolution to which the Soviets paid no attention and which the executive branch has largely ignored.

It is surprising to me that anyone in this country expects mere negotiations to get the Russians out of Cuba. It is even more surprising that those who advocate this course —at least among my constituents— are the same people who warn that we cannot trust the Russians in any treaty. If that is so, I do not see any value whatsoever in bringing in additional complication into the treaty which we would not expect the Russians to abide by and in which it would be a lot harder to discover and confirm cheating than in some purely scientific area such as nuclear fallout.

In my view, it would be a most serious mistake for the Senate to accept any of the unnecessary or ex-traneous proposals that have been offered as additions to the resolution of ratification.

With the clear understanding then that this treaty is a limited commitment, that it does not even bind the United States to further negotiations of any sort on any issue that we would not otherwise wish to discuss, and that it is interpreted by the United States in accordance with the points that are made in the report of the Senate Foreign Relations Committee, I support the treaty. What the treaty provides is in our interest and that of the whole free world. What it does not provide, both good or bad, should not be the object of present decisions, and should not be brought into the discussion to mislead or alarm our citizens.

APPENDIX VI

October 26, 1964

Hon. Robert F. Kennedy
Chatham Hotel
33 East 44th Street
New York, New York

Dear Mr. Kennedy:

I have your letter of October 2, for which thanks, which arrived by messenger on the morning of the 23rd simultaneously with Senator Keating's complaint. I gather you obtained the text of his complaint from the press, obviating the need for us to advise you of it formally.

We are interested in further documentation on the score of education. Specifically, could you tell us to which roll call your item 14 on page 4 of your release refers? Also, the description of this vote as involving a cut of $600 million from the bill has been contested. Would you please explain that characterization in detail? (We have been trying to get this information by phone from your headquarters.)

As to the Nuclear Test Ban Treaty, I say with deep regret that I read your statement with dismay. Mr. Keating has provided documentation for his complaint, enumerated in the enclosed copy of his letter to us, which demonstrates conclusively that your description of his position on the Test Ban Treaty is not only false and distorted, but also appears to be either a deliberate and cynical misrepresentation or the result of incredible carelessness, touched with luck.

As early as May 27, 1963, Mr. Keating strongly supported S. Res. 148 (on the day that it was referred to the Committee on Foreign Relations) expressing the sense of the Senate in favor of such a treaty (Congressional Record, page 8953). On September 5 (p. 15547), and September 9 (pp. 15680–2), and September 12 (p. 16017), and September 20 (pp. 16713–15) he spoke for the treaty in terms that flatly contradict your assertion that he "preferred to be an interested observer."

Whoever prepared for you the quotations purporting to state Senator Keating's position, "in part," as you say, had to pore through 240 lines of the Senator's Congressional Record speech of September 20, 1964, beginning at page 16713, before finding the first of three isolated passages which you lump together to describe his attitude.

The speech began with Keating reiterating his constant support for the treaty and his intention to vote for it. He observed that his mail was turning against the treaty, but that he still intended to vote for it. Then he proceeded to analyze the mail he had been getting, in spite of which he continued to support the treaty. It is from this anaylsis * that your totally misleading quotation comes.

I trust you will be able to correct the grievous flaw in your research operation that this dishonest and unfair distortion reveals.

With personal regards and deep regret at the necessity for this letter, I am

Sincerely,

BRUCE L. FELKNOR
Executive Director

BLF:h

* This was an error. Actually, Keating had finished discussing the mail and was proceeding to review other arguments against the treaty that he found "hypothetical and never successfully proved."

WESTERN UNION TELEGRAM

1:05 A.M., EST
October 27, 1964

THE HONORABLE ROBERT F. KENNEDY
ROOM 820
CHATHAM HOTEL
33 EAST 48TH STREET, NYK

WE REGRET AND APOLOGIZE FOR THE FACT THAT A COPY OF OUR PRELIMINARY CONFIDENTIAL LETTER TO YOU WAS OBTAINED AND COPIED SURREPTITIOUSLY * BY A NEWSPAPER AND PUBLISHED WITHOUT AUTHORIZATION AND OVER OUR MOST VEHEMENT PROTEST. IT WAS NOT A FINAL OR OFFICIAL JUDGMENT OF THE COMMITTEE. THIS OCCURRED THROUGH AN ERROR IN OUR PROCEDURES WHICH WE ARE REVIEWING TO ENSURE THAT IT CANNOT HAPPEN AGAIN. THIS COMMITTEE DOES NOT, NEVER HAS AND IS NOT PERMITTED TO ISSUE PUBLIC JUDGMENTS ON CANDIDATES OR CAMPAIGN TACTICS. ANY ATTRIBUTION OF SUCH JUDGMENTS TO THE COMMITTEE IS FALSE. THE LETTER REPRESENTED A PRELIMINARY OPINION AND WAS CONVEYED TO YOU FOR YOUR CONSIDERATION AND REVIEW IN STRICTEST CONFIDENCE. NATURALLY WE WILL REVIEW ALL NEW EVIDENCE SUBMITTED.

CHARLES P. TAFT, CHAIRMAN
BRUCE L. FELKNOR, EXECUTIVE DIRECTOR
FAIR CAMPAIGN PRACTICES COMMITTEE

* In retrospect, "surreptitiously" was revealed as too strong a characterization.

APPENDIX VIII

The following is the text of a statement issued late in the
afternoon of October 27, 1964, over the signatures
of Bruce L. Felknor and Charles P. Taft.

A charge of violation of our Code was made last week by Senator
Keating. Mr. Kennedy's reply was received by us almost simultaneously, based on newspaper accounts of Senator Keating's charges. We
reviewed these at once.

Our regular procedure is to insure that all the facts about such
charges are presented to the public, which, in the end, must judge
whether there has been a violation of the code or not. We are not
permitted to render judgments on such charges. In this process we
frequently communicate directly with both candidates in order to
eliminate and correct misinterpretations intentional or otherwise. In
this case our letter to Mr. Kennedy was such a communication, intended to be confidential, but unintentionally leaked to the press at
our end. It is not our function to render judgments.

The letter should not have been written and any accusations
in it were necessarily unfair to Mr. Kennedy at that stage. We hereby
withdraw it in full.

Additional material has been received from Mr. Kennedy which
raises quite different questions of fact.* We expect both candidates
to discuss this issue on the basis of facts they find and publish, with
such assistance as we can render, but the preliminary judgments in
our letter now withdrawn are not a proper basis for discussion and the
letter should not have been used.

* The new material was stated by Kennedy's aides to raise different
questions of fact. Actually, as noted on page 196, it did not.

BIBLIOGRAPHY

American Protestantism and Social Issues 1919–1939, Robert Moats Miller. Chapel Hill: The University of North Carolina Press, 1958.

A Catholic Runs for President—the Campaign of 1928, Edmund A. Moore. New York: The Roland Press, 1956.

A Choice Not an Echo, Phyllis Schlafly. Alton, Illinois: Pere Marquette Press, 1964.

The Costs of Democracy, Alexander Heard. Chapel Hill: University of North Carolina Press, 1960.

Danger on the Right, Arnold Forster and Benjamin Epstein. New York: Random House, 1964.

None Dare Call it Treason, John Stormer. Florissant, Missouri: Liberty Bell Press, 1964.

Ordeal of the Presidency, David Cushman Coyle. Washington, D.C.: Public Affairs Press, 1960.

Political Campaigning: Problems in Creating an Informed Electorate, Stanley Kelley, Jr. Washington, D.C.: The Brookings Institution, 1960.

Professional Public Relations and Political Power, Stanley Kelley, Jr. Baltimore: Johns Hopkins, 1956.

The Radical Right, Daniel Bell (ed.). New York: Doubleday, 1963.

Religious Liberty and the Presidency, Patricia Barrett. New York: Herder and Herder, 1963.

Richard Nixon, Earl Mazo. New York: Harper, 1959.

The Strange Tactics of Extremism, Harry and Bonaro Overstreet. New York: Norton, 1964.

A Texan Looks at Lyndon, J. Evetts Haley. Canyon, Texas: Palo Duro Press, 1964.

Shorter Publications

The Blue Book, the John Birch Society, Belmont 78, Mass.

Fact Magazine, October, 1964.

Fair Comment, the Fair Campaign Practices Committee, October, 1964.

Fair Play in Politics, the Fair Campaign Practices Committee.

Investigation into the 1950 Ohio Senatorial Campaign, Hearings of the Subcommittee on Privileges and Elections, U.S. Senate, 82nd Congress, 1951.

Maryland Senatorial Election of 1950; Report of the Committee on Rules and Administration, U.S. Senate, 82nd Congress, 1951.

Prejudice and Politics, Charles P. Taft and Bruce L. Felknor. New York: Anti-Defamation League, 1960 (revised 1964).

The Reporter (magazine), October 22, 1964: "New York: The Keating Record," by Meg Greenfield, p. 33ff.

The Reporter, November 5, 1964: "Kennedy vs. Keating (Con.)" in "The Reporter's Notes," p. 12ff.

State-by-State Study of Smear, the Fair Campaign Practices Committee. The studies for *1956, 1958* and *1960* are out of print; *1962* is in print and *1964* is due for publication in September 1966.

Western Political Quarterly, June, 1957 (University of Utah Press, Salt Lake City): "The Art of Political Dynamiting," by Frank H. Jonas. Also see special sections on the elections in western states, usually in June following Congressional and Presidential elections.

Note:

Most of the modern-day campaign literature described in this book is held either by the Fair Campaign Practices Committee or the Smithsonian Institution. The latter has an excellent collection dating back to the first days of the Union.

Also see assorted publications and articles on campaign finance by the Citizens' Research Foundation, Princeton, N.J., mostly written or selected by the CRF executive director, Dr. Herbert E. Alexander.

INDEX